LEAVING THE LIFE:
Lesbians, Ex-lesbians and the Heterosexual Imperative

Ann E. Menasche

Published in 1999 by Onlywomen Press, Limited
40 St. Lawrence Terrace, London W10 5ST

ISBN 0-906500-53-2

Cover Design © Tyra Till
Typeset by Chris Fayers, Lower Soldon, Holsworthy, Devon.
Printed and bound by Mackays of Chatham plc

To lesbians everywhere,
whose strength and courage are always an inspiration.

CONTENTS

ACKNOWLEDGEMENTS

This project was a long time coming and I would not have been able to complete it without the support, help, and encouragement of many people, some lesbians, some not.

First and foremost, I would like to thank my publisher, Lilian Mohin of Onlywomen Press for providing a voice to lesbian-feminists.

Thanks to Adrienne Rich and Alex Dobkin for their ideas about the heterosexual institution that I expanded on here.

Thanks also to Joan Nestle of the Lesbian Herstory Archives for providing me with invaluable historical material.

My deepest appreciation to the women who helped me with mailings and distribution of the questionnaire in the early stages of my research, especially Laura H. and Margie W; and also to Rick Chiofolo, my computer consultant, who spent countless hours running, correcting and re-running my statistics; and to my friend Cheryl Christensen for her financial generosity, and her early critical reading and meticulous editing of my work.

Other friends also were great sources of support and feedback: the members of my lesbian couples support group who listened to portions of my manuscript and cheered me on while I went through the frustrating process of finding a publisher and especially Kathleen C., Shelley Minden, and C.K.

The women who worked with me in my law office were frequently drafted into assisting me with this project and were a huge help, especially Francine Bartolotti, and my intern from Germany, Anne Rottke.

Thanks also to my parents, Sal and Mollie Menasche, and my two sisters, Irene Weiss and Reina Menasche, for their love and unqualified enthusiasm for this project, and for reading and critiquing the manuscript.

Thanks to my beloved partner and best friend, Rochelle Glickman, for her patient listening, her valuable insights, her constant love and encouragement, and for seeing this through with me from the beginning.

And finally, a special thanks to all the women who shared their life stories with me in the interest of greater freedom for all of us.

DANGEROUS TOPICS (aka Introduction)

All the top tunes tell us we need guys
We're nowhere without them they emphasize
all the TV, movies, book and magazines
They give us the same old dance,
    the same old routines
It's boy-girl—boy-girl sure get's tedious
Heavy-handed hetero harangue from the media's
tryin' to convince us a woman needs a man,
And they go on and on about it ad nauseam
They con us, bully us, guilt-trip, lie
They ignore us, ridicule, trivialize us
Why boys? What's the story?
What's the REAL story?

> – from the song "Boy-Girl Rap"
> by Alix Dobkin (1985) in *These Women*
> *Never Been Better*, Lady Slipper Music,
> Durham, North Carolina, USA, 1986

Women have been married because it was necessary, in order to survive economically, in order to have children who would not suffer economic deprivation or social ostracism, in order to remain respectable, in order to do what was expected of women because coming out of "abnormal" childhoods, they wanted to feel "normal", and because heterosexual romance has been represented as the great female adventure, duty and fulfillment. We may faithfully or ambivalently have obeyed the institution but our feelings – and our sensuality – have not been tamed or contained within it.

> – from "Compulsory Heterosexuality and Lesbian Existence"
> by Adrienne Rich
> This article first appeared in *Signs: Journal of Women in*
> *Culture and Society*, Vol.5 no.4, 1980, University of Chicago

In 1980, Adrienne Rich introduced to feminist scholarship a new and radical framework for understanding female sexuality and lesbianism. Her groundbreaking piece, "Compulsory Heterosexuality and Lesbian Existence" urged that we undertake the study of compulsory heterosexuality as a **political institution** that crushes, invalidates, and forces into hiding love between women. Since that time, not enough has been done to study how the institution of heterosexuality actually limits and controls women's sexual behaviour and identity. This is exactly what this book aims to do. By focusing on the lives and stories of the lesbians-who-left,[1] former lesbians who are now involved in or pursuing relationships with men, I hope to expand our understanding of the myriad ways that heterosexuality is imposed on women; the manner in which, almost three decades after the Stonewall Rebellion, we are not yet free.

How do we explain this long silence on an issue of central importance to both women's liberation and lesbian/gay liberation? Part of the answer lies in the relatively quiescent and conservative climate of the 1980's and 90's, which, while providing some increased visibility and other gains for lesbians, has reinforced a definition of lesbianism which is de-politicized and banalized into mere sexual practice. This "lifestyle" lesbianism may be "chic", but is certainly not a force to be taken seriously. Rather, this definition divorces lesbianism from the nascent feminist rebellion contained in a women-centered existence, rendering lesbians less of a threat to the status quo.

In addition, an unconscious assumption has begun creeping back into writings about sexuality, even those by feminists and progressives. Most are quick to recognize that lesbians and gays still suffer discrimination and stigma. Neither would they deny that gay people in the dark ages of the 1950's often engaged in heterosexuality, got married and/or denied their homosexual preferences, often even to themselves. However, most contemporary writers assume that today, people's sexual preferences can be more or less accurately measured by what they call themselves and what they do. In other words, that there is now something approximating free choice.

At the same time, essentialist concepts of sexuality – the idea that sexual preference is biologically determined and fixed at birth – have regained popularity. Hardly a month goes by without another study being published in the mainstream media about "gay brains" or "gay genes". This is closely related to the view that male domination as well as "masculinity" and "femininity" are natural, the result of our biology.

But it is not only establishment scientists and the straight media that have been advocating "born that way" theories of sexual preference. Sections of the Lesbian and Gay Rights Movement, faced with an anti-gay backlash and unprecedented organizing by the religious right, have also latched onto these theories in an attempt to reassure a deeply homophobic and lesbophobic population. These activists have argued that passing anti-discrimination laws, recognizing lesbian and gay parenting rights, permitting gay marriages, and taking other steps to make a homosexual life both visible and socially acceptable, would have no significant affect on the prevalence of homosexuality. Homosexuals, will, so they claim, always remain a small minority of the population. Of course, the opponents of gay and lesbian rights know better.

This defensive approach to winning basic civil and human rights for lesbians, gay men and bisexuals has led to a certain reticence to explore the question "what makes people straight"?

Because heterosexuality is indispensable for maintaining male access to, and control over, the bodies, lives, and productive and reproductive work of women, lesbianism is a dangerous topic. Heterosexuality is the sustaining force underlying the hierarchical division of labor between the sexes. To demystify this institution is to directly challenge the class and patriarchal structures of society.

This book has been over six years in the making: three years distributing questionnaires and doing interviews (1988 through 1990), and three years to write it. It then took considerable time to locate a publisher who understood both the nature of my project and its political importance. In choosing to conduct a study on the effects of the heterosexual institution on women's lives and choices, I had no "professional" researcher credentials on which to rely. Rather, I drew on over two decades of experience as a feminist, lesbian, socialist, and political activist and on my own insatiable appetite for every book on lesbianism, women's history, and female sexuality that I could get my hands on. I proceeded on the belief that, as lesbians and as women, we are in the best position to understand our own lives. Mostly, I hoped to provide a forum for women to tell their own stories in their own words.

How it all began: Is there a "trend" of lesbians leaving?
In 1984, I began noticing what appeared to be a disturbing trend among women I knew. Though this trend was and still is impossible to prove empirically, over the course of several years I accumulated considerable anecdotal evidence. I observed that many long-time lesbians, particularly those that had "come out" at the height of the second wave of feminism in the mid to late 1970's, were beginning to reject their lesbian identities and enter sexual relationships with men again (or for the first time).

Some of these women married, some became heavily involved with a boyfriend, some slept with a number of men, some dated men and women at the same time. They now saw themselves in various ways – some identified as heterosexual, despite their lesbian past, others bisexual; some were unsure of their sexual identity or rejected labels altogether; and a few still considered themselves lesbian despite primary or exclusive heterosexual involvements. But in each case, the direction was the same – away from a life exclusively with women and towards intimate relationships with men.

Soon, the issue of lesbians leaving began to be openly discussed in groups of lesbians and in lesbian and gay publications:

(a) The "Lesbian Connection", a national bimonthly publication "For, by and about Lesbians", composed mainly of contributions by the readership, contained a heated debate on the phenomenon of "ex-lesbians" through three issues – May-June 1986; September-October 1986 and January-February 1987. The debate began in the June 1986 issue when a lesbian from Minneapolis (who had been "out" for twenty-five years) noted:

> In the past year, I have seen at least a dozen women who have called themselves lesbians "go straight". Some of them have been lesbians for a very long time. I asked some of them why and they answered that they feel safer with a man. They told me of the pain of lesbian relationships and implied that if they are to suffer like that, they might as well be with a man. They said they needed a rest.

("Lesbian Connection" vol. 8, iss. 6, pgs. 3-4, May/June 1986)

She referred to this as a "phenomenon". Interestingly, she prefaced her remarks by writing that five years after she came

12

out, while involved with a woman, she found herself attracted to a man, and pursued the relationship out of both "curiosity" and "relief" that maybe she was "normal". She stated that she hurt "all three of us" very badly and never did it again.

In the next issue, several lesbians who were involved with men wrote back. They included one woman who considered herself "70% lesbian and 30% bisexual" and another who said she fell in love with a man after twenty years of lesbian identity and that she still considered herself a lesbian.

The lesbian readership reacted to this with anger along with some possible insights into the "phenomenon". In the following issue, one woman wrote, "How can lesbians allow a woman who fucks men to call herself a lesbian?". Another woman, responding to the 70% lesbian, wrote, "It must feel strange to live out only 15-30% of one's identity and what a coincidence that the 70% or more she is suppressing just happens to be socially despised". Another woman, with a little more sympathy for the women involved, wrote:

Lesbianism isn't something one DOES but something one IS...I had no choice as to the way I felt – I do have a choice as to whether I want to act on my feelings...I can understand Lesbians who opt for relationships with men. While heterosexual relationships can be horrid, they can have many advantages that even the best lesbian relationship cannot offer. There are financial and legal advantages, cultural support and often a lack of hassles. ("Lesbian Connection" Vol. 9, Iss. 4, page 19, Jan./Feb. 1987)

In the same issue, another woman observed:

Because women are expected to love, honor, and serve men in our private and public lives, we are trained to feel guilt, shame and an assortment of nasty feelings if we desire to live with and love women instead of men. The power of anti-lesbian feelings within women who feel drawn to women is proven by the vast majority of lesbians who have "tried men" before they were able to lead lesbian lives. In order to live happily as a lesbian, a woman must overcome the lesbian-negative feelings she has developed living in this culture.

("Lesbian Connection", Vol. 9, Iss. 4, page 21, Jan./Feb. 1987.)

Notably, one woman from New Zealand wrote that the same

set of "syndromes" was beginning in her own country.

(b) In the July, 8, 1986 edition of *The Advocate*, an article was published entitled "Yes, I'm still a lesbian, even though I love a man". The author accused the lesbian community of "a sort of reverse homophobia" for hesitating to accept her as a lesbian now that she had a boyfriend. Such accusations of "reverse discrimination" and bigotry became more common as the decade progressed and we entered the 1990's.

(c) Sometime in the 1980's, well known lesbian singers/songwriters Holly Near and Betsy Rose started dating men. In 1988, I heard Betsy Rose perform a song that describes attending her ex-lover's wedding as the "maid of honor" and how Betsy "ran out" on her lover first by going back with an old boyfriend. A few years earlier, lesbian singer/songwriter Alix Dobkin had begun singing about the same subject but from a more critical perspective in her song, "Crazy Dance".
(See quote beginning chapter II.)

(d) Lesbian comedian Kate Clinton told a joke about a support group for "lesbians without boyfriends" in the late 1980's.

(e) The September 1988 edition of *Coming Up!* a Bay Area lesbian/gay newspaper (now called the *San Francisco Bay Times*) featured an article called "Freedom or Betrayal? Lesbians Who Sleep with Men". Though the article was superficial at best, the fact that it was published at that time is, in my mind, indicative.

(f) Along the same vein, the Winter 1990 edition of *Out/Look, National Lesbian and Gay Quarterly* featured an article by lesbian novelist Jan Clausen on her transition to heterosexuality entitled "When Lesbians Fall for Men". Clausen claimed that "the lesbian-feminist way of life I knew was very hard on women" blaming a lot of the difficulty on lesbian "trashing" and a tendency to treat other lesbians as political symbols. Yet her disillusionment seemed as much political as personal: "I watched feminist institutions consume staggering quantities of energy and time and go under anyway...Of course, all of this happened in the context of oppression; I'm not saying we simply did it to ourselves. Yet I wish we could have been gentler with one another, and more honest about how hard and sometimes disillusioning it was".

(g) An article in the February 11, 1990 edition of *OUTWEEK* entitled "Lesbians Who Sleep with Men" quoted a 29 year old member of ACT-UP New York as saying "There are more obvious reasons now for lesbians to both be involved with men and also to acknowledge it because the political climate is shifting". Another ACT-UP New York member observed that more lesbians were sleeping with men during the past year, at least in her circle, than had done so in the last ten years. Lesbian therapist JoAnn Loulan stated in the same article that she believed many of the women "jumping ship" had come out as lesbians when it was "very trendy" to do so, and that they were "not really lesbians". She also reported that older former lesbians had told her that they had found it "too hard" being a lesbian, given our woman-hating and lesbian hating-culture.

(h) Friends who attended bisexual groups in the Bay Area in the late 1980's reported to me that many of the women in attendance *had* identified as lesbians, some for ten years or more. This was confirmed when I began sending out questionnaires – bisexual groups and publications proved to be a great resource for reaching former lesbians. As the new decade began, bisexual groups had become a larger and more outspoken part of the lesbian/gay community. In recognition of this fact, many lesbian/gay publications and organizations, added the word "bisexual" to their name. Although there are many young bisexual women in such groups who have never identified as lesbians, it appears that a good number of bisexual leaders and organizers are in fact lesbians-who-left.

As the evidence began to mount, I found myself both disturbed and intrigued by the phenomenon of lesbians leaving: What was going on here? Were women merely falling in love with people who happened to be men or acting on heterosexual attractions that they had suppressed in the interests of "political correctness" (as many publicly claimed)? Or did lesbian oppression and a more conservative, less hopeful political climate have something to do with the personal choices these women were making? I decided to find out.

Of course, I had read enough women's history to be aware that lesbians sleeping with men or getting married is nothing new. Rather, one could say that, historically speaking, only recently did a few of the more privileged among us, and only in certain areas of the world, have the option not to do so. As the results of this study confirm, a large majority of women who presently identify as lesbians have had at least some sexual experience with men. In addition, a significant number of lesbians have had sex with men after coming out, continue to have occasional casual sex with men and/or foresee some significant possibility of heterosexual involvement. Many women in their fifties, sixties and seventies have had lesbian experiences or (more rarely) embraced a lesbian identity when they were quite young, only to spend years or decades in heterosexual marriages before coming out again. Therefore, I felt that any coming to grips with this apparent trend of lesbians leaving needs to be rooted in its historical, social, and political context.

However, the question that I sought to answer is not so much "why now?" but "why at all?". Why do some long-time lesbians leave? The desire to know why, to understand more deeply our lives as lesbians, was the primary motivation for writing this book.

How I conducted this study

I began my research by drafting a questionnaire of multiple choice and essay questions, and distributing hundreds of copies to two main groups of women from around the country: the first consisted of women who had identified as lesbians for five years or more and who now identified as heterosexual, bisexual, were unsure of their identity or who continued to identify as lesbian but are involved in heterosexual relationship(s), the second group was composed of women who identified as lesbians and had done so for a period of five years or more, and at the time of the study, were relating sexually only to women or did not have a lover or sexual partner. The questionnaire was distributed: (1) in women's bookstores, at the Women's Building, and at the Pacific Center in the Bay Area of California; (2) to Bay Area lesbian and bisexual groups; (3) through advertisements in gay, lesbian, bisexual, feminist, and "straight" progressive publications, many with national (U.S.A.) distribution; (4) by mailing to *Lesbian Connection* – "Contact Dykes" around the country asking that women distribute questionnaires in their area; (5) at the 1988 West Coast Women's Music Festival. I also made a special effort to reach lesbians and former lesbians of color: I placed an ad in *Blackout*, a Black lesbian and gay publication, and distributed the questionnaire at lesbians of color support groups in San Francisco and New York City and at a lesbians of color conference in Southern California.

In addition, I relied on a large amount of networking to reach the "ex-lesbian" population. All women who completed questionnaires were asked to provide names of former lesbians they might know who would be willing to participate.

The design of this study and the questionnaire are mine and mine alone, though several other Bay Area women, both lesbian and bisexual, assisted me along the way, helping with distribution and mailings and providing me with suggestions and criticism.

My research was limited by a minuscule budget (no funding except for small sums that I could dig out of my own pocket or borrow from friends) and equally limited assistance. Even if I had had the resources and staff of, say, the Kinsey Institute, there are certain objective limitations in a study such as this one. It is virtually impossible to obtain a truly representative sample of a hidden population, and in the case of former lesbians, a doubly hidden population. With this in mind, a couple of weaknesses in the study should be noted. The women who participated were overwhelmingly white, more so than should have been the case, given the proportion of women of color in the population. In addition, my sample of heterosexual-identified former lesbians remained relatively small, as compared to the number of bisexual women who responded. This probably has more to do with the difficulty in reaching this group of former lesbians (many of whom may have severed all ties to the lesbian/gay community) than to their actual proportion in the "ex-lesbian" population.

After distributing the questionnaires, I conducted one to two hour long follow-up face-to-face interviews with a number of lesbians and former lesbians in California and on the East Coast, I also conducted shorter telephone interviews with women who lived in other locales. At the end of the process, 147 lesbians and 64 lesbians-who-left had completed questionnaires; of these, I had face-to-face interviews with 10 lesbians and 19 former lesbians, and telephone interviews with 4 lesbians and 7 lesbians-who-left.

Both the questionnaire and follow-up interviews sought to elicit as much personal, biographical and attitudinal information as possible in order to determine if a woman's experience of female and lesbian oppression, and her internalization of that oppression, affected her sexual choices. Some of the questions concerning lesbophobia were based on homophobia scales developed by other researchers. Other questions, aimed at measuring internalized sexism and lesbophobia, were more exploratory and experimental in nature. Some answers could be given both lesbophobic and non-lesbophobic interpretations and others might be directly affected by the degree of external oppression that a woman experienced. For example, a woman would be more likely to feel threatened walking down the street holding hands with a woman lover in socially conservative Kansas than in San Francisco. The multiple choice questions were thus most useful when viewed in conjunction with essays and personal interviews.

Not surprisingly, definite patterns did emerge in the responses I received from the lesbians-who-left. Certain reasons for leaving and certain attitudes and experiences came up again and again. Also, the lives of the self-identified lesbians paralleled in many respects that of the former lesbians. Hearing these stories of lesbian oppression, isolation, and despair was both moving and horrifying. It helped me to have a greater appreciation for the courage involved in lesbian survival.

I also arose from this study with a deeper understanding of the taboo against lesbianism. It is a taboo against women loving women that runs parallel to the even stronger taboo against women *not* loving men.

What was perhaps most shocking for me was the high degree of internalized lesbophobia and sexism that appeared not only among the lesbians-who-left – though, as expected, it was greater there – but also among the lesbians that I studied. What causes one woman who experiences deep self-hatred to conform to the expectations of straight society, while another woman with an equal amount of self-hatred still does not conform, remains a mystery. However, the answer is not necessarily that one woman is "more lesbian" than the other. Perhaps, because of complex differences in the two women's overall personalities and life experiences, one woman, at that time in her life, simply handles the pressure differently.

Finally, this book is not about condemnation of anyone. Rather, it is an attempt to increase our understanding of the institutions that limit and define our choices as women. Such feminist inquiry always forces us to look critically at our own lives and that of the women and men around us. This, in my view, is the original meaning of the phrase "the personal is political" and what feminism is all about.

[1] Throughout this book, the terms "lesbian-who-left" and "former lesbian" are used interchangeably.

I
HARD TIMES FOR INDEPENDENT WOMEN:
an overview

Lady poet of great acclaim
I have been misreading you
I never knew your poems
    were meant for me
You lived alone in a quiet den
Pouring passion through your pen
Weeping for your lady lovers
As they safely married men.

- from the song "Imagine my Surprise"
by Holly Near, 1976

What I wanted, needed, was a woman who would love me as I knew myself capable of loving and finding in her love for me, my love for her, completion, she not feeling herself incomplete if she did not have a male lover or husband. Would that ever happen? Were there in the world any other women like me – since Sappho?...Dear sisters and friends, you have asked me so often, "How was it then so long ago when you were young? How was it for a lesbian?" Well, as you can see, it was a desert, a desert of men.

– from *Elsa, I Come With My Songs, The Autobiography of Elsa Gidlow* by Elsa Gidlow (referring to her life in Montreal in the 1920's.) (SF: Bootlegger Press, San Francisco, 1986), pp.121-122.

Women throughout the ages have passionately loved other women. However, the freedom to live as a lesbian, to make one's life independent of men and marriage, is much more recent.[1] Being connected to a family was often the only way to survive, for men as well as for women. In colonial Massachusetts, for example, unmarried adults were prohibited by law from living outside family units.[2] Until the mid-nineteenth century, living under a father or husband's roof, joining a convent, or working as a prostitute in the cities, were the only economic options available to women.

In past centuries, women who loved other women were almost invariably condemned to leaving each other upon reaching what might be called a marriageable age. A few women from the upper classes might escape, like the Ladies of Llangollen who eloped with each other in 1778[3]; or a woman could acquire greater freedom for herself by passing as a man, as did Dona Catalina de Erauso in seventeenth century Spain who actively pursued other women[4]; but these were the rare exceptions.

As long as a lesbian life remained beyond the reach of all but a handful of women, individual men and the patriarchal social order had little to fear from women's attachments to other women. For hundreds of years prior to our own century, society not only tolerated but even encouraged female-to-female romantic friendships, though genital sex outside the marriage bond remained taboo.[5] In the context of a homo-social society, such relationships were not only commonplace, but were viewed as perfectly normal. As Lillian Faderman so successfully documented in *Surpassing the Love of Men*, romantic friendships were all-consuming and sensual, even if the women involved were frequently innocent of their genital potential. Many pairs of romantic friends would kiss, caress and fondle each other and sleep together in one bed, while dreaming of sharing their lives together. But because so few women had the economic independence to do so, society considered such passions a safe and transient outlet for young girls and a harmless source of comfort for unhappily married wives. Because heterosexual marriage was an inevitable part of life, women's attachments to each other did not threaten the status quo.[6]

Eighteenth Century Leaving
This did not mean that the losses and separations were easy for romantic friends to endure when duty or necessity intervened.

For example, Mary Wollstonecraft, the eighteenth century feminist and author of *Vindication of the Rights of Women* had fervently hoped to make her life with Fanny Blood, but instead, had to grapple with painful disappointment and loneliness. In 1779, Mary wrote to a friend, Jane Arden, that she loved Fanny "better than all the world", and that "to live with this friend is the height of my ambition".[7]

The following year she wrote to Jane of the strength of her resolve:

> ...this connection [with Fanny] must give colour to my future days, for I have now given up every expectation and dependence that would interfere with my determination of spending my time with her. I know this resolution may appear a little extraordinary, but in forming it, I follow the dictates of reason as well as the bent of my inclination; for tho' I am willing to do what good I can in my generation, yet on many accounts, I am averse to any matrimonial tie...[8]

Mary set about to establish financial independence by opening up a day school where she, Fanny, and her two sisters could work. However, the school was to be short-lived. Fanny was more timid than Mary, with less of the strength of character necessary to pioneer an independent life in the difficult environment of the late eighteenth century.[9] In addition, Fanny became ill with tuberculosis and doctors urged her to move to a more moderate climate though there were no funds with which to do so.

Thus, when Hugh Shreys offered to marry Fanny and take her to Portugal, Mary had no alternative but to urge her to accept. Fanny's leaving threw Mary into a deep depression. "I have lost all relish for life and my broken heart is only chear by the prospect of death,"[10] she wrote to Fanny's brother George.

Shortly after her marriage, Fanny became pregnant and Mary borrowed money to travel to Lisbon to be with her. Some days after she arrived, Fanny died in Mary's arms on November 29, 1785.

Mary herself eventually ventured into heterosexuality some seven years later. Though she was able to maintain financial independence for most of her life through work as a governess and through her writing (with assistance from male colleagues), all the women around her were married. The world in Mary's time, even more than in Elsa Gidlow's, was "a desert of men". As Godwin noted, "She felt herself alone as it were, in the great mass of her species; and she repined when she reflected that the best years of her life were spent in this comfortless solitude".[11]

Some of Mary's most productive years occurred after the loss of Fanny, including the writing of *Mary, A Fiction* (1787) based on her relationship with Fanny, and *Vindication* (1792); however, the impression obtained from reading Godwin's biography is of a woman who ultimately loses her spirit. According to Godwin, the "Amazonian" quality, "masculine" sentiments, and "harshness" of certain passages in *Vindication*, are missing in her later works, which exude a more appropriately feminine melancholy.[12]

Mary's affair with her first male lover, Gilbert Imlay, ended disastrously; he abandoned her as a single mother, an extremely precarious economic and social condition for a woman in the eighteenth century. Mary's bitterness and despair resulted in two suicide attempts. Shortly thereafter, Mary got involved with Godwin and when she became pregnant again, agreed to marry him. She reportedly told Godwin that "a husband is a convenient part of the furniture of a house, unless he be a clumsy fixture".[13] Mary died after giving birth in 1797 at the age of thirty-eight.

The Nineteenth Century - beginning of change

It was not until the second half of the nineteenth century that a developing feminist movement succeeded in opening up jobs and higher education for women. This made it possible for some women in the middle and upper classes to reject marriage and build an independent life without having to either pass as a man or endure stultifying isolation. However, this freedom touched only small numbers of women and remained limited, even for them.

Though there were pairs of college-educated career women who formed lasting "Boston Marriages" and remained spinsters, for the great majority of romantic friends, there were no such options. Marriage remained as inevitable as it had been for women in prior centuries.

In many ways, however, the nineteenth century was a time where the practice of romantic friendship reached its zenith. Numerous writers have commented on the strong emotional bonds women commonly formed with one another during this era.

But even among mid-nineteenth century suffragists, it took extraordinary courage to refuse marriage, while seeing so many of one's friends "leave the fold". Susan B. Anthony, who remained a spinster and whose closest relationships were with women, wrote to Lydia Mott in 1859, her only remaining spinster friend, about the powerful influence of compulsory heterosexuality on the lives of the women she knew:

> The twain become one flesh; the woman, "we" henceforth, she has no separate work, and how soon the last remaining monuments (yourself and myself, Lydia), will lay down the individual "shovel and hoe" and with proper zeal and spirit grasp those of some masculine hand, the mercies and the spirits only know. I declare to you that I distrust the power of any women, even of myself, to withstand the mighty matrimonial maelstrom![14]

Yet change was imminent as writer Geraldine Jewsbury intuited in a letter written in 1849 to Mrs. Jane Carlyle with whom she carried on a life-long passionate correspondence:

> I believe we are touching on better days, when women will have a genuine normal life of their own to lead. There, perhaps, will not be so many marriages, and women will be taught not to feel their destiny manqué if they remain single. They will be able to be friends and companions in a way they cannot be now...[15]

By the end of the century, romantic friends making a life together had become common among the educated classes. Such couples included novelist Sarah Orne Jewett and Annie Fields; writers Katherine Bradley and Edith Cooper; Emily Blackwell and Elizabeth Cushier, both physicians; and Jane Addams, the founder of Hull House and philanthropist Mary Rozet Smith.[16] Many of these women were graduates of the new women's colleges which became bastions of female independence and self-development. Between 1869 and 1900, only 51% of college-educated women married; in the female population as a whole, the percentage of American women who never married reached 10% during the last two decades of the nineteenth century, the highest it had ever been.[17]

Early Twentieth Century - Opportunity and Backlash

Between 1870 and 1900, employment began opening up for women of working class backgrounds, tripling the female labor force.[18] With more women gaining the opportunity for financial independence, love between women, previously tolerated, was seen as a threat to the heterosexual institution.

The backlash against women's new freedoms which reached heights in the late nineteenth century and again in the 1920's, took a number of forms: State legislatures (USA) criminalized abortion and passed restrictive divorce laws; Congress outlawed the distribution of contraception; the media attacked feminism as an evil influence causing female unhappiness and disease.[19]

In addition, an ideological offensive was mounted to marginalize and stigmatize women who stepped out of their traditional roles and/or who loved other women, thus ensuring that most women conformed. Women who passed as men or who were in love with their girlfriends were labelled by Kraft-Ebing, Havelock Ellis and other sexologists as abnormal congenital freaks, members of a "third sex," a condition that resulted from degeneration and hereditary neurosis. In order to minimize the number of women who might come to see themselves as lesbians, these defenders of the status quo, attempted to distinguish so-called "true inverts" from "spurious imitations". The latter were women led to homosexuality through their feminism (as many were), or who'd experienced school-girl crushes on other girls (as most girls did) and later left their friends in order to do what society expected of them.

In the 1920's, after World War I had brought more women into public life, Freud's views became more prominent and lesbianism began to be regarded as the result of childhood trauma and arrested development, thus amenable to psychoanalytic treatment and "cure".[20] At the same time that lesbianism was being portrayed as a "disease," companionate heterosexual marriage was promoted as representing the ultimate in sexual and emotional fulfillment.

Though there were small circles of lesbian friends in the early part of the century, the overwhelming sense of isolation that Elsa Gidlow described (see quote at the beginning of this chapter) was probably more typical. Among the radical feminists who belonged to Heterodoxy, a woman's club in Greenwich

Village that began in 1912, there were several lesbian couples – Katherine Anthony and her lover Elisabeth Irwin; Dr. Sara Josephine Baker and Ida Wylie, among others. But, more commonly, women who loved other women continued to live double lives. For example, Marie Jenny Howe, the founder of Heterodoxy, was said to be sadly disappointed in her relationship with her husband; she dedicated a book she wrote on George Sand not to her husband, but to Rose Young, a known lesbian.[21] The lives of these women were thus not fundamentally different from those of women who loved women in earlier centuries.

The same was true for Harlem nightlife in the 1920's which was a mecca for Black and white lesbians and gay men. For every Gladys Bentley who lived and performed openly as a lesbian at that time, there were many more like Ma Rainey and Bessie Smith who were married to men, a lifestyle that provided greater social acceptance in the Black community.[22]

Those few who managed to live as lesbians often internalized the views of the sexologists – that they were genetically different – more "masculine" and ambitious – than "normal" women. Yet prior to becoming lesbians many had lived heterosexual lives. In a study concerning a group of twenty-five lesbian friends in the 1920's and 1930's in a middle-sized American city, only six had had no heterosexual experience. Of the rest, six had been married (three of these were still married at the time of the interview) and four had been engaged to men.[23]

Lesbians in turn-of-the-century Germany recognized that most "contrasexuals," as they saw themselves, married men. E. Krause, writing in 1901, presents a clear picture of the societal pressures to marry in that era as well as the feminist sentiments underlying a woman's lesbian preference:

> We contrasexuals are often surrounded by suitors and admirers...And unfortunately, unfortunately, most of us give in eventually; almost all contrasexuals marry. You look at me baffled and you possibly want to contradict me heartedly? You few unmarrieds who are aware – be careful! Watch out! I've warned you in time. Maybe you too will have a turn some day. But I fear less for you, you who are knowing, initiated and have your eyes wide open. I'm sure you are courageous enough to earn

yourself that little bit of keep for which many thousands sell themselves. I'm also convinced you won't be petty enough to let the pitiful ridicule attached to the concept of "spinster" make you throw yourselves under the yoke of marriage with a being whom you can't understand and love, who will want to assert his "he shall be your lord and master" from the first minute of your union.[24]

By the 1930's, hard economic times had eroded female independence, pushing a lesbian life even further beyond the reach of most women. Not surprisingly, a "bisexual compromise", as Faderman describes it, became increasingly attractive and commonplace.

Two Lesbians Who Left

The stories of Vita Sackville West and Eleanor Roosevelt, two women whose lives spanned the first half of this century, are particularly revealing of the pressures on women to conform during this era. Both women came from wealthy prominent families in which social propriety was highly valued. Both left women-centered existences in their youth to marry, and settled on a double life, conventional in appearance, if not in reality. Vita, in her teenage years, had romantic friendships with two girls, one of whom became her lover, ironically at the same time that she was being brought out into high society for the purpose of finding a husband. She was aware, even then, that men didn't attract her "that way", while women did; and that while she was fond of Harold Nicholson, her future husband, it was Rosamund that she was in love with. As Vita's son Nigel Nicholson explains, "In love with Rosamund, she was teaching herself, willing herself, to love Harold too".[25]

Vita's autobiography, written in 1920, reveals that at the time of her marriage, she had internalized the anti-lesbian messages of her time:

> ...there has never been anything but absolute purity in my love for Harold...And on the other hand stands my perverted nature...I am so frightened of that side sometimes – it's so brutal and hard and savage...[26]

Describing the first few years of her marriage, Vita wrote:

> One side of my nature was so dormant that I believed it would never revive...How rescued I felt from

everything that was vicious and violent. Harold was like
a sunny harbor to me.[27]

Not long afterwards, however, Vita's lesbianism reemerged in
a passionate love affair with her childhood friend, Violet Trefus.
Vita, dressed as a boy and adopting the name "Julian," travelled
with Violet around Paris, until scandal and parental reproach
brought her home. Vita wrote:

> I didn't go back to the end of March, and everybody
> was very angry with me and I felt like suicide after those
> four wild and radiant months. The whole of that time
> is dreadful, a nightmare. Harold was in Paris and I was
> alone with Mother and Dada who were both very angry
> and wanted me to give Violet up. (There had been a lot
> of scandal by then)...[28]

Throughout their affair, Violet attempted to convince Vita to
run away with her, while Vita remained indecisive. In a letter
to Vita dated July 21, 1918, Violet pleaded:

> This can't go on. We must once and for all take our
> courage in both hands and go away together. What sort
> of life can we lead now? Yours an infamous and
> degrading lie to the world, officially bound to someone
> you don't care for [Harold!] perpetually with that
> someone. And I, who don't care a damn for anyone but
> you, am condemned to lead a futile existence.[29]

And, one month later, Violet, exclaimed:

> Mitya, do you think I am going to waste any more of
> my precious youth waiting for you to screw up sufficient
> courage to make a bolt? Not I. Damn the world and
> damn the consequences.[30]

Finally, in 1920, Vita made plans to abandon her husband,
home, and her two young children in order to elope with Violet.
However, with the help of Vita's mother, the two husbands,
Harold and Denys, intercepted the women and attempted to
bring them home. Vita at first refused to leave Violet, until Harold
suggested that Violet had been unfaithful to her. Unable to
forgive Violet, Vita returned to her proper role as wife and
mother, limiting her future conduct to casual affairs. However,
she never again shared a bed with her husband.[31]

But as Nicholson points out, it was really the pressures of family
and society that prevented Vita from fully embracing a lesbian life:

Let it not be supposed that Violet's infidelity (the infidelity of sleeping with her own husband) had destroyed Vita's love for her. They felt themselves defeated, not by each other, but by convention, by "them", by what today would be called the Establishment, the Establishment of two such totally un-Establishment figures as Harold and Denys.[32]

Though Violet was clearly the more defiant of the two, she also spent the rest of her life with her husband.

In the case of Eleanor Roosevelt, we do not have the benefit of such a frank autobiography. However, it can be surmised that she was not a stranger to romantic relationships between women when she married in 1905 at the age of twenty.

When she was fourteen, Eleanor was enrolled in Allenswood, a girl's finishing school outside of London. The headmistress, Mlle Souvestre, was a spinster and lesbian. Eleanor described her stay as Allenswood as "the happiest years of my life", noting that "whatever I have become since had its seeds in those three years of contact with a liberal mind and strong personality".[33]

At turn of the century boarding schools and colleges for young women, female romantic friendships were an almost universal phenomenon; even sexual relationships between women were surprisingly common.[34] It appears that Allenswood was no exception. Eleanor's cousin remarked on the passionate relationships that went on at the school and Eleanor's popularity among the students:

Saturdays we were allowed a sortie in Putney which has stores where you could buy books and flowers. Young girls had crushes and you left gifts in the room with the girl you were idealizing. Eleanor's room every Saturday would be full of flowers because she was so admired.[35]

Both Eleanor and Souvestre entertained dreams of Eleanor's future as a schoolmistress, a life dedicated to work and female friendship. For a short while after her return to the United States, Eleanor did settlement work on the Lower East Side. But very quickly, Eleanor was being pulled in another direction by the demands of her class and society to accept the conventional heterosexual life expected of her. She made her debut into society, attended dances and balls, and began looking for a husband. "I felt the urge to be part of the stream of life", she wrote, explaining her decision to marry.[36] Soon Eleanor quit her work and married Franklin. At the time of her marriage, she even opposed women's suffrage since women's duty was to care for husband and children, not make public policy. And duty was how she saw it: sex with one's husband was an ordeal to be borne, Eleanor once told her daughter.[37]

According to Eleanor's son, Elliott, after the birth of her last child in March 1916, Eleanor ceased sexual relations with her husband. Two years later, she discovered Franklin's affair with Lucy Mercer. After that, Eleanor made a commitment to herself to never share a marriage bed with Franklin again, but she agreed, for appearance's sake, to continue as his wife.[38]

After struggling to regain her self-esteem, Eleanor took advantage of her new freedom and quietly returned to the life she had known before her marriage. She became politically active, a leader in her own right, and surrounded herself with close women friends, many of them lesbians and veterans of the fight for suffrage. Eleanor's closest friends included two lesbian couples, Esther Lape and Elizabeth Read; and Marion Dickerman and Nancy Cook. In 1925, Eleanor convinced Franklin to build a separate cottage at Hyde Park for herself, Nancy and Marion; the monogram "EMN" eventually adorned the towels and linen there. The three women also became business partners in the running of Todhunter School, a girls' school in New York City, a furniture factory, and a political journal, the *Women's Independent News.*

Eleanor's mother-in-law, Sara Delano Roosevelt, disapproved of Eleanor's new companions' unorthodox behavior – they smoked, wore neckties and lived independently. She didn't understand why Eleanor wished to live with them in that "hovel".[39] Sara probably never suspected that Eleanor and her lesbian friends were more alike than appeared on the surface.[40]

Eleanor met Lorena Hickok, a reporter and lesbian, while Lorena was covering Franklin's 1932 presidential campaign. Throughout the 1930's they exchanged almost daily letters and phone calls, and planned weekends and vacations together. The record of their correspondence reveals a passionate love affair, which is undeniably lesbian.[41]

On March 7, 1933, Eleanor wrote:

Hick darling, All day I thought of you and another birthday, I **will** be with you and yet tonight you sounded so far away and formal. Oh! I want to put my arms around you. I ache to hold you close. Your ring is a great comfort. I look at it and think she does love me, or I wouldn't be wearing it.![42]

However, Eleanor's duties as first lady and wife to Franklin and the need to maintain appearances – meant the lovers could never really make a life together. This was painful for both of them, but particularly for Hickok. A place where they could live together at least part-time never materialized. (Of course, if Eleanor had left her husband, the President, to be with her woman lover, the scandal that ensued would have dwarfed any other government scandal either before or since.) Toward the end of their relationship, Eleanor wrote:

I never meant to hurt you in any way but that is no excuse for having done it. It won't help you any, but I'll never do to anyone else what I did to you.[43]

Eleanor was dealing not only with outside pressures to conform but also with her own internalized messages about "women's place". Thus, Eleanor was not adverse to blaming Hick's unhappiness on her choice to live independently of men:

I think you will remember that I once told you I wished you had been happy with a man or it might still be. I rather think that the lack of that relationship does create "emotional instability" but people do seem to weather it in time and who knows what the future holds…[44]

By the early 1940's, their relationship had cooled and Hickok had found a new lover. However, they remained close friends for the rest of their lives.

World War II and the 1950's – Community Building and Witchhunt

Ironically, it took a major war to improve the situation for women-who-love-women. During World War II, with men away at war, women's labor was needed by the burgeoning war industry – jobs even offered child care and paid high wages, previously reserved for men. Millions of young women, many of them single, were drawn away from small towns and families and a future as wives and mothers into all-female environments in the major cities. There, they became self-supporting. Thousands of others joined the military where they came to see other women as role models and mentors. Suddenly it was OK, or even admirable, for women to wear trousers, to operate heavy machinery, and to travel together without a man's "protection". Thus, significant social space was opened up, permitting the development of lesbian identity and culture.[45]

Some of these changes proved to be irreversible, even when the war ended and women were expelled from their high-paying positions and told that their "place" was again in the home. All through the 1950's, women continued to hold jobs, though they were usually low-paying clerical ones. More women were actually employed in 1952 than at the war's height.[46] Perhaps this explains why – despite McCarthyism, anti-gay witchhunts in the military and government, police repression, and a popular culture that stressed conformity to heterosexual norms – lesbian bar culture persisted. In addition, the first gay organizations in the U.S.A. were born during this era, including, in 1955, Daughters of Bilitis. This rudimentary political organizing among gays and lesbians set the stage for the powerful movements that emerged more than a decade later.

Yet, the reactionary nature of the times took its toll on many lesbians (as well as gay men) who sometimes found it easier to conform than to suffer ostracism. Large numbers of lesbians married for parental and social approval or in order to have children in the only way that seemed possible. Perhaps others were discouraged from an independent life by the prospect of subsisting on women's low wages and reduced status in the work place.

The September, 1959, edition of *The Ladder*, published the results of a questionnaire circulated by Daughters of Bilitis to *Ladder* subscribers. The 157 respondents were well-educated, enjoyed higher incomes, and were more likely to be professional workers than the average American woman of the period, making a lesbian life more of an option. However, while two-thirds considered themselves exclusively homosexual, almost the same number reported having had heterosexual relationships; only a third of the total never attempted to lead a heterosexual life. Twenty-seven percent of the respondents either were married at the time they completed the questionnaire or had been previously married. A slight majority of the once married group (24 persons) *knew* they were homosexual when they married. The reasons for marriage were quite revealing: "Wished to please parents and family"; "Concealment – hunger for social acceptance"; "To get away from home"; "To see if I could lead a normal or heterosexual life". Only five of the 24 persons mentioned love or physical attraction as a reason for getting married.[47]

Undoubtedly, it took an inordinate amount of self-confidence for a lesbian not to see herself as "sick" and "perverted" at a time when psychiatrists were working overtime to condemn and "cure" homosexuals. Typical of these psychiatrists was Frank Caprio, who, writing in 1954, described lesbians as "unstable and neurotic", suffering from "narcissism" and "arrested development" while having a pronounced tendency toward violence and criminality.[48]

Susan Madden Johnson who loved another woman during the 1950's, described her feelings then:

> This was 1958, and, as we all knew, there wasn't a Dyke in the land. Well, I wasn't one either. Ellen's and my love developed from friendship to inseparable friendship, to touching, to making love to an absorbing love according to its own dynamics…It felt very natural, but, deep down, I knew it was very unnatural.[49]

Ellen eventually left her lover to marry a man. Susan also made an effort to conform, though not as successfully: She began six years of heterosexual dating, while continuing her lesbian involvements and seeing a psychiatrist in an attempt to be "cured".

Another woman who ultimately succumbed to this pressure was Gladys Bentley, the well-known lesbian blues singer who performed in the Harlem of the 1920's and 30's. During the 1920's, she proudly acknowledged her lesbianism, even going through a highly publicized wedding ceremony with another woman. During World War II, Gladys moved to Los Angeles and began performing at gay nightspots like Mona's, a well-known lesbian bar in San Francisco.[50]

But by the 1950's, her career was floundering and Gladys decided to "go straight". She began wearing dresses during performances and in 1952, she published a story in *Ebony*

Magazine, "I am a Woman again", publicly proclaiming her conversion to heterosexuality. The article reveals the powerful impact that the homophobia of the outside world had:

> For many years I lived in a personal hell. Like a great number of lost souls, I inhabited that half-shadow no-man's land which exists between the boundaries of the two sexes...Society shuns us. The unscrupulous exploit us. Very few people can understand us...The censure which rages all about us has the effect of creating within us a brooding self-condemnation, a sense of not being as good as the next person...While I earned large sums of money and thrilled to recognition, I was weeping and wounded because I was travelling the wrong road to real love and true happiness...[51]

Gladys explained how hormone treatments for her "infantile" sex organs and her acceptance of "the true devotion of a man who loved me" had led to her salvation from the "extreme social maladjustment" that had characterized her lesbian life. She claimed to be "happily married" to J.T. Gipson and "living a normal existence".[52]

Gladys' marriage was soon revealed to have never taken place. However, in August, 1952, Gladys, at the age of forty-five, married Charles Roberts. That marriage ended in divorce. Despite Bentley's rejection of her lesbianism, her career remained at a standstill until her death in 1960.[53]

The Dam Bursts –
Stonewall and the Rise of the Second Wave

The decades of the 1960's and 70's were a period of deep radicalization among Black people, students, and large sections of the youth, not only in the United States, but on a world scale. This led to the development of dramatic protest movements challenging the status quo and a process of relentless questioning of every institution of society, however sacred. It was a time when visions of a peaceful, just, and egalitarian world captured the imaginations of millions of people. Though progressive movements were, of course, permeated with the same bigotry that plagued the larger society, messages of liberation also inspired new movements.[54] Ultimately, this favorable political climate gave birth to both Gay Liberation, with the 1969 Stonewall Rebellion, and the Women's Liberation Movement. From the interaction of the two, lesbian-feminism emerged as a distinct identity and movement. Lesbian-feminism contributed not only important leadership to the feminist movement as a whole, but also was largely responsible for creating a vibrant women's culture of music, books, magazines, newspapers, presses, festivals, battered women's shelters, rape crisis centers, bookstores, women's centers and coffeehouses that flourished during the late 1970's and 80's. This culture celebrated women's love and friendships with other women as well as women's resistance to oppression. Perhaps even more significantly, lesbian-feminism challenged the heterosexual institution both politically and ideologically in a way never done before.

Already, by 1970, lesbians were defining themselves in a new way. No longer were they internalizing the view that there was something wrong with them, physically or psychologically. Neither did they attempt to win acceptance on mainstream society's terms. Instead, they pronounced society "sick", and affirmed lesbianism as a positive identity and political rebellion against the oppressive limitations of the feminine role. One of the classic pieces written at the time was "Woman-Identified Woman":

> What is a lesbian? A lesbian is the rage of all women condensed to the point of explosion. She is a woman who often beginning at an extremely early age acts in accordance with her inner compulsion to be a more complete and freer human being than her society perhaps then, but certainly later, can allow her...She may not be fully conscious of the political implications of what for her began as personal necessity, but on some level, she's not been able to accept the limitations and oppression laid on her by the most basic role of her society – the female role.[55]

Many women became lesbians during the 1970's and early 1980's through the support they received in a Women's Movement which provided a significant counterbalance to the sexist and heterosexist ideology surrounding them.[56] Others embraced the lesbian choice they had previously made.

Under the impact of the Feminist Movement and the

progressive political climate, women's social and economic status improved substantially. Anti-discrimination laws and affirmative action policies opened up a number of "male" professions and skilled trades to women; abortion was legalized.[57] All this contributed to the ease with which a woman could choose a lesbian life.

The dramatic role played by feminism in expanding women's sexual and life options is apparent through many of the forty-six stories and poems published in *The Original Coming Out Stories*, most of them written in the 1970's. At least twelve of the contributors were women who had left a lesbian life to marry or "go straight" only to come out again at a later date, usually under the influence of feminism and gay liberation.[58] Another fifteen contributors indicated that they had been exclusively heterosexual prior to coming out (in most cases through the Women's Movement) and had had no conscious awareness of their lesbian potential prior to that time.[59]

Miriam G. Keiffer, who had previously been married to a man, wrote:

> I first realized I was a lesbian in 1968 when I was twenty-six years old. I had always known I was attracted to, was comfortable with women, but before the women's movement, I didn't have a word for someone who felt those feelings.[60]

Mary Lee Sargent was similarly affected by the feminist movement. Having been in love with her best friend for years, she described herself in 1966 as "desperate" to find a woman lover:

> I may have been desperate but I knew no lesbians...it was four more years – 1970 – before I came out sexually...That affair and the feminist movement jolted me into living with women. I left my marriage and became an official out-&-about lesbian.[61]

Paula Tree found that her experience in consciousness-raising caused her to lose interest in sex with her boyfriend. She began exploring her sexuality by reading feminist books and articles, while considering herself bisexual. Before that time, it had never occurred to her that lesbianism was even possible. Finally, she decided, for both personal and political reasons, that she was "no longer bisexual but a lesbian". Paula became sexually involved with a woman for the first time, observing, "I began to discover all the ways in which I had been unfree in my heterosexual relationships".[62]

Author Joanna Russ had been lovers with her best girlfriend during adolescence, but soon denied the nature of that relationship. Instead, she focused her energy on falling in love with inaccessible men and finally entered a dissatisfying marriage. The feminist movement changed her life, freeing her up to reclaim her lesbian preference:

> I knew that I did not really want to sleep with men – But that was sick. I did want to sleep with men – but only in my head and under specialized circumstances. That was sick. In short, I had – for close to twenty-five years – no clear sexual identity at all, no confidence in my own bodily experience, and no pleasure in lovemaking with any real person. I had to step out of the heterosexual institution before I could put myself back together and begin to recover my bodily and emotional experience. When I did, it was only because the women's movement had thoroughly discredited the very idea of a "real" woman, thus enabling me to become a whole person who could then pay some attention to the gay liberation movement...Whenever people talk about the difference between politics and personal life, I'm dumbfounded. Not only were these "political" movements intensely "personal" in their effect on me; I can't imagine a "political" stance that doesn't grow out of "personal" experience. On my own, I never would have made it.[63]

The Tenuous Hold of Compulsory Heterosexuality – The Hite Report

By the early 1980's, women's expectations for equality and freedom had risen along with a growing dissatisfaction with heterosexual relationships. A 1986 study by *Women's Day* found that four out of five women would not marry the same men if they were to live their lives over. Shere Hite documented similar disillusionment and frustration in the 4500 women she studied:

> Ninety-five percent of the married women in this study want to make basic changes in their marriages, and 84

percent of single women say that love relationships with men are more often than not filled with anxiety, fear of being "uncool" (by wanting commitment), and so on. Woman after woman says she is putting enormous amounts of energy into trying to make her relationship work, but that the man doesn't seem to be putting in the same effort. This makes women even more alienated, frustrated, and often angry.[64]

Large majorities of women complained about not being "heard or seen" by the men in their lives. They also described experiencing condescension and put-downs related to their gender, and emotional indifference from their male partners.[65]

Hite found that women's friendships with other women were highly valued and were often emotionally closer and more satisfying than their love relationships with men.[66] Not surprisingly, Hite also found a high percentage of lesbianism: 11% of the participants in her study were exclusively lesbian (including 16% of women over forty) and another 7% had had relationships with women at some time.[67]

Hite discovered that 32% of the lesbians had been previously married to men, while 61% of those lesbians over forty had been heterosexually married. Notably, the reasons the lesbians gave for leaving their marriages were identical to those given by the heterosexuals.[68]

Hite recognized that the need to be socially acceptable still affected women's sexual choices. Her study found that 8% of lesbians left a lesbian life and returned to heterosexual relationships; the most frequent reason given for this change was "a desire to fit in with society".[69] One former lesbian wrote:

I used to be a lesbian and although becoming one was frightening because of the label, it's the most comforting identity I've had since I was a cheerleader in junior high school. I am now with a man that I don't really love...I don't have the feeling of closeness with him that I had with my woman lover...[70]

Hite asked a provoking question about why, despite widespread dissatisfaction, most women continue to be heterosexual:

If one took away women's remaining economic dependence on men, and men's dominance in the larger society, would women still feel they "should" be "heterosexual?"[71]

This was one question that society was not eager to answer.

Hard Times Return: The Present Era

As Susan Faludi documented in her best-selling book, *Backlash – The Undeclared War Against American Women*, a reaction against feminism began gaining momentum in the decade of the 1980's. From the ideological assault on single career women as frustrated and unhappy; to the selling of marriage and motherhood and the renewed glorification of heterosexual domesticity; to the dismantling of affirmative action and civil rights laws; to the decreasing availability of safe, legal abortion, through anti-abortion laws and right-wing terrorism against clinics; to the weakening of the social safety net for single mothers; to the epidemic of male violence; to the increasing political influence of Christian fundamentalists spewing a misogynistic and homophobic ideology; the effect has been to make an independent life for women more difficult again.

Sometimes the attacks on feminism have involved more subtle attempts to blunt its radical edge. For example, the media have promoted a "family friendly" feminism that distances itself from lesbians and refuses to challenge gender roles, patriarchy or capitalism.[72] But whatever the tone of the proponents of the backlash, it appears that, the heterosexual institution, so threatened by the movements of the previous decades, has been at least temporarily salvaged.

Of course, none of this has occurred in a vacuum. Rather, the last fifteen years have been a time when radical change of *any sort* no longer seemed on the horizon anywhere in the world – every oppressed group, every progressive cause was being pushed back – from the Sandinistas in Nicaragua, to organized labor in the United States. By the early 1990's, the "new world order" of U.S. militarism and the "free market" stood unchallenged, while xenophobia, "ethnic cleansing" and religious fundamentalism – whether Christian, Muslim, or Jewish – set the tenor of the times. At the same time, world-wide economic recession has increased the numbers of people living in poverty. Yet that women suffered setbacks specifically *as women* is hard to deny.

During the decade of the 1980's, the gains in status that women made in the workplace and in society were slowly eroded. As Faludi pointed out, occupational segregation increased and many women were relegated to temporary positions without benefits or security. The pay gap between men and women in some occupations actually increased. The few women who had gotten into the trades or other traditionally male blue collar jobs were forced out through discriminatory layoffs, sexual harassment, and fetal protection policies.[73]

Moreover, in the face of economic crisis, those in power encouraged the placing of blame on the most vulnerable sections of the population. Thus, feminists along with lesbians and gays, immigrants, the homeless, welfare mothers, and poor African-Americans trapped in deteriorating inner cities, have served as convenient scapegoats to a frightened populace. And violent "hate crimes" particularly against women, gays, and people of color increased.

Lesbians began to find themselves increasingly isolated, demoralized, and depoliticized. Lesbian communities became less cohesive and politically active; the lesbian-feminist music industry fell into a rapid decline[74]; women's bookstores and feminist publications struggled to pay their bills and some were forced to cease operations entirely.[75] Even lesbian bars – that provided some sense of community despite their drawbacks - disappeared in favor of mixed clubs and "women's nights".[76] In addition, lesbians, particularly lesbian-feminists, became marginalized in the gay movement as a whole – subsumed in overwhelmingly male groups like ACT-Up and Queer Nation.[77] The mixed gay press, too, became more male-dominated. As the new decade began, most lesbians, like most straight women, were becoming so involved in the struggle to survive economically, that there was little energy for anything else.[78]

Of course, this is only part of the story; the picture is far more complex and contradictory than first appears. The feminist movement has shown a remarkable resilience in the face of this backlash: the late 1980's, for example, witnessed the largest demonstrations to defend abortion rights that had ever occurred. However, the women's movement has primarily been confined to such defensive struggles and became much more quiet as the 1990's progressed. And though the Courts and legislatures have mostly weakened women's legal position, it should be acknowledged that there have been a few important victories: In 1991, the U.S. Supreme Court struck down fetal protection policies. In addition, the Clarence Thomas -Anita Hill hearings during the same year raised national consciousness on the issue of sexual harassment in the workplace. In 1993, unpaid parental leave, was approved by Congress. In 1994, the Violence Against Women Act was passed (though, almost immediately, its constitutionality was challenged in the courts). However, these remain exceptions to the general trend.

Similarly, during the late 1980's and early 1990's, the Lesbian and Gay Movement mobilized in the face of the attacks by the far right.[79] And there have been a few modest victories for lesbian/gay rights – a handful of states passed gay rights bills; some courts approved second parent adoptions by lesbian and gay couples; domestic partnership laws were instituted in some cities; there were a number of openly gay and lesbian Judges and politicians. But President Clinton's modest proposal to lift the gay ban in the military and the ultimate betrayal of that promise has had greater public prominence; and while court decisions in Hawaii have opened up the possibility of same sex marriage in that state, that in itself has fuelled a virulent backlash.

Under these worsening conditions, some lesbians have chosen to leave. But many others have not. Women are still coming out as lesbians, even though in smaller numbers than a few years ago. Much of the changes in consciousness among women is difficult to reverse; many of the movements and institutions lesbian-feminists helped create remain. Women have secured a permanent place in the workforce that make right-wing fantasies of returning to eighteenth century family life only that – fantasies. Perhaps the next wave of feminist anger and organizing will open up new social space that will allow more women to lead lesbian lives.

Footnotes

[1] Andrea Weiss and Greta Schiller, *Before Stonewall: The Making of a Gay and Lesbian Community* (Tallahassee: The Naiad Press, Inc., 1988) pp. 12-13.

[2] See "Capitalism and Gay Identity" by John D'Emilio in *Powers of Desire* Snitow, Stansell and Thompson, eds., (NY: Monthly Review Press, 1983.)

[3] Lillian Faderman, *Surpassing the Love of Men* (N.Y.: William Morrow & Co., 1981) pp. 74-75.

[4] Charlotte Bunch, "Dona Catalina De Erauso" reprinted in *Women Remembered* (Baltimore: Diana Press, 1974.)

[5] This taboo usually caused no problem since society and often women themselves did not conceive of women as having any independent sexual desire.

[6] See Lillian Faderman, *Surpassing the Love of Men* (1981) (NY: William Morrow & Co, Inc, 1981.)

[7] *Collected Letters of Mary Wollstonecraft* Ralph M. Wardle, ed. (Ithaca: Cornell Univ. Press, 1979) p. 67.

[8] Ibid., p. 73.

[9] See William Godwin, *Memoirs of Mary Wollstonecraft* (NY: Gordon Press, 1972) pp. 30-32. Godwin was married to Mary for a short time before her death.

[10] Wardle, *Collected Letters*, p. 91.

[11] Godwin, *Memoirs of Mary Wollstonecraft*, p. 65.

[12] Ibid., pp. 84-85. Godwin found Mary's melancholy attractive and was pleased that she had "softened".

[13] Wardle, *Collected Letters of Mary Wollstonecraft*, Introduction, p. 48.

[14] Katherine Anthony, *Susan B. Anthony, Her Personal History and Era* (Garden City, N.Y.: Doubleday & Company, Inc., 1954) p. 143.

[15] *Selections from the Letters of Geraldine Endsor Jewsbury to Jane Welch Carlyle*, ed. Mrs. Alexander Ireland (London: Longmans, Green & Co., 1892.)

[16] See Faderman, *Surpassing the Love of Men*; See also Lillian Faderman's more recent book, *Odd Girls and Twilight Lovers* (N.Y.: Columbia University Press, 1991), pp. 22-39.

[17] William G. Shade, "A Mental Passion – Female Sexuality in Victorian America", published in *International Journal of Women's Studies, Vol I, No. 1*, Vol. 1, No. 1, (1975), p. 16.

[18] Faderman, *Odd Girls and Twilight Lovers*, p. 38.

[19] Susan Faludi, *Backlash- The Undeclared War Against American Women*, (NY: Crown Publishers, Inc., 1991), p. 49.

[20] See the discussion on the role of the sexologists in both of Faderman's works, *Surpassing the Love of Men* and *Odd Girls and Twilight Lovers*. See also, "Sexologists as Social Police", Chapter V, Part I, infra.

[21] See Judith Schwarz, *The Radical Feminists of Heterodoxy -Greenwich Village 1912-1940* (New Victoria Publishers, Inc., Norwich, Vermont 1986)

[22] Faderman, *Odd Girls and Twilight Lovers* p. 74.

[23] Vern Bullough & Bonnie Bullough, "Lesbianism in the 1920's and 1930's, A Newfound Study" *Signs: Journal of Women & Culture* Vol. 2, no. 4 (1977).

[24] "The Truth About Me" by E. Krause from *Yearbook of Intermediate Sexual Types*, Leipzig, 1901; reprinted in *Lesbian-Feminism in Turn of the Century Germany* Lillian Faderman & Brigette Eriksson, eds., (Tallahassee: The Naiad Press, Inc., 1980).

[25] Nigel Nicholson, *Portrait of a Marriage* (N.Y.: Atheneum, 1973), pp. 29-30.

[26] Ibid., pp. 34-35.

[27] Ibid., pp. 38-39.

[28] Ibid., p. 111.

[29] Ibid., p. 147.

[30] Ibid., pp. 147-148.

[31] Interestingly, Harold, too, had casual homosexual affairs throughout most of their marriage.

[32] Ibid., p. 174.

[33] Joan Hoff-Wilson and Marjorie Lightman, eds., *Without Precedent – The Life & Career of Eleanor Roosevelt* (Bloomington: Indiana University Press, 1984), p. 5.

[34] In a study of college women published in 1929, over half the women acknowledged experiencing deep sexual attraction to another woman and one in five had had a lesbian sexual experience leading to orgasm. See Katherine B. Davis, *Factors in the Sex Life of Twenty-two Hundred Women* (NY: Harper & Row Publishers, 1929.) In contrast, the Kinsey studies published in 1953 found only 28% acknowledged sexual feelings for other women and only 13% had reached orgasm with another woman. (Alfred C. Kinsey, et al., *Sexual Behavior in the Human Female* (W.B. Saunders & Co., 1953.)

[35] Wilson and Lightman, *Without Precedent*, p. 5.

[36] Joseph P. Lash, *Love, Eleanor: Eleanor Roosevelt and her Friends* (NY: Doubleday & Company, 1982) p. 42, quoting Eleanor's autobiography *This is my Story* written in the late 1930's.

[37] Ibid., p. 42.

[38] Ibid., p. 71.

[39] Blanche Wiessen Cook, *Eleanor Roosevelt* (NY: Penguin Books, 1992.), Vol. 1, pp. 325-326

[40] Blanche Wiesen Cook suggests that during this time period (from 1929 through the early 1930's), Eleanor was having a secret affair with her bodyguard, Earl Miller. Since all correspondence between the two of them have disappeared, there is no way of knowing this with any degree of certainty. Indeed, the eagerness with which her son, James Roosevelt, wishes to reconstruct such a heterosexual romance, in order to rescue her "normality" is at least suspicious. Cook quotes him as saying that Miller was "the one real romance" in his mother's life and that to deny the existence of this relationship so as to protect his mother's reputation was a great "disservice to her", since it suggested "that because of her hang-ups she was never to be a complete woman".

Even if Eleanor did have an affair with Miller, it was never exclusive (she actively encouraged his many romances, including two marriages) and it ultimately receded in favor of her relationship with Lorena Hickok. See Cook, *Eleanor Roosevelt*, pp. 429-447.

[41] Though some biographers have tried to deny the sexual nature of this attachment, Blanche Wiesen Cook dismisses this interpretation: "The fact is that ER and Hick were not involved in a schoolgirl 'smash'. They did not meet in a nineteenth-century storybook, or swoon unrequitedly upon a nineteenth-century campus. They were neither saints nor adolescents. Nor were they virgins or mermaids. They were two adult women, in the prime of their lives, committed to working out a relationship under very difficult circumstances". (Ibid., p. 479.)

[42] Lash, *Love, Eleanor*, p. 107.

[43] Wilson and Lightman, *Without Precedent*, p. 16.

[44] Lash, *Love, Eleanor*, p. 194. Perhaps even more shocking, Eleanor discouraged her daughter, Anna, from attending college because she feared that she might end up a spinster. (Cook, *Eleanor Roosevelt*, pp. 300-301.) To the end, Eleanor remained a woman in conflict.

[45] See Andrea Weiss & Greta Schiller, *Before Stonewall: The Making of a Gay and Lesbian Community* (Tallahassee: The Naiad Press, Inc., 1988) pp. 31-39.

[46] Faludi, *Backlash*, p. 53.

[47] Sept. 1959 *The Ladder* Vol. 3, Number 12 from the files of the Lesbian Herstory Archives, NYC. It is striking that a similarly low number of the former lesbians in this study gave love or heterosexual attraction as a reason for leaving. (See Chapter III)

[48] Frank S. Caprio, M.D., *Female Homosexuality, a Psychodynamic Study of Lesbianism* (NY: Citadel Press, 1954). For a more in-depth discussion of the ideas of Caprio and others like him, see Chapter V, Part I, "Sexologists as Social Police."

[49] Julia Penelope & Susan J. Wolfe, eds., *The Original Coming Out Stories* (Freedom, CA: Crossing Press, 1980 & 1989.)

[50] Eric Garber, "Gladys Bentley: The Bulldagger Who Sang the Blues" *OUT/LOOK* (Spring, 1988.)

[51] Gladys Bentley, "I am a Woman Again" *Ebony Magazine* (Aug., 1952) from the files of the Lesbian Herstory Archives in NYC.

[52] Ibid., Gladys' internalized homophobia struck a responsive chord in other *Ebony* readers. One reader wrote in a letter to the editor in October, 1952, "Thank you Gladys Bentley for at least telling the world that we hate ourselves too...I too want to leave...The price is too severe and I am unable to pay it". (from the files of the Lesbian Herstory Archives.)

[53] "Gladys Bentley, The Bulldagger Who sang the Blues", *Ibid.*

[54] As Audre Lorde pointed out, "The Black power and civil rights movement of the late 50's and early 60's was the prototype of every single liberation movement in this country that we are dealing with". *Before Stonewall*, pg. 61.

[55] "Woman-Identified-Woman" by Radicalesbians, 1970, republished in

For Lesbians Only, edited by Sarah Hoagland & Julia Penelope (London: Onlywomen Press, 1988.)

[56] For a fuller discussion about the role of feminism in the process of coming out as a lesbian, "Feminism, Social Climate and Women's Choices".

[57] Faludi, *Backlash,* p. 55.

[58] Throughout this book, these women are referred to as the "Lesbians-who-returned". See Chapter VII, infra.

[59] Penelope & Wolfe, *The Original Coming Out Stories.*

[60] Ibid., p. 84.

[61] Ibid., p. 97.

[62] Ibid., p. 145.

[63] Ibid., pp. 166-167.

[64] Shere Hite, *Women In Love, A cultural Revolution in Progress* (NY: Alfred A. Knopf, 1987), p. 134.

[65] Ibid., pp. 5-44.

[66] Ibid., p. 542.

[67] Ibid

[68] Ibid., pp. 631, 542. Those reasons included feeling uncomfortable with the "wife" role, and lack of verbal and emotional communication.

[69] Ibid., p. 631.

[70] Ibid., p. 567.

[71] Ibid., p. 643.

[72] See "Feminism Wears a New Suit" by Nina J. Easton, published in *This World Magazine, San Francisco Examiner* 2/23/92.

[73] Faludi, *Backlash.*

[74] Though a few women in mainstream music have "come out" as lesbians and independent women's music and culture continues to exist in weakened form, there are many disturbing trends. Explicitly lesbian and feminist lyrics are virtually non-existent in the mainstream and has become increasingly rare in what is left of the independent women's music industry as well. Mainstream music is at most only slightly less male dominated than in the past, while women's music is no longer made and produced exclusively by women, thus providing less opportunity for female musicians and engineers.

[75] Some lesbian writers have celebrated the "new life-style oriented lesbianism" of the late 1980's and 90's that is no longer dependent on radical feminist politics or community for its identity. However, for most women, the loss of community support and validation has made a lesbian life harder.

[76] Of course, part of the reason for the folding of lesbian bars is the growing sobriety of the lesbian community. However, the economic recession has had a major impact as well since women have even less money to spend than do men. Gay men's bars, on the other hand, have continued to thrive. Notably, no other community institutions have taken the place of the bars to provide a place for lesbians to be together. For a look at the social role of lesbian bars, see the documentary film *Last Call at Mauds,* released in 1993.

[77] Socialist and gay activist Peter Drucker, writing in the March/April, 1993 edition of *Against the Current* on "What is Queer Nationalism?" observed that "for all the talk about inclusiveness, Queer Nation groups have been overwhelmingly white and male". He went on to state, "issues of racism and sexism have been key to Queer Nation splits in several cities". Lesbian invisibility and the subordination of lesbian and feminist concerns has remained generally a problem.

[78] Despite this general depoliticization of the lesbian community since the 1980's, lesbians continue to be disproportionately involved in the feminist movement and in all progressive social struggles. However, they have often been invisible as lesbians. In 1992 and 1993, lesbian voices made themselves heard again through the formation, in New York City and a few other cities, of a militant direct-action group, "The Lesbian Avengers". However, this group has remained small.

[79] The two largest demonstrations for lesbian/gay rights ever to occur took place in Washington D.C. in October, 1987 and in April, 1993. In the 1993 action, over one million gays, lesbians, bisexuals, and their heterosexual supporters participated. Also, as part of that weekend's activities, 20,000 lesbians demonstrated in a night-time "Dyke March". However, after 1993, the level of lesbian/gay political activism was also in decline.

[80] The so-called "Defense of Marriage Act," denying federal benefits to same-sex couples and allowing states to refuse to recognize such marriages, received overwhelming support in Congress and was signed into law by President Clinton in 1996. As of this writing, similar bills have been introduced in a number of states and some have become law.

II
WHY DID THEY GO:
the Lesbians who left

Remember that woman from way back when
She was a radical man-hating Lesbian
Crew cut hair, mean and righteous,
More pure, correct, hard-line than I was
Lately I hear she's reborn, yeah
Living with a boy in California
    Too hard, I guess
    This must be part of a process
One step forward, two steps back...
– from "Crazy Dance" song by
Alix Dobkin (1983) in album
These Women Never Been Better

It certainly must be recognized that being involved with a man is to receive heterosexual perquisites, but that desire for "het" acceptance is not the reason why I, or other sisters have chosen to be involved with men... Personally, it is despite the fact that I would be receiving heterosexual benefits that I have been involved with a man for six years.
– "To Bi or Not to Buy, That is the Question.." by Patti Chung
Phoenix Rising Feb./March 1990

A slew of articles and letters have appeared during the last several years in the feminist and gay press written by former lesbians. Almost universally, they have claimed that institutionalized heterosexuality had nothing whatever to do with their decision to leave a lesbian life and pursue sexual involvements with men. Instead, they simply fell in love with a man or began experiencing powerful heterosexual attractions. And that was all there was to it.

The stories I received in dozens of handwritten pages and in hours-long taped interviews revealed, with few exceptions, a strikingly different picture.[1] Many lesbians-who-left frankly acknowledged the impact of societal, work, and familial pressures to conform to heterosexual norms. Others demonstrated that they had internalized society's messages that a woman without a man is incomplete or somehow unhealthy and that something had gone wrong to cause them to become lesbians in the first place. So these women conformed, partially or totally, temporarily or permanently, and with varying degrees of ambivalence. Some adjusted well to their new lives, or at least appeared to; others were clearly miserable; many were simply making do. But their leaving was always in some sense incomplete, since once a woman has lived a lesbian life, she is changed, permanently.

The degree to which the lesbians-who-left are like the self-identified lesbians I studied was surprising even to me. The sixty-four former lesbians who shared stories of their lives with me come from all over the USA and are distributed between rural and urban areas in almost identical proportions as the lesbians. Most age groups are also represented in similar proportions to the lesbians. However, only one lesbian-who-left was over fifty, while close to 10% of the lesbians were from that age group. In addition, there are slightly more women of color among the lesbians-who-left – 19% versus 12% women of color among the lesbians – the difference being made up primarily of Asian-American women. There is also one Native American former lesbian included in this study.

The lesbians-who-left are as well educated as the lesbians. Slightly more of the former lesbians – 32.8% – had graduate degrees compared to 28.6% of the lesbians. The income levels of the lesbians-who-left are also comparable – though somewhat more lesbians than former lesbians earn more than $40,000 per year (10.5% versus 6.2% of the lesbians-who-left); slightly more lesbians than former lesbians earned under $10,000 per year (23% of the lesbians compared to 18.7% for the lesbians-who-left); and more lesbians than former lesbians earned between $20,000 and $30,000 per year (22.4% versus 29.7%.)

The type of employment held by lesbians and former lesbians is extremely similar: almost the same high percentage reported that they were self-employed (21% of lesbians compared to 20% of lesbians-who-left); there is also almost no difference in the percentages of lesbians and former lesbians who were in blue collar or male dominated professional jobs. A slightly higher percentage of lesbians (23.8%) are in traditionally female professions such as teacher, nurse or social worker, as compared to 18.7% of the lesbians-who-left.

One important difference between the two groups is that the former lesbians tended to have been lesbians for a shorter period of time. Close to 60% of the lesbians-who-left had been lesbians for five to seven years as compared to one-third of the lesbians.[2] The percentages of lesbians and former lesbians who had been gay for seven to ten years was similar – 22.2% of the lesbians compared to 26.6% of the lesbians-who-left. The difference becomes dramatic after ten years – only 9.4% of the former lesbians (as compared to 23.6% of the lesbians) had been gay for eleven to fifteen years; and only 4.7% of the former lesbians (as compared to 20.8% of the lesbians) were lesbians for more than fifteen years. It thus appears that the "risk" of leaving a lesbian life decreases significantly after more than ten years of lesbian identity.

Heterosexual Histories
The difference in the heterosexual histories of the lesbians-who-left compared to the lesbians is small, with the large majority of both groups having had at least some heterosexual experience. While 17.8% of the lesbians had never had sex with a man, 4.7% or three of the former lesbians had no such experience either. Though these three women had never slept with a man, they no longer identified as lesbians (or exclusively as lesbians) and were actively pursuing, or newly open to, heterosexual involvements.

In addition, a similar percentage of lesbians and former lesbians had never been married – 68.7% of the former lesbians compared to 69.4% of the lesbians. About 12.5% of the lesbians-who-left are presently married to men.[3]

Of the forty-eight former lesbians, 70.8% had significant heterosexual histories prior to first coming out.[4] This compares to 56.3% for the lesbians. To look at this result in another way, close to 30% of the former lesbians had little or no heterosexual experience prior to their decision to leave a lesbian life.

New Sexual Identities and Behavior
The lesbians-who-left, in grappling with their change in lifestyle, adopted a number of different sexual identities: 6.2% (4 women)

continue to identify themselves exclusively with the lesbian label despite being married to a man or being in a primary relationship with one. One-fifth or 20.3% now identify as heterosexual.[5] Approximately 8% adopted what I call a "dual identity" – they are "lesbian-identified bisexuals", or they are lesbians "emotionally" and bisexuals "sexually". Another 15.6% are unsure of their sexual identity or reject labels altogether. And the largest sub-group, exactly half, now identify as bisexual.

Many of these women, were, at the time the study was conducted, still in transition, and had not yet found regular sexual partners. Thus, 34.4% of the former lesbians as compared to 21.8% of the lesbians had no sexual partners of any gender; and 40.6% of the lesbians-who-left compared to 32% of the lesbians were not in a primary relationship. Of those former lesbians who had sexual partners, their sexual behavior had dramatically shifted toward the heterosexual side of the spectrum: 61.9% had only male sexual partners, 16.7% had only female sexual partners and 21.3% had both male and female sexual partners. When primary relationships are measured, the nature of this change becomes more apparent: 78% were in primary relationships with men (56% of the total living with their male partners), while only 22% continued, at least for the time being, to be in primary relationships with other women.

There were some differences in lifestyle worth noting between the sub-identities of former lesbians. The "unsure" and "dual identity" groups were least likely to have sexual partners (50% of the "unsure" and 77.8% of "dual identity" women had no sexual partners). The "unsure" women were also the most likely to be presently involved with only women partners – 30% as compared to 10.3% of the bisexuals, none of the lesbian-identified or heterosexual-identified former lesbians and only one or 11.1% of the dual identity women. The bisexual and heterosexual former lesbians were equally likely to be in primary relationships with men – 55.2% and 53.8% respectively – though, not infrequently, the bisexuals carried on casual affairs with women as well (27.6% of bisexuals reported presently having both male and female sexual partners). At the same time, 20% of "unsure" women had male-only sexual partners. Only one "dual identity" woman (11.1%) stated that she had both male and female sexual partners, while none of the "unsure", heterosexual or lesbian-identified women so indicated. All three of the lesbian-identified former lesbians were in primary relationships with men.

Conflicted Sexual Preferences

Most of the lesbians-who-left remain strongly female-oriented emotionally, despite predominantly or exclusively heterosexual behavior in their present lives. Consequently, their sexual preferences tend to be conflicted and ambivalent, lacking the bodily and spiritual integration that exists, by and large, among the lesbians.

This conflict is reflected in the answers to multiple choice questions designed to elicit sexual preference. When asked whether they prefer intimate relationships with men, women, or men and women equally, the former lesbians appear quite bisexual – 42.2% chose "men and women equally," while the remainder break down evenly between men and women. The same is true for the question of which gender they prefer making love with: 54.7% say both genders equally; however, of the balance, more say they prefer women (28.1%) than prefer men (15.6%).

When questioned about their deepest feelings of love or who they prefer for close friendship, companionship, and as a confidante, the responses were significantly more lesbian. Only 4.7% said their strongest love relationship had been with a man; 45.3% responded women, and 48.4% said men and women equally. For close friendship and companionship, the female preference is overwhelming – a whopping 71.3% prefer women; 7.8% prefer men and a little more than one-fifth or 21.9% prefer men and women equally.

There were also some differences in reported preferences between sub-identities. The lesbian-identified former lesbians showed the most ambivalence toward heterosexual relationships and the biggest contradiction between their emotional preferences as indicated in the multiple choice responses and their sexual behavior. All three stated that they preferred intimate relationships with women, that their deepest love had been for women and that they preferred women for friendship and companionship. The heterosexual former lesbians showed the least ambivalence about their move toward male lovers: 76.9% stated that they preferred intimate relationships with men as compared to none of the unsure, 20.7% of the bisexuals, and 22.2% of the dual identity women. Second only to the lesbian-identified sub-group, the dual identity women acknowledged being women-oriented emotionally – 55.6% stating that their deepest feelings of love had been with women, compared to 46.4% of the bisexuals, 40.7% of the unsure women and 30.7% of the heterosexuals. Merely 23% of the heterosexuals and none of the other lesbians-who-left stated that their deepest love had been for men.

This emotional preference for women among the former lesbians was even more apparent in the essays and interviews than in the multiple choice responses. Of the 50 lesbians-who-left who completed the essays and/or were interviewed, 72% or 36 women gave strong indication that they were emotionally closer to women than to men and that their most passionate love relationships had been with other women. In addition, many of their comments demonstrated considerable ambivalence toward heterosexual relationships.

One bisexual-identified former lesbian in her forties living with her boyfriend in the San Francisco Bay Area, described her feelings after experiencing her first woman lover:

> ...it was so great with women. God, she was so soft. And we cried together. And we knew each other's feelings...Everything felt familiar – like I had always been with women. How magical. I loved it...It's so different, the sex...You kiss and kiss for hours and you touch and touch for hours...With men, even if they are really good, it's a lot briefer...It takes forever to be soft with a guy...With women, we go to bed once and it's like we've been together all our lives...I felt that women were definitely better.

At another point during the interview with the same woman, the following interchange took place:

> Lesbian-who-left: I can't handle rejection from women. I get so hurt. It hurts a lot more than with men.
>
> Question: Could that be because you get closer to women on some level?
>
> Lesbian-who-left: Definitely. Definitely.

Another former lesbian, Jewish, in her thirties, and living on the east coast, was asked why she preferred women as friends. She responded:

Because men are often jerks…Whatever I look for in a friend, that's the default place to look; even without thinking, you have your friends and how you structure the sexual part of your life is almost a separate question. To me, friends and lovers are not in the same category…I think women are more interested in the things I would talk about…more willing to hear the long version of the story – all your feelings, the day-to-day events, a more intertwined, trivial, relaxed thing. I don't share the long version with men. I would package up a summarized version and here it is.

Her ambivalence about relationships with men was also obvious in other ways. At the time of the interview, she had been involved for a number of years in what she described as a "delicious and brief" relationship with a married man. I asked her more about that involvement:

Question: You seem to like the fact that he's not around all the time. Is that true?

Answer: Yes – that's definitely the case. If he moved in with me permanently, then our relationship would be worse, would not be as good. I really like to have privacy…

Q: So would you say you like the fact that he's not totally free?

A: Yes, definitely…

In contrast, her former relationship with a female lover was extremely intense:

We were inseparable. We were so close. I loved her passionately…It was the most intense relationship I have ever been in and ever hope to be in again…[6]

As in the case of the two former lesbians mentioned above, many other women in this study had similar difficulty coping with their extremely close and passionate feelings toward women lovers, especially during the inevitable hard times and break-ups.

This was often a direct consequence of the social isolation (closeted existence) in which many relationships between women existed. Another lesbian-who-left described her feelings after the break-up with her girlfriend:

> I was totally nuts...It was the kind of thing where you
> walk down the street and break out crying. I couldn't
> see anybody or anything for six months.

Soon thereafter, she started seeing men again, but acknowledged that her relationship with her female lover had been the most intense relationship – both emotionally and sexually – that she had ever experienced.

As one former lesbian explained:

> I have a lot more in common with women...I'm more
> supported in who I am by women. I can be seen – all
> of me – a whole person, for my strengths and my ideas
> and my power and really be acknowledged and
> appreciated with women, whereas with men, an eighth
> of me is seen and that they have trouble with or is
> misinterpreted...All my interactions with women had a
> depth and realness that my interactions with men never
> had.

A Jewish lesbian-who-left (from Atlanta) who now sees herself as heterosexual had this to say:

> After three and one-half years of going out with men,
> I sort of wish these [heterosexual] feelings hadn't
> occurred because it is much harder to find men who
> have the depth and caring – they can't compare with
> women...Straight men are not comfortable talking
> about their emotions...

Another former lesbian, a bisexual from Washington, D.C., described her own ambivalence about men:

> I like men a lot, really enjoy their company, just not
> too close...Women are easier to live with...I feel more
> respected, I feel safer, I feel less distracted, less hassled..

It is not surprising then that most of these women found leaving a lesbian life to be a painful and difficult process. Many felt deeply nostalgic toward their past female lovers or toward the lesbian community in which they no longer completely belonged.

A Latina former lesbian (in Colorado) continued to pine for her woman lover despite her marriage to a man:

> I love my husband though I am not sure I am "in love"
> with him...I still love Joanna deeply and would like to

be again involved with her...The only problem with the transition from woman to man has been letting go of her. I accept that I will always love her and I go on. I am working on a novel concerning her and our life together

Another woman in her thirties (from a small town in the midwest) suffered similar longing:

I met my current lover, a man, about four and one-half years ago...I miss women desperately. I have very close friends but little chance for a woman lover whom I am sure would want more from a relationship than I can give...Life is pretty OK, but not as dynamic as my lesbian life...I frequently think that in San Francisco or a more liberal area of the world than the midwest, I could have survived as a Dyke and found the woman of my dreams.

Twenty-four former lesbians (over 89%), reported that they continued to feel attached to or had problems separating from the lesbian community.

One bisexual-identified former lesbian in her thirties (from the Boston) area was asked why the lesbian community continued to be so attractive to her, though she no longer identified as a lesbian. She replied:

My lesbian community was a lesbian-feminist community...I was part of a group of people who had similar perspectives...It was something so central to me.

Our dialogue continued as follows:

Question: Why was it so central to you?

Answer: It resonates. Feminism and lesbianism are for me very tied together.

Q: Why is it that lesbian-feminism resonates for you? There are other ways of being a feminist.

A: It's who I am. It's what feels most comfortable...It felt good being a lesbian. I loved being political. Just everything fit together.

Another bisexual (also from Boston, in her twenties) expressed similar sentiments:

When I first moved to Boston, I was really looking to meet women – that's the base for me – women's community, feminism, women's culture. The hard part of my transition was that it was harder to find feminists in the bisexual community than in the lesbian community.

However, she continued her relationship with a married man. Like many other lesbians-who-left, she felt ambivalent toward involvements with men while continuing to pursue them. And, like many other former lesbians, the fact that her heterosexual relationship could only be part-time was seen as an asset:

> I don't envision myself living with a man because I like my living space to be women-centered, women-only space…Your feminist connection can only go so far with a man.

An African-American former lesbian (from New Jersey, in her late twenties) described her own transition to male lovers:

> Adapting from being a lesbian into being one man's woman was very difficult, very strange, and very time consuming emotionally. I eventually did feel that I loved him, but I missed the gentleness and softness of being touched by a woman. Men don't love like women do…My involvement (in the future) will certainly be with another woman.

Similarly, a New York lesbian-who-left (Jewish and in her thirties, unsure of her identity) explained her present conflict:

> I feel fairly ambivalent about my "new" life. The person [man] I am involved with is better than any other lover ever has been. Our relationship is much healthier, more supportive, more loving and way more sexual than any relationship I've had in the past. However, I miss feeling like I'm part of the lesbian community, although I'm having trouble figuring out exactly what I miss. It's not the bars that I miss, and it's not my friends (since I still have them) and it's not the politics (since I'm still active) and it's not the literature (since I still read it). It's an amorphous feeling of belonging.

For some former lesbians, this was not the first time they had attempted to leave a lesbian life. One Jewish bisexual in her thirties who was now actively looking for a boyfriend, explained how, following a couple of flings with women she had "gone back in the closet" and entered a long-term relationship with a man. Five years later, she returned to lesbianism. I asked her why she had come out the second time:

> I couldn't help it; I was freaking. I stayed in the house for a year – I got really fat. I knew the truth of the matter was I was still a lesbian. I would look in the mirror and go "I am a lesbian..." And my roommate at the time, a straight woman, said, "for god's sake, will you come out...Just get on with it".

So Why Did They Leave?

If the lesbians-who-left miss their lesbian lives so much and are so women-oriented emotionally and spiritually, why did they choose to leave in the first place? Is it merely, as many have claimed publicly, that they unexpectedly fell in love with an individual who just happened to be a man, or was there something else? Did the change have anything to do with lesbian oppression? To determine the answer to this question, I asked all of the former lesbians who filled out a questionnaire to write an essay explaining all the reasons for and circumstances of their change to male lovers. (48 former lesbians or 75% filled out the essays.) I also went into this subject at length during face-to-face and telephone interviews: personal interviews were conducted with 19 of the lesbians-who-left; in addition, another seven were interviewed by telephone.

Only 28% of the lesbians-who-left gave falling in love with a man or experiencing a compelling heterosexual attraction as even one of the reasons for their leaving. Thus, for close to three-quarters of the lesbians-who-left, heterosexual attraction played no role whatever in their initial decision to leave a lesbian life. And even more rarely did former lesbians state that such attractions were the only reason – 4% so indicated.

For the vast majority of lesbians-who-left, there were a number of other factors involved:

(1)   hoped to win approval from family members – 24.%;

(2)   desired to raise children in a heterosexual family – 16%;

(3)   felt that heterosexual involvements were necessary as a form of "therapy" in order to heal child sexual abuse or rape experiences or to get over their "fear" of men – 18%;

(4)   wished to avoid job discrimination – 20%;

(5)   wanted to be able to express affection publicly -20%;

(6)   religious reasons for changing their lifestyle -4%;

(7) found the lesbian community too small or claustrophobic – 22%;

(8) found the lesbian community narrow-minded – 26%;

(9) wished to fit in better with the heterosexual majority – 48%;

(10) inadequate role models for successful lesbian relationships and/or for their future as a lesbian – over one-third – 34%;

(11) wanted economic security or privileges – 14%;

(12) felt they were "missing something" – 44%;

(13) relationships with men seemed easier, less painful, less emotionally demanding – 20%;

(14) difficulty finding a satisfactory long-term woman lover – 42%;

(15) problems functioning sexually with a woman – 20%;

(16) problems finding women as partners for casual sex, while finding men more sexually accessible – 12%;

(17) believed heterosexual relationships were more stable, lasting, and emotionally secure – 24%;

(18) became demoralized because they discovered that lesbian relationships weren't perfect; – 28%;

(19) And finally, only one former lesbian (2%) indicated that she hoped to be "cured" or have her lesbianism go away.

In most cases, the lesbians-who-left found their former lives too difficult because of social isolation, lack of role models, and the absence of validation and support from the outside world - precisely because of lesbian oppression. But why did the former lesbians leave, while the lesbians (who also experience such oppression) did not (or did leave and later returned)? Did the former lesbians have a harder time of it because they were on the receiving end of more rejection, isolation, harassment, and discrimination? Or were the lesbians-who-left more likely to internalize the messages of mainstream society? And, if so, why?

Outside Pressures on the Lesbians-who-left

Part of the answer to these questions lies in the fact that the former lesbians tended to have led more closeted lives and receive less acceptance for their homosexuality than did the lesbians. With the exception of parental acceptance, however, the difference between the two groups is quite small.

While 74.1% of lesbians were "out" to their parents, 71.4% of the former lesbians had also been "out" to their parents, almost identical figures. But when asked if they were actually accepted by their parents, the difference becomes statistically significant. Only 60.4% of the former lesbians reported receiving parental acceptance, compared to 77.6% of the lesbians.

Similarly, while the difference in the percentage of lesbians and former lesbians who were "out" at work is small (57.3% of the lesbians compared to 50% of the former lesbians), the difference is somewhat greater for those who stated they were actually accepted as lesbians at work: 88.3% of the lesbians for whom the question was applicable, compared to 77.5% of the lesbians-who-left.

At the same time, a slightly higher percentage of lesbians reported being fired or threatened with job termination or denied a promotion because of their lesbianism (17% of the lesbians compared to 10.9% of the former lesbians) This 6% difference may be because the lesbians-who-left were more likely to have been closeted at work.

The percentage of lesbians versus former lesbians who were "out" to their straight friends is approximately the same (89.5% of the lesbians versus 88.7% of the former lesbians), while the difference in acceptance by straight friends is very slight (95.2% of the lesbians compared to 91% of the former lesbians). Likewise, there is only an extremely small difference between the two groups in the rate of acceptance by siblings: 84% of the lesbians compared to 80.7% of the lesbians-who-left.[8]

The lesbians-who-left were, however, somewhat more likely to have been subjected to harassment on the street. While 33.6% of the lesbians indicated that they had never been harassed on the street for being lesbians, this was so for only 25.4% of the former lesbians. Similarly, while almost 15% of the lesbians had never been harassed on the street for being women, merely 3.2% of the former lesbians had never had such experiences.[9]

These statistics only tell some of the story. For example, many of the former lesbians participating in this study come from Jewish or other ethnic backgrounds where strong familial ties are highly valued and parental rejection may, therefore, be more difficult to cope with. Others were raised in religious families where the stigma against homosexuality is particularly powerful.

Unfortunately, I neglected to include questions about religious and ethnic background in the questionnaire; however, all those who were interviewed were asked such questions. The percentage of lesbians-who-left from Jewish backgrounds is extraordinarily high – 46.1% – as compared to 26.7% of the lesbians and 2% for the general population. I would therefore tentatively conclude that Jewish women found becoming lesbian easier than keeping that identity.

The lesbians-who-left were also disproportionately from Catholic backgrounds (34.6% of the former lesbians compared to 26.7% of the lesbians; the population as a whole is 22% Catholic.) Still, there is no question that both the lesbians and former lesbians experienced considerable oppression from family and society for choosing to love other women. The reasons such pressures resulted in partial or total conformity in the case of the latter (at least for now) while the former continue to live as lesbians (at least in the present) is a complex question that this book can only begin to address.

Nevertheless, it is fairly clear that the lesbians-who-left were more dependent on outside support and validation (such as the burgeoning women's movement of the 1970's and early 80's provided) and also were less able to locate and maintain such systems of support in the more conservative climate of the past decade. Though both the lesbians and former lesbians I studied overwhelmingly considered themselves feminists (89% of the lesbians and 91.8% of the former lesbians) and the percentage who described themselves as presently active in some aspect of the women's movement is essentially identical (approx-imately half), there are some important differences. Only 29.9% of the lesbians as compared to 54.7% of the former lesbians indicated that feminism played a major role in their original decision to identify as a lesbians. Moreover, 28.1% of the lesbians-who-left compared to 10.2% of the lesbians reported a decrease or cessation of feminist political activity.

During the first three years of lesbian identity, the former lesbians were more likely than the lesbians to have had close lesbians friends (79.4% versus 71.3%); more likely to have participated in lesbian/feminist organizations and political and cultural events (73.4% versus 54.3%); more likely to have regularly read lesbian and feminist books (76.6% versus 69.3%); and to have frequently listened to women's music (69.8% versus

57%). The same percentage of both groups usually had women lovers (approximately 70%).

Yet, for the last two years of lesbian identity, something had changed for the lesbians-who-left. While the lesbians had become **more** connected with the lesbian community and less isolated from other lesbians, the former lesbians had begun to lose ground. It is unclear how much of this was because the lesbians-who-left had already begun drifting away from a lesbian life, and how much of the leaving itself was due to less outside support actually being available to this group of women. Yet, whatever the cause, the difference between the two groups is striking: 68.9% of the former lesbians usually had women lovers as compared to 80% of the lesbians; 84.7% of the former lesbians had close lesbian friends compared to 92.8% of the lesbians; 61.4% of the former lesbians were involved in lesbian/feminist political or cultural activities compared to 74.3% of the lesbians; 64.4% regularly read feminist and lesbian literature as compared to 75.3% of the lesbians; and 67.3% frequently listened to women's music compared to 72% of the lesbians.

Essential elements to lesbians survival – political and social support and close ties with other lesbians – had begun fading from the lives of the former lesbians at least two years before they actually left.

Internalized Lesbophobia and Sexism

The greatest difference between the lesbians and the lesbians-who-left, however, was the degree to which the latter internalized the anti-female and anti-lesbian prejudices of the larger society.

The former lesbians were much more likely to feel that they needed a man for physical "protection" and personal validation: Approximately 38.7% (compared to merely 16.5% of the lesbians) stated that they usually feel safer walking down the street with a man than by themselves or with another woman.[10] In addition, 37.1% of the former lesbians as compared to 13% of the lesbians stated that they had felt like a failure when unable to make a relationship with a man work.

There is other evidence of greater dependency on male approval among the lesbians-who-left. More former lesbians than lesbians had problems saying "no" to men when they didn't want to have sex with them (45.3% versus 38.3%). And 34.9% of the former lesbians (compared to 20.4% of the lesbians) responded "yes" to the statement, "It is important to me to know that men like me and find me physically attractive even when I am not interested in a particular man or men".

The lesbians-who-left were also more likely to believe that marriage to a man was the preferable lifestyle for women – 94.5% of the former lesbians compared to 82.8% of the lesbians gave an unqualified "false" response to the statement, "A good marriage to a decent loving man offers women a greater possibility of satisfaction and security than any other lifestyle".

There was a tendency on the part of the former lesbians to be more traditional or "feminine" women. While 51% of the lesbians denied being "feminine" or "straight-looking" outside of work, only 29.7% of the former lesbians denied being "feminine" or "straight-looking". Yet approximately two-thirds of both groups felt that they were neither "butch" nor "femme" in relationships with other women. However, of those who identified with one role or the other, more lesbians than former lesbians were "butch" (19.2% versus 8%); and more lesbians-who-left compared to lesbians were "femme" (21% versus 14.4%).

Specifically lesbophobic attitudes were also more evident among the lesbians-who-left: 93.2% of the lesbians compared to 85.9% of the former lesbians gave an unequivocal false response to the statement, "Most lesbians hate men". Additionally, more former lesbians internalized the view that heterosexual relationships are more "natural" for the vast majority of women – 39% responded "true" to such a statement, while only 25.8% of the lesbians responded "true". Along the same vein, more lesbians than former lesbians (90.4% versus 73.4%) unequivocally disagreed with the statement that the women who became lesbians during the women's movement are not "real" lesbians.

The former lesbians also tend to be more critical of lesbians as a group – 64% of former lesbians as compared to 46.9% of lesbians agreed with the statement, "A lot of lesbians are just as macho and just as oppressive and objectifying of other women as many men".

In addition, the lesbians-who-left were more likely to have doubts about raising children in a lesbian household: 72.8% of the lesbians compared to 60.9% of the former lesbians disagreed with the statement, "It is a lot easier on children to be raised in a heterosexual family than in a lesbian one". And although the overwhelming majority of both groups agreed that most lesbians are happy and fulfilled, there were some differences here as well – 93.2% of the lesbians agreed with this statement, compared to 85.9% of the former lesbians.

There were a couple of statements in the questionnaire that functioned as litmus tests for anti-lesbian bigotry. In both cases, the differences between the two groups were significant. The first statement, "Women who look obviously lesbian or who publicly flaunt their lesbianism make me uncomfortable" received these responses: 12.2% of the lesbians, compared to 28.1% of the former lesbians agreed. The second incorporates the idea put forward by a large number of homophobic sexologists who identify heterosexual trauma and a morbid childhood as root "causes" of a lesbian life. Half of the former lesbians agreed with the statement, "Traumatic experiences with men such as rape and childhood sexual abuse are one reason that many women become lesbians", while 34.7% of the lesbians (still a distressingly high number) so agreed. At the same time, 54.4% of the lesbians unequivocally disagreed with this statement compared to only 35.9% of the lesbians-who-left – almost a 20% difference.[12]

Five True Stories of Lesbians-Who-Left[13]

Bisexual Barbara
Barbara is an outspoken bisexual activist who had identified as a lesbian for the previous five years. She's in her forties, comes from an Anglo-Saxon Protestant background and resides in a large city in the east. At the time of the interview, she was involved with two men in relationships which she described as "primary" and had a very occasional involvement with another woman. She stated that she's not interested in monogamous relationships. "I just have a very high need for freedom," she told me. Barbara lives with women roommates because she

finds women easier to live with. "We can read each other's minds", she said.

Barbara described herself as 70% hetero and 30% lesbian. She told me that she found it easier being with men as lovers. When I asked her why, she responded:

> I think it's a lot of early conditioning ...I feel like the part of me that's lesbian has been crippled...I tried when I was younger to force myself to be more sexually active with women faster than worked...I think I feel safer, more confident, more nurtured and more approved of by men and that has a lot to do with my sexual choice.

I then asked her why she felt more approved of in heterosexual relationships. Barbara replied:

> Because women are not taught that it's right or safe or exciting to be sexual with each other or to be each other's primary partner for life.

Barbara explained how she doesn't think she would ever have had the nerve to explore her lesbian feelings without the support of the feminist movement. She remembered having a lesbian dream and feeling frightened and repulsed by it:

> I think it was a conditioned response to society's homophobia that is internalized in me.

I asked Barbara what her lesbian life had been like. "It was very exciting and it was very scary," she replied.

And why was it scary?

> Because I was doing something that most of society really disapproved of and really misunderstood... Because there wasn't any role really, I didn't understand what I was doing...

In addition, her mother's response when Barbara first came out to her had been quite negative: "Well I hope you aren't doing it to avoid dealing with men".

Barbara explained why she chose a bisexual identity:

> I feel uncomfortable being straight...They're sick, most of them. It feels limiting to me.

But she didn't feel comfortable being totally lesbian either:

> I feel like a failure as a lesbian...mandatory heterosexuality has crippled me.

She described not feeling as free, or able to be creative or relaxed, when sexually intimate with another woman.

As reasons for her transition, Barbara mentioned heterosexual attraction, but also explained that she didn't want to feel cut off from the rest of the world. She also had hoped for parental approval, though it didn't work out that way.[14]

Barbara also felt that she was "missing something" by living a lesbian life, that she needed a man for personal validation:

> On the top of my head, I would say that's bullshit, but from my internal conditioning, I would say it does affect me...it is hard as a bisexual not to be affected by looking to get male approval.

She remains, however, very attached to the lesbian community.

Dual Identity Doreen

Doreen is an African-American in her twenties who lives in a small city in Colorado. She "sometimes" identifies as a lesbian, but "mostly" as bisexual. Though she acknowledges she has a "strong preference" for intimate relationships with women, preferring both making love to a woman and women for close friendship and companionship, she is presently living in a common law marriage with a male partner (who is white) and raising children with him. At the time of the interview, she had just begun a part-time relationship with another African-American woman.

Doreen explained her dual identity as follows:

> "I have to admit I'm living with a man. That makes me bisexual, right? But my social interactions are with women; who I find most attractive is women. And I don't think bisexual says that".

Though Doreen had experienced crushes on other girls as a young teenager, it wasn't until she attended a progressive college where lesbians and gays were openly organizing, that she became aware of lesbianism as a possibility. Almost immediately, she came out as a lesbian and eventually became president of the Gay and Lesbian Alliance on campus.

When she was twenty, Doreen converted to Buddhism and transferred to a Buddhist university. (She had been raised Catholic but became disaffected with Catholicism as a young child.) There, she found no support for a lesbian life:

> When I went there I was still identifying as a lesbian...I put up this card on the bulletin board that said that if

anybody [gay] wanted to get together, call me and we'll do something. I put my name on it and didn't get any responses. Much later I got feedback that it wasn't appropriate...Lesbianism wasn't accepted, but more than not accepted, it wasn't supported. And there were some lesbians around, but they didn't talk to you.

I asked Doreen how this affected her. "It drew me away from the lesbian community", she answered. "I was having a relationship with a woman at the time, but when that fizzled out, I didn't pursue any more".

Doreen told me that while at the Buddhist university she had become more religious and certain "spiritual experiences" convinced her to give men another try:

I was coming from this man-hating. I had had bad experiences with men so I didn't want to deal with them...I got the message very strongly that I couldn't **not** want to deal with men because of these experiences...that I had more work to do with men.

Did she feel that by being a lesbian, she wasn't being "fair" to men?, I asked. Doreen replied:

Yeah, kind of like that, but not just that – you know how you get a plate of food and your mother says you haven't tasted it – or you say you don't like liver and they say you just haven't had it cooked properly, and then later on the more concrete thing was this teacher actually said I should get married and have a baby.

Doreen had her first child while she was still attending school. And three years after she received her teacher's "advice", she began living with her present partner.

Doreen mentioned a number of other factors that had influenced her to get involved with men again. First was her mother's rejection of her lesbianism:

I told her [about being a lesbian] and she was like, well no, forget it, I don't even want to talk about this...I think that definitely affected me in a negative way...It was hard on me and it did affect my subsequent behavior.

Doreen was also disturbed by how hard and even dangerous it was to be publicly affectionate with another woman:

It's the kind of thing where you can't walk the streets

holding hands because somebody will throw a pop bottle at you...I'd say that might even be the single most hard thing for me.

I asked if this was because she liked being really open and affectionate. "I'd like to have that option", Doreen said.

She also emphasized that she didn't see any role models for a lesbian life, especially one involving children:

I like having kids and I like having someone to share them with and up until recently, I've never seen any Lesbian couple in a long-term relationship. I might have read about them but I never related to any...I don't relish the thought of being a single parent trying to raise two children. So that makes me more conscious of wanting a partner...there's no paradigms where a lesbian partner would fit into their [children's] lives...

Doreen added that if she were to raise children with another woman, it would be hard to make it work with her extended family. They would be much less accepting. She pointed out that family ties among African Americans are very important – more so than in white Anglo-Saxon cultures – and that the opinions of elder members of the family are particularly valued. She also said that there are even fewer role models for Black lesbians than for white.

I asked Doreen if falling in love with a man or experiencing a compelling heterosexual attraction played any role in her leaving an exclusively lesbian life. She answered, "no". She also stated that if the world had been different and totally accepting of lesbianism, she would never have left.

Leslie the Married Lesbian

Leslie is a woman in her thirties from Anglo-Saxon parentage who has struggled with her lesbian feelings and identity since she was in junior high school. She lives (monogamously, at least for now) with her husband, Ed, and their young daughter in a rural area in the east.

I probably spent more time with Leslie than any of the other women in this study. I ate meals with her, met her husband and child, and stayed overnight in her barn. We talked extensively -at least two and one-half hours of which was on tape.

Despite being married to a man and having every intention

of staying that way, Leslie emphatically continues to identify as a lesbian. I asked her why she remained so attached to her lesbian identity:

> If you put me in a room with a hundred women and if you put me in a room with a hundred men, I would start being sexually attracted to 75 to 90 of the women and maybe one of the men. And to me that doesn't constitute bisexual. In general, the male persona, body, doesn't attract me, women attract me. It's just a fluke of nature that I happen to be married.

The story I got from Leslie's written responses to the essay questions contrasted sharply with what I later learned in the personal interview. According to the essays, Leslie was having a wonderful, very "out", and totally fulfilling lesbian life when all of a sudden she met Ed and fell passionately in love:

> I was very blatant and obvious...I had been living in that town for five years and was well known and respected, so it was OK to come out. I started having women lovers left and right...My life felt complete, whole... Then I met Ed. The connection was instant and puzzling. There was wild eroticism in my head and a lust I had never felt before. The more time we spent together, the more I knew this was the love I had been looking for all my life...The first time we made love and each subsequent time was cosmic and beyond words.

Yet, in reading her essays, I was struck by something unreal about her descriptions and an ambivalence that came through clearly in her continuing lesbian identification and in some of her other statements:

"Many times I wish Ed were a woman (and sometimes he wishes he was one too). This has not been easy for me", she wrote.

In the interview, Leslie revealed that far from being wonderful, her life prior to meeting Ed had been fraught with isolation, loneliness, despair, rejection from parents and community, and economic difficulties. In addition, the "cosmic" sex with her husband had already fizzled:

> Making love with Ed is wonderful because I love him, but if I wanted to get clinical about this act and that act, I would say I prefer being with women. I have a very

hard time having sex with him because he's a man and it's a real struggle for both of us...I don't get real aroused. I used to, in the beginning.

As I discovered in our long talks, Leslie's internal conflict was not new; rather, she had struggled with her lesbian identity since she was a young teenager and had "left" and "returned" on several occasions prior to her marriage to Ed. Leslie's personal history is a powerful and disturbing example of how lesbian oppression can sometimes succeed in exacting conformity.

Leslie's first sexual relationship was with a best girlfriend starting in the seventh grade and lasting through her sophomore year in high school. She knew that she shouldn't be doing what they were doing together, but couldn't understand why, since it felt so nice. She had already developed a strong preference for female companionship:

> I remember writing in my journal, "why do I have more fun with my girlfriends than going out with boys, it seems so much trouble and not nearly as much fun..."

Yet, at the same time she was discovering that a lesbian life was not an easy choice to make. "All I remember is the taunt of me being a lesbian" she told me.

But the hardest part for her was the requirement of secrecy - that it was not possible to share her joy and her pain with the rest of the world:

> The biggest thing I was aware of was that it couldn't be public. That we couldn't go to the prom. There was still all that pressure to have a boyfriend to be accepted...We would double date and then go home and spend the night together. We couldn't talk about it to anyone – that seemed sort of sad...Then when we broke up, it was private – we couldn't talk about it.

Leslie started sleeping with men in college, and it wasn't until 1973, in the context of a rising feminist movement on campus, that she fell in love with a woman in her dorm and began calling herself a lesbian. However, when her lover asked Leslie to come to California with her, she declined:

> I was nineteen and real scared...I was going to be a lesbian. I was going to be away from my liberal college where it was OK because half the campus was doing that and I was going to be in the real world.

So, instead of following her lover, Leslie agreed to move to the country with a man she hardly knew. That man turned out to be physically abusive but she stayed with him for a year and a half. Another boyfriend followed, also a stormy and unsatisfying relationship, this one lasting three and one-half years.

"Part of the storminess", Leslie explained, "was due to my inability to come out – again – to myself".

She also returned to school and attempted to connect with other women:

I fell in love with several women... while I lived with him. When I attempted to turn each of those relationships into sexual ones, I lost the friend and the friendship.

It was not until Leslie was in the supportive environment of nursing school that she came out a second time:

Nursing school was a delight. All my professors were lesbians.

There, Leslie found a woman lover and made plans to move with her to Seattle upon graduation. But again, the "real world" proved too much to handle, this time for Leslie's lover, and they separated:

We had been in this real insular world of nursing school...By the time we got to Seattle...I think she got too afraid, we had a lot of fights about it.

In Seattle, feeling disillusioned and depressed over the loss of her lover, Leslie found herself again isolated. "I felt who am I, am I really a lesbian and am I always going to be by myself?"

Finding other lesbians seemed too difficult for her.

"It was such a struggle trying to find lesbians", she told me. "I felt very shy and scared".

Besides attending occasional women's events, her only close connection with the gay community was a gay male roommate. When he died, she felt even more disoriented and alone.

Leslie had no women lovers during her two years in Seattle. Toward the end, she briefly considered heterosexuality. "I had sex with a couple of men very unsatisfactorily and called it quits on men".

She then returned to her home state in the east to be nearer her family and to follow her dream of a life in the country. She settled in an isolated rural community where everyone was in heterosexual couples. There, Leslie worked at a birthing center at the local hospital. Though she was now more determined to live a lesbian life, the outside obstacles were greater than they had been in Seattle. For five years, Leslie knew no lesbians nearby – neither friends, lovers, nor acquaintances. She described her life during that time:

> ...pretty much my relationship was with my job...I went on vacations to Key West to women's retreats and had hot week-long affairs...I had long distance friends I would write and call...I was on everybody's mailing list and read every lesbian romance and periodical that existed and fantasized about meeting lesbians. I would drive to one gay bar, a two hour drive, and sit in the corner and be very scared.

How did it feel being confined to having little affairs long distance?

"It was awful", Leslie explained. "I always read and answered ads and never got anywhere".

Other outside pressures began mounting in Leslie's life. She started experiencing homophobia at work:

> People would try and fix me up and want to know why a nice girl like me wasn't married. They made your basic queer jokes but mostly I was suspect because I was single.

Leslie had also recently come out to her mother. Her mother's reaction was far from accepting:

> Her response was not to tell my father because he would die if I told him, and she wanted to know what it was really like, the sex.

Her mother also made it clear that Leslie's lovers were not welcome in her parents' home. At the same time, her mother tried to convince Leslie that she was not really a lesbian:

> She mostly talked about it around babies, because at the time I was working at the birthing center...She'd say you'd be much happier...you haven't met the right man yet...

To escape the oppressive environment of the hospital, Leslie opened up a restaurant with a heterosexual female roommate. "The whole town thought we were lovers", Leslie said.

The restaurant didn't last long. Soon, she was in the midst of a severe financial and personal crisis – her business partner had been found stealing money and the restaurant was not making it financially.

Immediately prior to this crisis, Leslie had met a woman through a personal ad who lived two hours away and they had begun seeing each other on weekends; but they simply didn't "click" – she was the only woman Leslie had been with where the spark just wasn't there. But she was to look no further.

Leslie had now given up on ever being able to find a satisfactory woman partner. "It felt pretty impossible", she said. Perhaps Leslie had already decided that trying to forge a lesbian life for herself in the face of job and financial problems, social isolation, parental rejection, and community hostility was too difficult and too frightening. In any case, after only two months with her woman lover, Leslie started pursuing a relationship with Ed.

She was also particularly susceptible to lesbophobic messages at this time:

> I went to a psychic and she said to me, now dear,
> don't be so afraid of men. You know there's somebody
> out there if you would just hold out your hand to him.

"Did you think you were afraid of men?" I asked.

"No. I'm joking in a way. I was the strong feminist. I wasn't afraid of men, I wasn't afraid of anything. But maybe she was right", Leslie said.

I asked Leslie how her parents had responded to her involvement with Ed:

> My mother was ecstatic…It was my father,
> he'd known him for five minutes and wanted
> to know when we were getting married…It was
> the first time I felt like I had done something
> right in his eyes.

Why did she often wish Ed was a woman?

> Well, because I prefer women. For sex is a big one. I
> miss a lot of the lesbian community stuff that I used to
> do…It's hard to think maybe I'll never be with a woman
> again and that kind of makes me sad…The big reasons
> that I'm glad he's a male is that it's OK with my father
> and also the reduced hassle.

Unsure Una

Una is close to forty and is from a devout Italian Catholic family. She had been a lesbian for fifteen years and is one of only three former lesbians I studied who had never been sexually intimate with a man. Una was also unusual in that despite her very conscious personal rebellion against the "feminine" role and strong sympathy with the goals of the Women's Movement, she did not identify as a feminist.

"There's a lot of anger in that movement and it's justified but it scares me", she told me.

Una stated that she was unsure of a label for her sexuality since she was very close to a man with whom she had sought a sexual involvement. However, the man was homosexual and not interested in more than a friendship. Una explained her sexual identity as follows:

> It's not that I don't identify anymore as being a lesbian but I also identify as not being a lesbian. My definition of being a lesbian has expanded to include deeply romantic sexual relationships with men.

Una's preference for women, which she continued to acknowledge, was clearly based on her refusal to accept a subordinate role for herself. She stated that she preferred women for intimate relationships because, "I can be myself; there's no role".

Una described "fitting in" with her peers until all the girls she knew started dating boys:

> It felt that in order to do that [date boys] you had to be lesser...I felt equal to the boys. I felt like one of them.

Her continued desire to excel in sports and in her studies as she had since early childhood rendered her an outcast.

Una's coming out experience in college was extremely traumatic. She fell in love with her best friend who was repulsed and cut off the friendship. To cope with her despair over this incident, Una began to abuse alcohol:

> The look she [the friend] gave me never left me. It felt like something was terribly wrong with me. That's why I started to drink. It was a painkiller.

For fifteen years, the alcohol acted as a buffer against the full weight of society's anti-lesbian messages. Una confessed that she would drink daily and would get "really ripped" several times a week. In such a numbed state, she lived a life centered around lesbian lovers and friends, became active in the Homophile League at College and even contended with rejecting parents.

When Una and her sister (also a lesbian) came out to their parents in 1982, the response had been strong condemnation:

> They were mortified...My father accused me of corrupting my sister. He brought up the Bible and mainly that they were afraid of what other people thought...The worst thing was that he accused me of causing him to have a nervous breakdown...It was really, really awful...Now, we just don't talk about it.

When Una finally got sober, approximately three years before the interview, "the day of reckoning had arrived", as she put it. All the old pain came to the surface.

Almost immediately (and prior to getting close to her gay male friend), Una's identity started to change. Though she had never experienced sexual or physical violence from a man, she began blaming her (exclusive) lesbianism on her "fears" of sex with men and her parents' sex-negative attitudes. "I've got to make sure I'm not with women to escape", she explained.

She told me that it was "very unhealthy" for a woman to rule out the possibility of relationships with men, as she had, and that lesbians may be "stunting their spiritual growth" by doing so. Una also had begun going to a therapist who was "supportive" of changing her identity and did not encourage her to examine her internalized homophobia.

I asked Una if she ever felt like a failure as a woman because she hadn't had a relationship with a man.

"Yes, I do get those feelings from time to time", she answered.

Una acknowledged that she sometimes felt guilty about being sexual with a woman, though she described that guilt as not "religious" but "societal" and "familial" guilt.

She also admitted that the prejudices of the outside world had affected her strongly:

> I definitely internalized society's views [of homosexuality] because when I felt attracted to this young man and we were holding hands, I felt so liberated...I felt, my God, I'm normal.

Every once in a while I get tired and I want to surrender. I feel like I'm on the front lines all the time.

Heterosexual Helen

Helen is a woman in her late thirties who lives in a small city in Northern California. At the time of the interview, she had been living monogamously with a man for several years and they had set the wedding date. They were also planning to have children together.

Though she had identified and lived as a lesbian for approximately twelve years, Helen presently considers herself heterosexual. At the same time, she continues to prefer women for close friendship and companionship.

Helen comes from a very traditional Polish-German Catholic family where girls were discouraged from higher education. She confided that she was physically and emotionally abused by her father and may have been sexually abused by an uncle.

The message Helen got from her family was that she should be "pretty, quiet, unassuming, not make waves". It was assumed that she would get married and have children.

Helen, however, was a rebellious child and soon became a disappointment to her parents. "I have always been the bad one, I was the hippie and the drug user, dated Black men as a teenager", she said.[15]

Helen had her first lesbian relationship when she was twenty but did not identify as a lesbian:

I thought of myself as not necessarily a straight person but I certainly wasn't a lesbian. I just happened to be in this relationship with a woman.

Around the same time, Helen became involved in feminist activities. Feminism began changing her view of herself and her future, and influenced her to begin identifying as a lesbian:

I think it [feminism] gave me the message that it was OK not to get married and have kids. Not doing that didn't mean that you couldn't have a happy, full life, there were other possibilities.

Helen was soon in a long-term relationship with a woman and moved with her to California. During a visit back east, her mother discovered her lesbianism accidentally[16] and "just totally lost it".

> ...she hit me with every horrible judgment, stereotype, criticism there is about lesbianism...They're all bulldykes, you'll never be happy, society is against you, it's sick, not normal, not natural, you're a freak...

Helen sank into a deep depression where she tortured herself with her mother's judgments. "I bought all her stuff", she told me. Helen claimed, however, that with the help of a lesbian therapist, she recovered quickly from this episode of self-hatred. Yet, her mother's rejection persisted:

> After two years, whenever we talked on the phone about it, she would say how could you do this and are you really happy, you really ought to reconsider.

Helen acknowledged that after the crisis had passed, her mother's approval "continued to have some importance". She explained that she felt "sad" that her mother "reacted in the way she did to the choices I made".

Meanwhile, Helen's relationship was in trouble. "I was smoking a lot of pot...I was scared to open up emotionally and be real". After four years together, they separated.

Her last two lesbian relationships were of much shorter duration. Helen became increasingly ambivalent about her lesbianism. She had also begun thinking about having children and made a conscious decision to do so in the context of a heterosexual relationship. I asked Helen why she decided to have children with a man rather than with a woman partner. She answered:

> I felt it would be easier in the world...being an acknowledged recognized couple...to be able to be totally "out", to have a relationship acknowledged and supported and validated in a way that gay relationships are not...What comes to mind is having a kid and visiting my relatives and what that would be like if I left my woman lover at home because my relatives don't know. I would be seen as a single mother, but I'm not a single mother. How much easier it would be to go with my kid and somebody I'm married to, that kind of acceptability.

Through most of her years as a lesbian Helen had smoked pot on a daily basis. When no longer under the influence, being different was less tolerable:

I remember that I went on a date with a man... and I really liked feeling normal... it's just harder to be in the world not following the program.

She was also surprised to feel physically safer on the street with a man:

I think some of it is socialization crap, some of it that men are physically stronger...The sort of irrational and neurotic part is the socialization that a woman needs a man.

Helen's mother was "excited" about her return to hetero-sexuality and this was a huge relief for Helen:

I was glad that what I was doing was helping her feel happy instead of contributing to her feeling awful.

I asked Helen if heterosexual attraction played any role in her decision to leave a lesbian life. She answered "no". She had moved toward men, she explained, "for the baby stuff, the acceptance stuff, and the ease of being in the world".

Footnotes

[1] This difference may be explained by the former lesbians' greater reluctance to publically acknowledge that their choices had been affected by societal pressures, as compared to what they are willing to say privately in questionnaires and interviews where their identities would not be revealed.

[2] Anyone who was a lesbian for less than five years was excluded from this study.

[3] Any woman who is presently married to a man and living with her husband was excluded from the lesbian group.

[4] I defined "significant heterosexual history" as either marriage, a long-term boyfriend (of one year or more), or three or more years of sexually active heterosexual dating.

[5] The small percentage of heterosexual-identified former lesbians in this study is probably more a result of the way participants were obtained – through ads in gay, lesbian, feminist, and bisexual presses and through lesbian contacts – than a reflection of the proportion of heterosexuals among all lesbians-who-left in the population at large. Women who now identify as heterosexual despite their lesbian past are more likely to have severed all contact with the lesbian/gay community than those who now identify as bisexuals. This is particularly the case since bisexuals have become a larger and more vocal component of the gay community.

[6] This same woman later explained to me that while she was a lesbian, she had lived an extremely insular and closeted existance with her lover. She believed that this put extra stress on their relationship and

was the principal factor leading to the breakup. She also said that she "probably would" still be a lesbian if the world were a freer place.

[7] For a more thorough discussion of this issue, see Chapter IV – "Pressures to Conform: the World," especially Part I(A) – "Partners".

[8] Ironically, a higher percentage of former lesbians actually reported that they were out to their siblings (82.3% of lesbians versus 85.4% of former lesbians), but again we are dealing with very tiny and statistically insignificant differences.

[9] With the exception of childhood sexual abuse, the former lesbians reported experiencing somewhat more male violence than did the lesbians. The issues raised by this experience – whether such violence "causes" lesbianism or can, alternatively, actually enforce traditional "feminine" roles – is discussed at length in Chapter V – "She swallowed the lie".

[10] It should be noted that both groups were equally likely to live in urban areas and thus probably faced similar dangers.

[11] 83.3% of the former lesbians (25 out of 30) showed evidence of gender non-conformity in childhood (defined as tomboyishness or non-traditional intellectual interests or ambitions), compared to 100% of the 32 lesbians.

[12] A few of both groups wrote equivocal responses such as "unsure" or "some" women to this question.

[13] These are not composites but actual stories about five individual former lesbians. All five women completed questionnaires and were interviewed between 1988 and 1990. Only the names have been changed.

[14] Barbara's mother is not very happy with her present lifestyle either, since Barbara refuses to settle down and her boyfriends are Black.

[15] Helen's present fiancé, interestingly enough, is white.

[16] Her mother had put on Helen's Theresa Trull album, not knowing what it was, and listened in horror to the lesbian lyrics.

III
THE LESBIANS

So many of us do find our way to each other, in spite of the silence, in spite of the denial. We are each a miracle of self-creation and self-validation! These are stories of our survivors, the wimmin who are coming home.

– from the Introduction to the First edition of *The Original Coming Out Stories* by Julia Penelope & Susan J. Wolfe (The Crossing Press, Freedom, CA: 1980, 1989), p. 8.

But now we reach problems. Am I a "real" Lesbian?
There is immense social pressure in our culture to imagine a Lesbian as someone who never under any circumstances feels any attraction to any man, in fantasy or otherwise...I have been attracted to men; therefore I'm not a Lesbian. I have few or no fantasies about women and do have fantasies about men; therefore, I'm not a Lesbian. This idea of what a lesbian is is a wonderful way of preventing anyone from ever becoming one, and when we adopt it, we're simply doing the culture's dirty work for it. There are no "real" Lesbians – which is exactly what I heard for years, there are only neurotics, imposters, crazy virgins, and repressed heterosexuals. You aren't a Lesbian. You can't be a Lesbian. There aren't any Lesbians. Real Lesbians have horns.

– from "Not for Years But for Decades" by Joanna Russ, published in *The Original Coming Out Stories* p. 161.

Pouring through the personal stories of the 147 self-identified lesbians[1] who participated in this study, I was struck by how ordinary these women are and, at the same time, how very extraordinary. Their lives have been woven with struggle, pain, passion, the miracle of transformation, considerable joy and, most of all, courage. Because even in the best of times, it takes an unusual amount of courage to publically embrace a lesbian life.

These lesbians come from all over the U.S.A. and from both rural and urban areas. Approximately 53% are from the West, 21% from the east coast, 14% from the midwest and 6% from the south. One woman lives in Fairbanks, Alaska. The majority – 57.1%- live in or near major metropolitan areas. Though at the time the study was conducted, almost half – 44.9% – were in their thirties, all age groups are represented: 25% were in their twenties; 21% were in their forties; and 8.8% were fifty or over.

My attempts to obtain a racially representative group were only partially successful; thus, the lesbians are somewhat dispro-portionately white – 88.4%.[2] Of the women of color, there are eight African-Americans (5.5%); five Latinas (3.4%); one Asian; no native Americans; and three who indicated "other". In comparison, U.S. Census Data for 1989 indicates that 12% of the U.S. population is Black and 3.4% "other". In addition, the total Hispanic population, many of whom are persons of color, is 6.7%.

This is a highly educated group of women. There are no high school dropouts and only five women (3.4%) who did not attend at least some college. Almost three-quarters – 72.8% – completed four or more years of higher education – 29.9% of this total having only gone far enough to obtain their bachelor's degree; 14.3% having attended some graduate school; and 28.6 having received a graduate degree. In contrast, the U.S. census for 1991 indicates that only 18.8% of the female population twenty-five years or older completed four or more years of college and a paltry 6% attended five or more years of college.[3]

The lesbians in this study benefit as well from higher incomes than the average American women: 23.8% earn an income of $30,000 or more per year and 10.5% earn over $40,000. According to the U.S. Census for 1990, only 9% of the female population over fifteen years of age receives incomes of over $30,000 a year. In addition, while 23% of our lesbians earn less than $10,000 per year, 54% of the female population as a whole have this small an income.[4]

With regard to employment, there are also significant differences between our group of lesbians and the U.S. female population: 21% of the lesbians are self-employed, compared to only 4% of the female population at large, according to the U.S. Census statistics of 1987. This may reflect an attempt to

82

escape a work environment that, because of sexism and homophobia, is doubly oppressive to lesbians. Only 8.2% of the lesbians are employed in female-dominated jobs such as clerical, retail or household worker, while 23.8% are employed in female-dominated professions such as nurse, social worker, or teacher. This compares to 69% of the female population in clerical or service jobs and 14% in female-dominated professional occupations according to the 1991 U.S. census.

In addition, the percentage of lesbians in non-traditional employment is disproportionately high – 5.5% work in the blue collar trades and 17% are employed as doctors, lawyers, college professors or in other male-dominated professional or managerial positions. In contrast, the U.S. Census for 1991 indicates that only 2% of the female population twenty years and older work in the trades and only 9.7% are employed in male dominated professional or managerial positions.

One can infer that women who become lesbians expect to be self-supporting and that they therefore emphasize education and pursuit of career goals somewhat more than do heterosexual women.

Overwhelmingly, the lesbians in this study prefer women in every way – emotionally as well as sexually, not only as lovers, but also as friends. Approximately 95% responded that their strongest and deepest feelings of love had been for another woman, and 83% prefer women for friendship and companionship. Only 15% of the lesbians prefer men and women equally as friends; merely three women (2% of total) indicated that they prefer men as friends.[5]

Numerous comments from the lesbians further demonstrate that a lesbian preference is not primarily sexual, but a wholistic preference for women as people. One African-American lesbian in her forties, when asked what she preferred about women, responded:

> Everything. Their bodies, their minds. Intimacy. I could be more intimate with a woman than I ever could with a man. A sense of being totally accepted and understood.

Similarly, a white lesbian in her thirties explained:

> I really like the emotional part of a woman a lot and the physical tenderness and softness...Women are much more honest about their thoughts and feelings

than men are. They don't have to live up to a macho image.

Another lesbian in her thirties wrote:

A love relationship with a woman is overall the most satisfying for me. I can enjoy sex with men but I never feel complete...My lover is my best friend and the best lover I have ever had.

A lesbian in her twenties summed it up like this:

I have decent relationships with men but I would not choose to be intimate with them because I prefer the company of women.

Two-thirds of the lesbians in this study reported that they were in primary relationships with other women – 51.7% of the total living with their lovers, and another 15.7% in primary relationships where they do not live together. Less than 22% indicated that they had no female sexual partner.

Most of the lesbians described their intimate relationships with other women in positive and even glowing terms. One lesbian in her twenties wrote:

My personal life is wonderful...I'm in love and it's going strong.

Other lesbians expressed a similar sense of satisfaction with their lesbian lives. A young lesbian who had been "out" for over a decade, wrote:

I have such independence and freedom from the burdens of raising children, having a husband and planning my life around family and serving others...I have a wonderful lover who, like myself, values her alone time as much as the precious time we spend together. We make our own relationship "rules", not using anyone else's model. I have sensitive, intelligent women and men and yes, mostly gay, friends...My life is full and lacks nothing.

One lesbian in her forties favorably compared her lesbian relationship with that of her parents:

Especially when I look at my parents and their relationship, I am filled with joy at how good Rita and I are together. We are supportive of each other in so many ways.

An older woman who had previously been married to a man

also considered herself lucky:

> After several years of attraction to women, I was fortunate to have a neighbor friend who shared so many experiences with me that we eventually just flowed into a relationship. We are still together after eighteen years. We raised (if one can call it that) six children together. For that, we deserve a medal...For me, my life with this woman I love has been happy, sad, intimate, and distant but always with so much more potential than most heterosexual possibilities because we have a common base (being female). I feel sorry for so many married women I know who always seem to be looking for something intangible.

Another lesbian mother, white, and in her thirties, who is presently co-parenting a child with her partner, wrote of her happiness:

> Identifying as a lesbian is a healthy, joyful, fulfilling place for me... *This* woman doesn't need a man...What I need I get from women, I give to women, I share with women. Its a beautiful synchronicity.

Yet, for most of the lesbians, it was not easy getting to that place and often a sexist and homophobic society continued to take its toll. Many spoke of years of isolation; of thinking they were the only ones; of painful rejection by family and friends; and of experiencing the traumas of breakups with lovers with no one to turn to for support. One women in her twenties told the story of the death of the first woman she loved:

> I really liked Diane and wanted to be much more than friends with her but I was afraid it would make me perverted or something...Over the months, our relationship grew stronger and she continued to see her boyfriend. I got more and more depressed over the situation. One night, I jokingly told her that if she would dump her boyfriend, I would be with her the way we both wanted. The next night she told me over the phone that she had broken up with him and wanted me to come over...I said I needed time to sort out my feelings...The next day, I was told that she had been in a terrible car accident and was in intensive care. She died before I was ever able to see her. The accident was

investigated as a possible suicide and I blamed myself for it.

As a result, this lesbian became extremely depressed and went into hospital. Fortunately, she made a gay male friend there who helped her work through the coming out process and the guilt she felt for her friend's death. She was also blessed with unusually supportive parents.

Other women had to struggle with their lesbian feelings in the face of severe parental hostility:

> One summer, when things with my family had been going pretty well for quite a while, my lover and I decided to go to the Michigan Women's Music Fesital...I wrote to my folks in Wisconsin and suggested that we could meet there for lunch...I got a letter that fairly burned through the envelope. I was "vile, disgusting, sick, perverted" – a long list. We didn't go to Wisconsin that summer.

Rejection by one's peers could also be deeply disturbing. A college student reported leaving her dorm because of the harassment she encountered:

> I was the talk of the dorm...My lover and I would be stared at constantly and the administration was no help. I commuted my last semester – much better.

One young woman in her twenties who loves her lesbian life described her previous ambivalence:

> There was a time when, if I could have somehow made myself straight I would have. The world I knew – my family, my friends, my teammates, and my community, everyone I cared about was STRAIGHT.

Coming to a comfortable lesbian identity was almost always a struggle:

> I worked/fought hard to develop a sense of pride as a lesbian...I now love being a woman who is a lesbian. But I wish to change the frustration and challenges, hurts and loneliness (difficulties finding a lover and lesbian friends) for others and especially for isolated types (old, physically challenged, etc.) We need to help each other survive.

However, this struggle often led to greater self-awareness and a sense of personal integrity for the woman involved:

...to be where I am today, I had to do a lot of self-examination. Nothing about my circumstances is accidental...I have chosen to live the life I have and I found my examined life is worth living. I don't just follow the crowd and do what is expected and safe. I blaze trails and have highs and lows, but plenty of passion.

One lesbian in her forties commented:

I think its hard to build a life outside of mainstream acceptability and not everybody is able to put up with the societal pressures...For me, it would be much harder to create a life in the mainstream. I think my own internal discomfort would heavily outweigh the external discomfort.

Heterosexual Histories and Behavior

Most of the lesbians in this study had at least some heterosexual experience – 82% had had sex with men and almost one-third (30%) had been married to a man at one time. Of the 119 respondents who provided adequate information about their early heterosexual history, slightly more than half indicated that prior to first coming out as a lesbian they had had significant heterosexual involvement, i.e., they had either been married to a man, had a long-term boyfriend of a year or longer, or engaged in three or more years of sexually active heterosexual dating.

The Kinsey Institute found a similarly high rate of heterosexual experience among the lesbians that they studied: More than one-third of the white lesbians and almost half of the Black lesbians had been married at least once. Of those lesbians that married, the Institute found that almost one-half of the white lesbians and about a quarter of the Blacks did not consider themselves homosexual prior to marriage.[6]

Likewise, many lesbians in this study had no awareness of a lesbian preference or even a lesbian potential in themselves until after many years of heterosexual experience. One white woman in her forties who lives in the deep south described her several marriages and late coming out:

I got married at sixteen. This was the one and only guy I ever loved...I found out when I was in labor that he was screwing my best girlfriend. I couldn't handle that, so we split up. Then about nine months later, I met my second husband. We were married fifteen years, I had three children...I was a doormat...I didn't have a life of my own...When I was thirty-three, he left me for a younger woman...I got everything – the kids and all the bills...So when this older man came along that was going to take care of me and my kids, I jumped at the chance. That lasted five years...Toward the end of the five years, I met my first lesbian encounter and it made me realize that I was missing out on a lot and had been all my life.

An African-American woman in her thirties didn't discover her lesbian feelings until graduate school:

My heterosexual history consisted mostly of a search for a man to make me OK. When I was growing up, I wanted a boyfriend like all the other girls...In graduate school, I started to make lesbian friends. I was dating men and still considered myself straight...It was in graduate school that I had my earliest conscious sexual attraction to a woman...

A white lesbian in her forties wrote:

I grew up very heterosexually-identified. I had no inkling that I might be attracted to women until I was nineteen...I had good sex with men, good relationships with men. My marriage of seven years broke up for other reasons...

Another white lesbian, this one in her twenties, told a similar story:

I was seriously involved with one man for seven years. I don't recall having any lesbian fantasies or thoughts when I was straight. But once I went out with a woman, I realized how much I *had* thought about it.

Even after she met her first woman lover, however, she still did not consider herself a lesbian:

We both felt we were "straight" and would stay together until we met the men we would marry...

Other lesbians reported that they were conscious of lesbian attractions and/or a lesbian preference at very young ages; many lesbians' first sexual experiences were with other women. However, the pressures to be heterosexually involved – to have a boyfriend or husband – were often so overwhelming, that some lesbians, for a time, conformed. As one lesbian in her thirties explained:

> My heterosexual contacts did not occur until after my first affair with a woman...My affairs with men were an attempt to be "normal"...

An African-American lesbian described why she got married despite her conscious preference for women:

> When I was thirteen, I had a mad crush on a senior woman. I wrote her poetry and letters and dogged her footsteps like a puppy... Nothing ever happened... They called me a "Lezzy"... it didn't even occur to me to accept that label... After that, I continued to have crushes on women and prefer the company of women, but I was raised a Catholic... I mean, it was not done, darling... I married because it was expected of me. It was pressure from my family... He was the guy next door... and he loved me so that was enough.

Of the 121 lesbians who provided sufficient information to be able to categorize them, 27 or 22% indicated that they had had lesbian relationships and/or identified as a lesbian in their youth, later got married or otherwise pursued heterosexual relationships (sometimes adopting a bisexual lifestyle or identity) and then came out as a lesbian a second time. In other words, these lesbians were at one time lesbians-who-left. The reasons for their leaving, temporary though it was, provide considerable insight into the motivations of the former lesbians, whose lives, after all, are not yet over. Throughout this book, this sub-group of lesbians are referred to as "lesbians-who returned". Their stories are the focus of Chapter VII.

The Kinsey Institute also found that a significant minority of homosexuals – about one-third (and more lesbians than gay men) – had seriously considered leaving. A majority of these – again more women than men – made at least one serious attempt to do so.

Notably, very few of the lesbians-who-returned in my study saw any significant possibility of heterosexual involvement in the future. Six percent of the 121 lesbians (seven women) stated that they engaged in occasional casual heterosex[7]; only 7% (8 women) predicted future heterosexual involvement. The rest, 67% (or 79 of the 121 lesbians) predicted that future heterosexual involvement was highly improbable or precluded[8].

As one lesbian-who-returned explained:

> I suppose I'd consider sexual involvements with men again, if I fell in love with one…but 'tis highly unlikely and I'd sure be wary about what/why was I feeling what I was feeling. I cannot "stop" being a Lesbian, Lord knows I tried. Didn't work – just made me miserable.

A woman over fifty who had been married and has been out for fifteen years described her commitment to a lesbian life:

> I am very pleased to be a lesbian now… I really like women!.. I feel men have value etc. but I don't want them in my personal life. Occasionally, I have a forlorn hope to retire and cruise the world with a husband to have social acceptance and ease of movement, but why would I want an old man?

Ultimately, it is women's passions for themselves and other women that keep them rooted to this place, despite the pull of compulsory heterosexuality. A white lesbian in her forties put it this way:

> When Jill (my first lover) and I were rolling around on the floor the first night, I said, I never knew how much I wanted to be loved by a woman; this is total – more than I ever imagined. This is what I am, where I belong, what feels right and fits.

And an African-American lesbian, who came out after seven years of marriage, exclaimed, "I enjoy being in the company of beautiful Black women".

Footnotes

[1] For purposes of this book, "lesbian" is defined as a female who, at the time the study was conducted, self-identified as lesbian and had no male sexual partners.

[2] This was probably due to the difficulties I had as a white person in locating high numbers of lesbians of color. Because so many of the women in this study are white, in order to avoid repeating the word "white" a dozen times per page, I do not always indicate the race of the white women I quote or refer to. However, I do mention the racial background of all the women of color, and in addition, I have included religious or cultural background information when it appears useful to do so.

[3] Kinsey also found that the incidence of homosexuality in women was positively correlated with education. At thirty years of age, he

found 18% of those with only high school education, 25% of those who had attended college and 33% of women who had attended graduate school had been erotically aroused by other females. (See Alfred C. Kinsey, et al. *Sexual Behavior in the Human Female* (W.B. Saunders Company, 1953) Similarly, JoAnn Loulan's study of 1566 lesbians found that 38% were college graduates and 32% had advanced degrees. (JoAnn Loulan, *Lesbian Passion: Loving Ourselves and Each Other* (Spinsters/Aunt Lute, San Francisco, 1987)

[4] This does not mean that the lesbians were necessarily more financially well-off then heterosexual women; the opposite may even be the case. Most straight women (at least those married to employed males) have the benefit of a man's income as well as their own, while lesbians usually do not. In addition, because lesbians are often estranged from their families of origin, they are less able to rely on them for financial assistance.

[5] The Kinsey Institute likewise found that the lesbians' friends were more apt to be women and that they had more close friendships than did their heterosexual counterparts. See Alan P. Bell and Martin S. Weinberg, *Homosexualities: A Study of Diversity Among Men & Women* (Simon & Schulster, New York, 1978.)

[6] Ibid., pp. 166-167.

[7] Women who had any on-going male sexual partners were excluded from the lesbian group as was any woman who no longer considered herself a lesbian.

[8] If the 27 lesbians-who-returned are removed from this group, 84% of the remaining lesbians expect to remain exclusively lesbian.

IV
PRESSURES TO CONFORM

...due to the nature of my world view, I find I'm not good in narrow spaces...The doors must always be open...I do not live well apart from society. It is more my nature to be inclusive even at great risk and women know all too well how risky it can be to relate to men.

> – Holly Near, explaining her return to male lovers, from her autobiography, *Fire in the Rain; Singer in the Storm* (William Morrow & Company, Inc., New York, 1990), pp. 205-206.

Women's love for other women has been pushed into narrow spaces on the margins of society and smothered in stigma and silence. To be lesbian has been to be cast out from the world, to be condemned, and worse, to be ignored. We, as lesbians, have been removed from the common, ordinary, every day rhythm of life, and become the "queer" ones, the "odd girls out", the "perverts", the unusual, the unnatural, the invisible.

What do we need, as women and as lesbians, to live complete and fulfilling lives?

(1) We need "Family"[1] not in the traditional sense of the isolated heterosexual nuclear family or even a lesbian version of that – but in the sense of an inner circle of love, caring, and intimacy, a circle made up not only of sexual partners and perhaps children but also composed of our families of origin and close friendships that endure. Lesbians need legal and social support and recognition for our partnerships, our parenting (whether we are biological mothers or not) and for all our close relationships equal to that given heterosexuals[2]; we need a culture that celebrates as well as recognizes our love. We need to be free to express affection to other women publicly without fear.

(2) Our economic survival in a patriarchal capitalist society depends, for most of us, on our ability to work, i.e., to obtain paid employment, or else to be in a family with someone who does. Many things have been said by socialist and progressive writers about how work and class relations should be transformed for everyone, ideas that I share; but here I will focus

on some bottom-line survival issues for women in general and lesbians in particular. We need our economic independence - meaning not only a living wage, but a working environment free from harassment and discrimination where we don't have to be secretive about our personal lives; where we don't have to fear losing our jobs because we won't sleep with our male boss or co-workers, or just because we are lesbians.

(3) Despite the large numbers of women presently in the workforce, women's economic dependence on men remains a bulwark of compulsory heterosexuality.[3] As long as men have more access to money than we do and are to one degree or another necessary for our economic survival, or the survival of our children, women will not be completely free to love other women.

(4) We all need the world; none of us do our best in narrow spaces. Lesbians need to be part of the whole, a recognized, valued and fully accepted part, no longer cast out or required to deny the truth of our lives as the "price" of admission. We need community.

Here in the United States, our culture encourages individual competition over group effort – the valuing of money and material success much more than other human beings. We should thus not be surprised at how many people suffer from isolation and loneliness. I think the current appeal of religion (as well as that of xenophobia and patriotic militarism) is primarily explained by this thwarted desire for meaningful connection to other people.

Lesbians have often created family and community support systems among ourselves. But while we are forced to live and love "apart from society" as Holly Near puts it, some among us will find the price too great and leave.

Partners
Because lesbians presently constitute a marginalized, and partially hidden minority of the female population, extra effort (seeking out the lesbian sub-culture) and a good bit of luck is needed to locate compatible women for intimate partnership.

Not surprisingly, then, many former lesbians mentioned difficulties finding a lover as a major factor in their leaving. Slightly more than half (51%) of the lesbians-who-left stated that immediately prior to their change in identity/lifestyle, they had experienced such problems.

And only a slightly lower percentage – 42% – indicated that difficulty in finding a satisfactory long-term woman lover was one of their reasons for turning to male lovers.

One Jewish bisexual former lesbian (in her forties, from the Bay Area) now living with a man, described her frustration and despair in searching for a woman partner:

> All three of the women ended up leaving me...These and other repeated failures (plus my last woman lover dying of cancer last year) brought me to a place of extreme agony. I wanted to kill myself I was so frustrated with the search for intimate partnership. I began to see myself as a martyr to lesbianism...I had no hope...I felt I would either be alone or be with a man.

A considerably smaller number of lesbians-who-left – 16% - complained about difficulty finding women partners for casual sex. Some pointed out that men were more "sexually accessible", while others stated that men were easier to be casual with because there was less emotional involvement on both sides.

One heterosexual former lesbian told me how she had mourned the loss of her woman lover in isolation from sources of lesbian support. Under these circumstances, male attention began to seem attractive:

> Whereas I was used to being ignored by lesbians, men at least paid attention to me as a possible source of sex.

Yet there was often more to a decision to reject one's lesbianism than problems locating compatible partners. Former lesbians as well as lesbians-who-returned repeatedly emphasized that being with men seemed "easier" because, with women, there were no boundaries, no structures, no rules, and few, if any, role models for relationships.

An Anglo-Saxon bisexual from New Mexico told me that she became involved with a man after being "really, really burnt out" in a painful lesbian triangle. She stated that being with a man was "safer" for her . When I asked her why, she explained:

> In the lesbian community, there was a real lack of boundaries and everyone getting involved with everyone else. There was a part of me that wanted things to be really clearly defined.

One Jewish former lesbian from New York described it this way:

> I feel relationships with men are less emotionally demanding, easier, and less painful for me than those with women. There is less hard work, just between the two people, probably because there are well-established norms which can either be followed or not, whereas, with women, you create your own from scratch. Although with women the benefits are tremendous and your life can feel whole and not partitioned, sometimes the "quick fix" [with a man] is just the thing.

Often, lesbians-who-left had found it difficult to imagine their futures as lesbians, because they had no examples of successful relationships between women. Movies, books, television, their families of origin, the entire dominant culture was heterosexual.

A bisexual former lesbian explained her dilemma as follows:

> This has been a very difficult time for me because I feel like a lesbian, love women, and have enjoyed sexual relationships with women. My desire to explore relationships with men came out of my questions/fears about what type of family or future I could look forward to. I am Jewish and have a strong intact nuclear family. I like this and want to "fit it". It is difficult for me to imagine what my life will be like in the future (as a lesbian)...I have no role models of really secure, stable long-term relationships, except heterosexual ones...I'd love it if I could have that with a woman, but I think it's so hard.

She believed lesbian relationships are less stable and long-lasting than relationships with men.

Many other lesbians-who-left agreed. Over a third (34%) gave lack of role models as a reason for leaving and 20% said that relationships with men seemed "easier". Almost a quarter (24%) said that heterosexual relationships seemed more stable and emotionally secure.

Along a similar vein, a heterosexual lesbian-who-left explained why she preferred men as sexual partners, even though her deepest feelings of love had been for other women:

> Men are a whole different category for me...A heterosexual man's role is not to be my friend but my boyfriend...with women they are friends too – there's

no clear distinction...I prefer making love to a man because...I know how things are supposed to go..

Quite a few former lesbians described difficulties being sexual with a woman or sexual problems in their long-term lesbian relationships (lack of desire on one or both sides or infrequent love-making) as a factor in their leaving. (Interestingly, none of the lesbians-who-returned mentioned this difficulty.) Male and heterosexual definitions of what is "sex" and what healthy long-term sexual relationships should entail[4], may have affected these perceptions.

Women have been conditioned by the dominant culture to respond erotically to male sexual aggression. Lesbians may thus find ourselves at a loss if neither partner is more aggressive than the other. As one former lesbian explained:

I think for men and women there are a lot of sexual stereotypes – that there are ways of behaving sexually, like who is going to be more aggressive in the relationship or who is going to want sex more, or who is going to pursue it, whereas between two women, they are kind of waiting around for the other one; you don't have those role models.

This may explain the recent attempts to revive "butch-femme" roles, as well as the popularity of sado-masochism (which sexualizes unequal power and violence) as more culturally familiar ways of feeling sexual.

Another factor that can interfere with sexual intimacy is the compulsion to remain closeted from the outside world. One lesbian-who-left described the strain this placed on her lesbian relationship:

It's like you almost had a split personality – the way you are on the street and the way you are at home. You almost have to create barriers – you don't want people to sense that you're lovers and then have this violence or potential violence inflicted on you. And then you go home and you have to take off your armor to be able to relax. And I think this is very hard to do.

The lack of lesbian images in the popular culture is felt most strongly when we experience problems with our lovers. We can rarely turn to our parents, our co-workers, or the larger community at those times. Thus, many lesbians leave after such personal crises: close to half – 46% – of the former lesbians in this study experienced painful break-ups of lesbian love relationships immediately prior to a turn to male lovers. Because there is no outside validation for our relationships and heterosexuality is so strongly encouraged, we may "give up" on women when an individual woman betrays or disappoints us or simply blame the problems on lesbianism.

One Portuguese lesbian-who-returned told me why she tried to be heterosexual after her first lesbian relationship broke up:

> When Louise and I broke up, I thought well maybe with a man you get married and you get to have kids, and you may be unhappy, but at least it's lasting.

All told, the lack of visible role models, the denial of recognition for lesbian relationships, and the stigma against public displays of affection, can add up to a tremendous pressure to leave a lesbian life. As one former lesbian from the Bay Area who eventually succumbed to that pressure explained:

> Somehow my fortieth birthday, my sister getting pregnant and my mom being surprisingly pleased by that, working with kids and families in a real straight work environment with people who seem happy in heterosexual relationships and seeing very few happy lesbian relationships have added together to make being straight appealing…It seems attractive now to have a regular settled heterosexual relationship like everyone else.

I asked a number of the women that I interviewed – both lesbians and former lesbians – a question: If they could imagine living in a world which was at least 50% gay and lesbian; where it was totally normal and acceptable to be a lesbian; where there were role models for lesbian relationships all over the mass media; where lesbian partnerships were given full and equal recognition with heterosexual ones, did they think their sexual choices would have been any different? Some stated that it wouldn't have mattered, but many others conceded that their choices might very well have been different. Here are some of the responses I received:

> (*from a Jewish former lesbian in her forties, now heterosexual*) I guess it would have helped. I mean right now what do you have? Gertrude Stein and Alice Toklas?

I don't consider that some ideal lesbian relationship... For example, television shows about real life experiences would make a lot of difference; not just educating heterosexual people but pushing gay people to feel good about themselves.

(*from a Jewish former lesbian in her thirties unsure of her identity*) You're saying that being with men would no longer be easier...Those would be really good, wonderful things in the world and my choices would probably be the same. I can't say that I would definitely be a lesbian...I don't know. I probably would.

(*from a bisexual woman in her forties, also Jewish*) Oh yeah. For sure. It's much more likely that I could slip into a partnership with a woman with all that backing. For sure...

(*from an Anglo-Saxon lesbian over fifty who came out after three marriages*) I think I would have followed my natural inclination as a young girl of eight or nine when I had so much fun sexually playing with other girls and just didn't like it with the guys at all. I think I would have continued with the girls and been a lesbian my whole life. Oh, yeah, my life would have been a lot different, a lot happier.

Families of Origin

"In the final analysis, parents do matter", wrote Ann Muller in her important study, *Parents Matter – Parents' Relationships with Lesbian Daughters and Gay Sons*. "Lesbian daughters, as women outside the social and financial security available to heterosexual women, need the recognition and approval of their parents..."[6]

Muller's study found that few parents of lesbian daughters – only 5% of the 58 families she studied – accepted their daughters' lesbianism, and that the rate of such acceptance was less than one-third that of parents toward their gay sons. In addition, Muller discovered that only 46% of the parent-daughter relationships were generally positive, as compared to 72% for gay men and their parents. Muller postulates that this greater negativity is because a lesbian is going against the primary social expectation placed on women – that they be wives and mothers.

Though men, too, are expected to be heterosexual, the most important expectation of the "masculine" role is that a man achieve success in the work world, something a gay man can still do[7].

Experiences of parental rejection were also extremely common among the women I studied. Such rejection (and, to a lesser extent, rejection by siblings, grandparents, and other blood relatives) had had a particularly devastating effect on the lesbians-who-left. Not only did the former lesbians report a significantly lower rate of (at least partial) acceptance by their parents than the lesbians (60.4% of the former lesbians compared to 77.6% of the lesbians) but, in addition, close to three-quarters of the lesbians-who-left (74% compared to 40.9% of the lesbians-who-returned) described a lack of acceptance from family members immediately prior to leaving. And 24% of the former lesbians (as well as 31.8% of the lesbians-who-returned) stated that a desire to win approval from family members was one of the reasons they had left a lesbian life.

Negative parental responses ranged from bitter condemnation to denial and everything in between. One Jewish bisexual from Connecticut experienced extreme hostility from her stepfather and avoidance from her mother when she announced her lesbianism:

> When I came out as a lesbian at nineteen to my stepfather, he made his feelings known to me very clearly – I was a freak, I was an animal, I was not a human being...Once, he hit me...When I came out to my mother, she started crying...She said maybe there's a part of me that always assumed you would fall in love with a man, get married, and have kids...I think deep down she felt it was a phase.

Several women reported being asked to leave the house as teenagers. A Latina bisexual in her twenties from Colorado described what had happened:

> When I came out as a lesbian at eighteen, I got no support from my family. They said I disgraced them and I was told to leave.

A similar experience led one lesbian-who-returned to consider suicide:

> When my parents suspected what was happening, I was

kicked out of the house. I still had three weeks of my Junior year of High School to finish...I moved in with one of my friends and her family for the remainder of the year...My mother and I were (and now are) very close...I had always been her perfect child...I felt I had let her down. It was terrible and I became suicidal.

An Italian-Catholic bisexual (in her twenties from New York) was mocked by her father:

My father makes no bones about it – he refers to me as "the man-hater".

Her mother's response was not much better. She simply refused to talk about it:

My mother's reaction to my coming out [as a lesbian] was that she doesn't think it's right...After that, it was not something we discussed.

I asked this same woman if it bothered her that her parents disapproved of her lesbianism. She responded:

It made me feel like a non-person.

Even though many parents did not completely withdraw their love, they would often hope for their daughters' eventual heterosexuality. As one lesbian in her twenties from the Bay Area described it:

My family was basically horrified...My mother repeatedly reminds me that she loves me, but I know she's constantly hoping I'll change. We fight and yell and cry...I could write a forty page or more essay on the topic of guilt alone.

Notably, this woman was one of a minority of the lesbians in this study who considered future heterosexual relationships a significant possibility.

Lack of full acceptance often meant that lovers were not welcome in the family home. Leslie, the married lesbian, described to me what happened when her mother visited unexpectedly:

I was in bed with somebody...My mother was blown away; this was my Boston bus driver who is six feet tall and into leather...Then I remember my mother asked what was going on. I said don't worry about it, it was just a fling. My mother said, you're not bringing her home.

Of course, such coercion can sometimes make sure that relationships between women remain just that, "flings".

For example, a lesbian-who-left, a woman who still considers herself a lesbian despite her present marriage to a man, tried unsuccessfully to talk to her mother about her lesbian feelings while still in college. Her mother's response was disheartening:

> She pretty much acted as if I was talking about the
> weather and nothing really happened.

So why didn't she press the point?

> If I pushed for them [her parents] to see what I was
> about and what was going on with me, I was afraid that
> it would be ugly.

A parent's quiet suffering over a daughter's lesbianism could also be devastating. A heterosexual-identified former lesbian living in Vancouver wrote:

> Eventually I told my family...They took it really well
> and never said a word (a bad word) about it for ten
> years...But I do know that after I left the state, my
> mother had a really bad time...My family was also the
> target of gossip and ridicule from people in their small
> mid-west town. I regret so much that they were hurt.

Clearly, a parent's concern with what other people might think can make it harder to accept a lesbian daughter. This was a factor in the case of a thirty year old Latina lesbian from Chicago who wrote:

> My father really gets perturbed when his friends ask
> him, "Why does your daughter wear short hair, she'd
> look better in long-hair".

Rejection by siblings can also be extremely painful. This same Latina lesbian also had problems with her brother:

> My brother is aware, but he always has negative things
> to say...He once said to me, "When I have kids, I won't
> let them come around you because you'll turn them gay
> like you".

Whether familial rejection affects the behavior of lesbian daughters depends not only on the severity of the response but also on how close the family is, both emotionally and geographically. For example, I interviewed a heterosexual-identified former lesbian in her forties who comes from an extremely traditional and close-knit Sephardic Jewish family;

both parents are immigrants from the island of Rhodes off the Greek mainland[8]. Like quite a few other women I studied (28.6% of the former lesbians and 25.9% of the lesbians), she had never come out to her parents. Though highly concerned about parental approval, she was able to manage living a lesbian life secret from her parents as long as she lived in a distant city. When she moved to the same southeastern city where her parents lived, it was a different story:

> I was around my family, I was more in the Jewish community...My younger brother was getting married and the hoopla over that was just phenomenal – I mean the whole town was involved – a reception party with 1,000 people...My Dad has said to my sister, if you get married, I'll give you the house that we live in...As a single person, that option is not there...It is definitely easier to be closer to my family as a heterosexual...

Similarly, a lesbian-who-left (in her forties, from Atlanta) waited until she had moved to Europe before attempting to explore her lesbianism. And another former lesbian did not come out to her family until she had joined the Peace Corps. When I asked her why, she explained:

> That's 10,000 miles away and that's pretty safe...It was far from my family and I could write to people who I was close to and agonize a long time over what to say...I didn't have to deal with anyone face to face.

Eventually, this woman came home and married a man.

For many other former lesbians, the pressure to conform to family expectations became overwhelming. One Jewish bisexual described how important it was for her to please her grandmother:

> Because I am the oldest, because I am the absolute hands-down favorite grandchild and the daughter of my dead father...the fact that I would be queer and not producing – would cause family craziness. And if I had a child without a man and being married it would be holy hell[9].

Another Jewish lesbian-who-left found it difficult to imagine her future as a lesbian:

> I find it difficult to envision myself being settled and happy and fitting into my nuclear family in that type of

relationship [lesbian]. I want to fit into my nuclear family – my parents, brothers, sisters, their partners, spouses, their kids – that whole thing…I want to feel part of that.

One woman who has identified as a lesbian on and off for more than a decade, and is now unsure of her identity, had been through six marriages in response to family pressures:

My mother repeatedly said to me, "It would kill your father if he knew…" When my father died, it was the final blow…I left my lover though not before my mother disowned me…Married my first husband…as an attempt to regain acceptance from my mother – lasted less than a year. Marriages #2,3,4, and 5 all lasted less than a year. Marriage #6 lasted five years…I was having to drink more and more to be able to tolerate sharing space with him.

Other lesbians, were able to escape their parents' control. An African American lesbian in her forties who came out at age twenty-eight after two marriages, described this struggle to establish her independence:

It took me until my late twenties to get out from under the influence of my parents. I was very conformist – I definitely wanted to please my parents and they are definitely pro-heterosexual. I don't think more inform-ation or role models would have helped me…I needed her (mother's) support and approval desperately – that is what I think retarded my coming out as a lesbian.

But for some women, it took the death of their parents before they were free to come out or to come out a second time.

For those concerned about winning the approval of homo-phobic parents, it was easier by far to be bisexual than to be a lesbian. This was both because of the greater acceptability of bisexuality (a bisexual could still fulfill the feminine role by dating men, marrying, and having children) and because it was easier for a bisexual to remain closeted. One Jewish hetero-sexual who had identified as a lesbian on and off for over fifteen years (though she had dated men or been married for most of this time) described the advantages of bisexuality:

As a teenager, I dated alternately men and women…I was really looking for female friends that you could be bi with. That would be real convenient…I'd get my mother off my back if I was appearing to date men.

Most parents were "thrilled" and "relieved" at the prospect of their lesbian daughters becoming bisexual. Wrote one bisexual lesbian-who-left:

> As far as the transition (to bisexual) my parents are relieved because they think I'm over my fifteen year "phase" of lesbianism and will be normal again.

Another woman wrote:

> My family is thrilled at the possibility of my being bisexual – they want me to find the right person and hope it's a man.

Another bisexual lesbian-who-left (from an Italian Catholic background) found it easier to tell her parents she was "bisexual", even though she expected to be involved exclusively with other women:

> I put it that way because, there was a part of me that wasn't totally sure and I just couldn't say the word "lesbian".

Did she think it would be more acceptable to her mother if she used the word "bisexual"?

> Of course...I softened it, definitely.

Almost universally, the turn toward male lovers was greeted by parents and other family members with unbridled enthusiasm. One former lesbian from Ontario, Canada wrote:

> At first family, friends and co-workers were puzzled at the change. How can my primary relationship be with a woman and yet I flirt with men, can conceive of and achieve relationships, even sexual relationships with them? But it also seemed to make them more comfortable. Perhaps I was normal after all.

Another lesbian-who-left described the support she received when with a man:

> Certainly, it's easier to take him to family gatherings, where myself and my woman lover always stood out as being "different"...My grandmother...never one to hold her tongue, always let me know that she wished I would meet a man and settle down, even when she was being polite to my woman lover...Now she is thrilled...she hears wedding bells and is glad I'm out from under the influence of my ex-lover.

A lesbian-identified former lesbian told me how pleased her mother was about her marriage:

> Today, my mother is ecstatic about the outward appearance of my life.

Children

"Being a mother in this society is in fact no more a free choice than being a heterosexual", wrote Nancy D. Polikoff in her essay, "Lesbians Choosing Children: The Personal is Political Revisited".[10] "The cultural pressure is enormous, the propaganda overwhelming. Women who never have children are considered empty, barren, selfish, peculiar...As the biological clock ticks, women without children are told they will be sorry, sorry, sorry."[11]

Polikoff observed:

> "My own introspection has forced me to recognize that I wanted a child in part because I wanted to be 'normal', because I wanted to have more in common with other women, and because I didn't want a life that seemed so clearly on the fringe of society".[11]

Yet at the same time, society is far from neutral on how motherhood is to be carried out. Proper mothers are expected to have husbands. And, until very recently, a lesbian mother was an unthinkable concept.

Now that lesbian motherhood has become more possible, anti-lesbian bigotry has become considerably more rabid when we propose to be involved in the care, raising, and/or teaching of children.[12] Despite studies that have been done to assure homophobic Judges and others that children of lesbians are as likely to turn out heterosexual as the children of heterosexual parents, many defenders of compulsory heterosexuality are not entirely convinced.[13] And neither am I.

While certainly no lesbian-feminist parenting can completely counteract the influence of the dominant culture, what of the impact on a little girl raised by a woman like the late Pat Parker, an "out" and proud African American lesbian feminist poet and activist who wrote, "One major difference in Anastasia's life is that she is not being raised 'heterosexual'"?[14] Is it not possible that such a child may be somewhat freer to follow her heart even if it leads her to other women?

Not surprisingly, then, pressures to conform to increase for women who have or wish to have children. Almost a quarter (22%) of the former lesbians I studied indicated that they began thinking about having children immediately prior to their move toward male lovers. And 16% of the lesbians-who-left (as well as 22.7% of the lesbians-who-returned) stated that at least one of the reasons for their leaving was that they wished to have or raise children in a heterosexual family.

One Jewish former lesbian in her thirties with a dual identity, described how these concerns drew her toward heterosexual relationships:

> I want to have children and have a hard time imagining bearing children outside a traditional heterosexual relationship. When I thought of having children as part of a lesbian couple, it scared me because I wasn't sure how I would go about it; how would it work; who would have the children; what the relationship of the other person would be; the legal implications; what would people think on the outside; how would I talk about it to my parents and siblings; all of those sorts of things made me think, oh my god, could I ever do this...As I was getting closer to my thirtieth birthday, I realized that these questions weren't going to disappear and it was time for me to explore alternatives. I had never had a sexual relationship with a man and I didn't know whether it could be satisfying for me sexually and/or emotionally. So I decided to explore relationships with men...

Another lesbian-who-left, this one heterosexual-identified, wrote that after failing to convince a woman partner to parent with her, she decided to pursue men:

> I made the choice to return to men because I felt the goal of sharing children would be realized more quickly.

An Asian-American bisexual explained her heterosexual interest in a similar fashion:

> I would like to be in a permanent relationship with someone and as I want to have children, question whether I should be with a woman.

A number of lesbians reported that they knew several former lesbians who had left in order to have children. As one African-

American lesbian from Connecticut explained:

> They wanted children; not necessarily the MEN involved
> in making this a reality, but the LOVE a child gives more
> unconditionally than any mate.

Yet there was little difference between lesbians and former lesbians with regard to having children. Approximately 36% of both groups planned to give birth, adopt and/or co-parent children in the future. And the lesbians were only slightly more likely to already have children (27.9% of the lesbians as compared to 23.4% of the lesbians-who-left.) This small difference may be explained by the fact that more of the lesbians were over fifty and thus unable, or unlikely, to give birth. It also appears that the overwhelming majority of both groups of mothers had had their children in the context of heterosexual relationships.

In fact, having children often delayed a women's coming out process. Most commonly, lesbians stayed married in order to avoid the economic hardship and stigma of single motherhood, and what they felt were the uncertainties of a lesbian life. In addition, many had internalized the prejudices of society, and were concerned about the effects of their lesbianism on their children.

One lesbian mother (over fifty from Tucson, Arizona) explained why she decided to stay in her marriage for five years after first identifying as a lesbian:

> I made a decision to stay in the heterosexual marriage
> because I didn't want the responsibility of raising my
> children alone and I didn't want them to live with their
> father alone. It seemed I could bide my time until they
> were grown.

She also felt that a straight relationship would provide a more "stable" family environment and be "easier" on the children.

Interestingly, former lesbians were more likely to hold such prejudices against lesbian motherhood than were the lesbians. In response to the statement, "It is a lot easier on children to be raised in a heterosexual family than in a lesbian one", 72.8% of the lesbians chose false compared to only 60.9% of the lesbians-who-left.

The pressure on mothers to marry was often overwhelming. One lesbian in her fifties from the Bay Area reported that she had married three times and had four children before coming

out. She got married the first time, she told me, because single
motherhood was socially unacceptable:

I really did have a true desire to have children. I was a
very good mother...And, of course, to have babies I had
to get married...I got pregnant when I was nineteen...I
had to leave my home town of 21,000. You didn't stay
in a town that small when you were pregnant. It brought
shame on your family and you had to leave. That was
the atmosphere in the early 50's.

I went to a different state and I met this man where I
was working. I told him that I was pregnant. He married
me simply to give my baby a name. I never even stayed
one night with him. With that marriage "diploma", I was
able to go back to my home town.

Her second marriage, was motivated by her need for economic
support:

My twins and I were living with my sister and her
husband and they had wanted me to move out as soon
as possible...So I had to find another place to live. And
though I was working as a secretary, I could not have
afforded a place on my own...When he first asked me
to marry him, I said "get out of here". I wasn't even
considering it. But then the more I thought of it and the
more the pressure built up, the more of an answer it
seemed to be.

She also hesitated to embrace a lesbian life because she didn't
want to cause her children hardship:

I had put my children through a lot of hell during my
bad years when I was sleeping around and smoking a
lot of pot. Then I had settled down and become more
stable and a good mother again. I didn't want to ask
them to accept anything else.

Sometimes, it was fear of losing custody of her children that
would keep a lesbian in her marriage, at least for a while. One
heterosexual lesbian-who-left reconciled with her first husband
after he threatened to take her children away. I asked her why
she had gotten back together with him. She replied:

In the 60's, father was God. All you had to say was my
wife is having a relationship with a known lesbian –
BINGO – take those kids – that's it...Later, he was

incarcerated, and I was able to divorce him.

Lesbians who made the decision to leave their husbands were often dragged into bitter custody battles and either lost their children or endured restrictions on their personal lives (such as not being allowed to have their partner in the house when the children were present) – restrictions that no heterosexual couple would tolerate.

Such experiences were extremely commonplace in the women I studied. Of those women who were mothers, 38.7% of the lesbians and 30% of the lesbians-who-left had been threatened with, or experienced a loss of, custody because of their lesbianism.[15]

Sometimes, in addition to threatening a legal battle for custody, a father would try to turn the child against the mother. One bisexual in her thirties, now living in Canada, wrote:

> My estranged spouse threatened a custody fight because of what he thought was (but wasn't) a sexual relationship between me and a female friend. Then he told my son that two women sleeping together was "wrong". My son eventually decided to go live with his Dad.

Other women voluntarily relinquished custody because they felt guilty about their lesbianism. Wrote a lesbian over fifty from the Northern California area:

> I did not fight for custody of my children. I felt guilty for breaking my marriage vows with a woman and gave in to my husband's demands.

A former lesbian explained how she decided to enter what she termed a "relationship of convenience":

> I went through initial adoption proceedings with the County when I was still in law school. At the time, I was living with five other lesbians in a real stable lesbian household and had a couple of preliminary interviews. And it didn't work – I kept getting rejected. The given reason was my economic situation wasn't strong enough. But that didn't hold up with other determinations that the same county board was making...I felt I was being discriminated against as a lesbian.

Soon afterwards, she entered a relationship with a man and they had a child together. She told me it was a lot easier this way:

> We just look like this straight family and people can handle that.

I asked if falling in love with a man or heterosexual attraction played any role – even 1% – in her decision to marry. She said "no" and laughed. She still identifies as a lesbian.

Frequently, children of lesbians had a difficult time accepting their mothers' lesbianism. A large part of that difficulty was abuse from their peers. One lesbian in her thirties from Missouri described her experience:

> By the time I came out, I only had custody of my daughter. She was young enough that she had really grown up with me being gay. At times this was very difficult for her. We lived in one neighborhood where she would be beaten up going to school every day because her mother was "queer". We moved out of that neighborhood.

Sometimes the children themselves discriminated against their mothers. Wrote a lesbian mother in her forties from Alabama:

> At the time of my divorce, my children were "brainwashed" to live with their daddy because I was living with a "woman". Now my children will not see me at my home because that "woman" is there...They don't want to accept my lover as a person.

A former lesbian told me that both her son and her daughter were very unaccepting of her lesbianism, but for her daughter, the issue came closer to home:

> She said, "Just because I'm sleeping with my girlfriend doesn't mean you can sleep with your girlfriend". She said", I don't want you to be a lesbian...didn't you read it's normal for teenage girls to have sex with their friends? We're just fooling around..." My daughter got married with her best friend holding her hand...And that was the end of her intimate relationship with her friend.

For some lesbians-who-left, becoming heterosexually involved was a way of winning acceptance from their children. As a former lesbian in her thirties from Northern California explained:

> My daughter is now schoolage and likes me to date men. She feels less threatened (they don't consume my attention), is nicer to them than she was to my

girlfriends, likes to tease me and talk about boys in a coy, giddy manner. She definitely likes this.

Despite all the pressure to have children with men, a growing number of women, including several in my study, have children as lesbians. I had the opportunity to interview a lesbian-who-returned in her thirties who, along with her lesbian partner, is co-parenting two children. She told me that after coming out as a lesbian, she became bisexual for a time largely because she wanted children:

> I thought for a long time that the only way I would have kids was to be in a relationship and to be in a relationship meant being in a heterosexual relationship.
>
> …And then about seven years ago it dawned on me that I don't have to be with a man or be alone, that I could have kids and be with women and be a lesbian.

Once she made that realization, she got involved with a like-minded woman and embraced a lesbian identity again. I asked her if she had any fears about having children in a lesbian relationship. She answered:

> Not exactly fears because my experience has been so positive so far…I think I have some concern about what it'll be like for these kids to grow up and have two Moms…I trust so deeply that we're great parents for these kids…My fear is more how they are going to handle what comes at them.

I asked her if there are any advantages to having and raising children in a lesbian couple. She replied:

> To be able to have the relationship that nurtures me and be a lesbian is the best in the world – to not feel like I had to be with men just to have kids. Another advantage is that I've been able to do some wonderful education along the way – both through panels we've been on and talks we've given and just by our example…The growth I've seen on my mother's part has been phenomenal…Our commitment to raising children is definitely equal. I feel very lucky to be in a relationship that's working and that these kids are thriving in…I had given birth, so I could go into it with my lover from a very different standpoint than with a man who does not know what the experience is. And that felt precious…

Work

Lesbians at work are in double jeopardy: as women, they are usually segregated into the lowest paying, lowest status jobs and are expected to exhibit "feminine" deferential behavior. Often this includes being (or at least appearing to be) sexually accessible to men as well as refraining from challenging their authority. Though such subtle and not so subtle sexual harassment and sex role stereotyping can be devastating to any woman, it is perhaps even more so for lesbians. In order to fit in at work, in order to keep their jobs, lesbians must live a double life, must pretend to be who they are not. To fail to comply with heterosexual expectations, to refuse to play the role expected of them at work, is to risk being ostracized by co-workers and supervisors and being denied the possibility of promotion, or simply fired.

The few researchers who have examined the extent of anti-lesbian discrimination in the workplace have found it to be both significant and widespread. In a 1984 study, "Discrimination against Lesbians in the Workplace", the two authors, Martin B. Levine and Robin Leonard, conducted a computer analysis of their own research (involving 203 lesbians from New York City)[16] alongside three previous studies on this subject. They found that 31% of the lesbians surveyed anticipated employment discrimination because of their lesbianism; 13% reported having experienced such discrimination; and 8% had lost, or almost lost, their jobs for this reason. The authors also discussed "coping strategies" for lesbian survival in the workplace – the most common of which was staying closeted. They discovered that 72% of the lesbians in these studies remained at least partially closeted at work, with 28% reporting that they were completely closeted. Other coping strategies to avoid discrimination were self-employment and "job tracking", i.e., seeking jobs in fields which tolerated lesbianism, or in feminist, lesbian or gay organizations.

The great majority of lesbians – almost two-thirds in Levine and Leonard's study – found staying in the closet at work psychologically stressful and dissatisfactory. Of those who reported being "pleased" with their decision to remain closeted, most (59%) stated they could thereby avoid job discrimination.

The studies reviewed involved lesbians from large urban

113

areas; the situation is probably worse for lesbians who live in smaller cities or in suburban or rural parts of the country and worse still for those in military jobs. The General Accounting Office has reported that 1500 gays and lesbians are discharged from the military, with women more requently targeted than men for investigation. Many women in the military, both straight and gay, find it difficult to resist male sexual demands because they are vulnerable to accusations of homosexuality. Lesbians in government positions have known that their sexuality was considered a "security risk" and subjected them to automatic dismissal if their sexual preference was discovered.[17] The irrationality of this policy is readily apparent, in that many such lesbians are in the closet solely at work, and only the government's discriminatory policies make blackmail possible.[18]

The participants in my study, who are spread out through much of the United States, reported somewhat higher rates of discrimination than in the Levine and Leonard research. A full 17.4% of the lesbians and 11.4% of the lesbians-who-left had been dismissed, threatened with termination or denied a promotion because of their lesbianism. Harassment on the job was even more commonplace: almost half – 49.6% – of the lesbians, and 37% of the former lesbians reported at least occasional anti-lesbian harassment at work.

These statistics seem to indicate that the lesbians suffered more discrimination than the lesbians-who-left. However, given both the fact that more lesbians than former lesbians stated that they were usually out at work (57.3% compared to 50% of the former lesbians) and that the lesbians-who-left had significantly shorter periods of lesbian identity than the lesbians, it is possible to conclude that the lesbians-who-left actually had higher rates of discrimination per year of lesbianism. A smaller percentage of former lesbians than lesbians were usually accepted at work (77.5% of the former lesbians compared to 88.4% of the lesbians).

Exactly one-fifth – 20% of the former lesbians (and 9.1% of the lesbians-who-returned) stated that a desire to "fit in" at work and/or to avoid job discrimination was at least one of the reasons that they turned toward male partners. And identical percentages reported experiencing workplace discrimination immediately prior to leaving a lesbian life.

Typical are the experiences of a Jewish bisexual former lesbian in her twenties:

I was a temporary secretary and an employer that I was temping for found out that I was a lesbian by going through some of my mail that was in my knapsack at work...The employer refused to pay my agency's fee and so my agency was going to withhold my salary because I was a lesbian...I had to hire a private lawyer in a progressive labor law firm and we finally got a contractual settlement... It ended up costing me $2,000 out of my own pocket...It really showed me how deep homophobia was...

She found little support from a depoliticized lesbian community:

The lesbian community at that time was not politically astute enough to know how to deal with it...there was a real shying away from activist behavior...I felt disgusted and very discouraged – I ended up writing all the articles about my case. No one wanted to start a fund for me. They were oblivious.

A year after this incident, she changed her identity to bisexual, even though at the time of the interview three years later, she had yet to have sexual relations with a man.[19]

Similarly, another lesbian-who-left, also Jewish, told me that she was not hired by Hillel (a Jewish student organization) in her home city because the director thought she was a lesbian. Three years later, she began dating men.

A bisexual from a small town in the midwest wrote, "I lost my job as a carpenter because of homophobia". Subsequently, she too, ceased identifying as a lesbian.

Likewise, a heterosexual from Vancouver described being fired from "the job of my dreams" as the "final straw" in her decision to leave a lesbian life.

Sometimes, rather than leave, a lesbian was able to make adjustments in her career to accommodate her lesbianism. One lesbian-who-returned reported that after being fired from a job with the federal government for being a lesbian, she made sure she worked where there was legal protection. She wrote:

I now work for the city of Philadelphia which has a protection clause for city workers. I cannot be fired on the basis of sexual orientation.

Many lesbians absorbed an appalling amount of abuse at work, yet still refused to conform to heterosexual expectations. However, such experiences add a great deal of stress to a lesbian's life.

A Latina lesbian from Chicago described her work situation:

> At work, I always am harassed. At one time a co-worker would ask me to go to bed with him and he'd "talk dirty" to me. I reported him to administration and I later found out that he only wanted to find out if I was a lesbian with a "tight cunt"...I feel uncomfortable being on the defensive all the time...

All too often, in order to avoid harassment and possible job loss, lesbians had to either remain extremely secretive, or to stop being a lesbian.

One lesbian in her forties from Phoenix, Arizona who considers future heterosexual involvement a possibility, wrote:

> A male supervisor at work threatened to "rape me straight". I went to personnel and they said it "wasn't any of their business" and we should settle our differences between ourselves. I quit. Since then, I've been in the closet at work.

Another lesbian, a woman in her twenties from the Bay Area, who also considers future heterosexual involvements possible, described how she had to hide her lesbian relationship at work.

> When I fell in love, I had to make up a fictional man to tell my boss and co-workers because they could all tell how happy I was and wanted to know all about it.

Remarkably, some women managed to remain closeted under oppressive conditions, yet stayed lesbians. A lesbian from the mid-west who has a government job requiring a security clearance described the level of fear that she lived with:

> At work, you can't do your job as well. Instead of communicating directly, there is always a screen and you have to be careful that it might come out on the other side incorrectly filtered...And you have to be careful how you react to the queer jokes your co-workers make, so they don't suspect anything...Even at home, you can't hug in front of open windows because the FBI could be asking neighbors questions at any time.

She told me that she wouldn't even go into a women's

bookstore in her hometown because of the possibility of discovery. She otherwise loves her work; it is a "trade-off" that she "puts up with". However, she remained committed to her lesbianism. "I would rather be alone than be with a man", she said.

Others proved less resilient. For almost one-quarter – 22% – of the lesbians-who-left, a move from a college campus or movement-type job (where lesbians are accepted) to the straight work world precipitated their change in lifestyle. One Italian bisexual-identified former lesbian from New York described the situation:

> I had to learn to reassimilate into the straight work world...The woman I was with, she liked to walk into a room and have people know she was a Dyke. She liked that – being picked out as one. In college, that was kind of fun because then you had your support group right there. But when I got into the professional world, I didn't want that...I made the decision that I wanted my career.

In her first job after college, she wore the "hose and heels" required of women professionals and stayed totally closeted. She reported feeling extremely isolated as a lesbian:

> It seemed easier to find men to go out with – to date....There weren't many other gay people, especially gay women...It was like either you were going to do nothing or you were going to go out with straight people.

She also was concerned that her female co-workers could not "handle the information" that she was a lesbian and might make it impossible for her to function at work.

It didn't take long for her to become convinced that staying closeted wasn't enough; that ultimately, she would have to choose between her lesbianism and her career. For a while, her lesbianism was sacrificed: she broke up with her woman lover and began dating a man she met at the office. However, by the time of the interview one and one-half years later, she was at a new job that provided a slightly less oppressive environment. Though she was still, of course, required to dress "straight" at work, she could be more open about her sexuality. In addition, she had already split up with her boyfriend. Her attitude, too, had begun to change again; she no longer believed that her lesbianism and her career were necessarily incompatible. Thus, she was now quite emphatic about her preference for women and referred to her bisexuality (a label which she still embraced) as a "phase". She was clearly in the process of returning to a lesbian life.

As bad as many corporate and white collar jobs can be, work in non-traditional mostly male fields often puts even more pressure on women to be heterosexual. Lesbians, if they wish to survive in such positions and win even a modicum of acceptance, have to not only increase their tolerance for large groups of (usually) hostile sexist and homophobic men but also tone down their feminist politics. In addition, "getting along" in such a work environment often means becoming heterosexually available. Sometimes, all these changes can amount to one and the same thing.

I interviewed a Portuguese-American bisexual from the Boston area who works in electronics. The overwhelming majority of her co-workers are male. Prior to entering this field, she had worked for progressive organizations where it was easy to be a radical lesbian-feminist. When she took her lesbian politics and identity with her to her first electronics job, the men she worked with were antagonistic:

> I was definitely harassed...I was one of few women doing the work that I did and I was being very outspoken as a feminist – and that made a lot of the men really uncomfortable so they made my life very difficult...

An attempt to accommodate the men at work coincided with her move toward bisexuality:

> I felt I had to learn how to work with men, be with men, and know how to deal with them forty hours per week...how to have positive relationships if I was going to do my job well...As a result, there are men who are my friends, there are men who I trust, there are men who I'm interested in being sexual with...I think there was a definite shift in attitude and politics from myself as a lesbian and myself as a bisexual...My tolerance for men is definitely greater...As a bisexual I don't think I'm less of a feminist but I feel I'm less of a radical

feminist...After my first job where I was harassed for being outspoken, I felt I needed to tone it down if I was to survive in this field.

She acknowledged that if she had the option to pursue her chosen field in a female work environment, her sexual choices might have been different:

I chose to put myself in that position [working with men]. I wanted to earn a certain amount of money and wanted to do this particular kind of work and there aren't a lot of women there and that's how the situation is. I think if I chose to work at a job where we were women together as a women-owned business and I came only in contact with women, I wouldn't miss men...I'd feel a lot more free and more comfortable.

Would she miss men sexually in that situation? "I don't know", she answered. "Probably not".

An Anglo-Saxon former lesbian from Colorado in her forties who now identifies as heterosexual told a similar story. While still a lesbian, she worked in a feminist bookstore and also in a daycare center where most of the employees were lesbians. She then took a job working as a photographer for the geological survey. She found this new work environment exceedingly stressful:

I never knew who I should come out to and completely separate from my lesbianism, it was just stressful as a woman being around large groups of men...I always felt not OK somehow, the fact that I was also a lesbian probably intensified that feeling, but even my lesbianism aside, I just felt uncomfortable as a woman being around so many men.

Soon, she, too, began dating men.

Money

A desire for the financial benefits associated with heterosexuality was mentioned as a reason for a turn toward male lovers by 14% of the lesbians-who-left (seven women), as well as by 9% of the lesbians-who-returned. In addition, 20% of the former lesbians (and 4.5% of the lesbians-who-returned) reported economic distress and/or job dissatisfaction immediately prior to their change in identity.

However, it is unclear whether the former lesbians had in fact experienced more economic distress than did the lesbians. As indicated earlier, the present gross incomes of the lesbians and former lesbians are virtually identical, both groups enjoying, on average, greater incomes than the typical American woman. At the same time, the lesbians-who-left were somewhat more likely to have worked as prostitutes (20.3% compared to 12.4% of the lesbians) and to have worked as models in the sex industry (14% of the former lesbians compared to 4.8% of the lesbians). This may be because the lesbians-who-left had experienced more severe economic hardship than the lesbians, forcing them into prostitution, or it may be that working as a prostitute simply reinforced beliefs that heterosexuality is essential for a woman's survival. Or perhaps both propositions are true. In any case, many women in both groups reported being pulled toward sexual involvements with men because they needed money to pay their bills or to support their children.

One lesbian in her forties from Alabama explained why she married again after her divorce:

> When I was thirty three, my husband decided that I was too old for him and left me for a younger woman. I got the house; the $500 per month mortgage payments; I got the car; I got the kids; I got all the bills. I was making about $150 per week managing a service station. So when this older man came along that was going to take care of me and my kids, I jumped at the chance.

It was not uncommon for heterosexual dating to also include an element of prostitution. A lesbian over fifty from the Bay Area told the following story:

> One time I couldn't pay the rent. This man never said I'll pay the rent if you go to bed with me. He just said, "I'll pay your rent; let's go out to dinner". A man pays your rent and you're obligated. I was obligated and I did not enjoy it. And I did that a dozen times with that same man.

A heterosexual former lesbian in her forties explained that one of her marriages was "strictly for security" and that later, when she was supporting her three children on her own, she would sleep with men for money, "to pay the gas bill so they wouldn't shut off the heat".

Similarly, a bisexual lesbian-who-left said that right after she ceased identifying as a lesbian, she had problems paying for necessities so she slept with men "who gave me money for things".

Another bisexual also indicated that she considered heterosexuality necessary for her own economic survival:

> I decided to learn how to fuck men in case I ran out of money travelling and had to barter for meals.

Sometimes a heterosexual relationship provided the only possibility of getting an education. Wrote a lesbian in her twenties from Alabama:

> In college, I slept with a guy on a regular basis just so I could move in with him and be close enough geographically to attend school. I moved into a dorm later and slept with a security guard so I could get food.

A lesbian from Arizona who considers future heterosexual relationships a possibility described how financial considerations might affect her sexual choices:

> If I get any poorer, I might consider marrying a man for money. I'm 41 years old and each year I make less money. Most of the jobs I have don't have medical insurance...I'm afraid I can't make it alone as a woman. I'm terrified I'm going to become a bag lady.

I asked an African-American lesbian in her forties from Southern California if she thought the specific economic problems African-American women face – job discrimination, lower pay, etc. – might make it more difficult to come out as a lesbian. She replied:

> I think economics definitely plays a role...I knew several African-American women who were married and had lesbian affairs – they weren't able to live with their lovers...They had bought homes and their economic life was intimately tied with this man. They couldn't make their mortgage payments without that check and income.

Sometimes it was the "finer things" in life that attracted lesbians to heterosexual relationships. A former lesbian from Marin County (a county in California that enjoys a relatively high average income) explained her own transition, motivated in part by the desire for the material benefits of heterosexuality:

For five years (after coming out) I had very little attraction to men in any form and was entirely with women. After three relationships...I shut down again... feeling not too successful with women either... fantasies of men began to resurface. "If I can't have a healthy relationship – I might as well have some financial support", I thought. And three months after my lover of three years split, I was with this yuppie male architect...home, cars, vacations, social approval...I can have great sex (in my domineering bitch mode), go out to expensive restaurants and have a good old superficial time of it...The hard part was risking the bonds I have in the lesbian community...I want their support; I also want the uncomplicated (hetero) sex...in an emotional sense there is freedom in it...and the economic perks are nice.

Community

Difficulty in finding others like oneself and social ostracism from the larger community can provide a powerful impetus toward conformity. Thus, almost half (48%) of the lesbians-who-left did so because they had felt isolated from other lesbians and/or the rest of the world and wished to fit in better with the heterosexual majority. And almost a quarter (22%) explained that they had found the lesbian community "too small" or "claustrophobic".

Isolation from other lesbians

Given the nature of institutionalized heterosexuality and lesbian oppression, it is not surprising that finding compatible lesbians for friendship, intimate partnership and social support was often a struggle for both groups of women I studied. One lesbian over fifty from the Bay Area, a veteran of three heterosexual marriages, described how, after recognizing her preference for other women, she continued having relationships with men because she was unable to locate other lesbians:

> For years, I considered myself a bisexual and was; but again, I had so little experience sexually with a female because there was no opportunity. But it got to a point when every time I had sex with a man it became more and more repugnant. I just couldn't do it any more...

Yet, despite being out as a lesbian for several years and living in a community with a relatively large lesbian population, she had problems connecting with lesbians her age:

My problem is an inability to find women in my age group...Am I fated to always be alone, unloved and unloving?

Likewise, a heterosexual former lesbians in her forties got involved with a man after being unable to find a compatible woman who was not an alcoholic:

It seemed that every woman I dated was an alcoholic... other women were saying the same thing. You meet a woman in a bar, you're likely to meet somebody who likes to drink...I went to Camping Women and then I started having back problems so I couldn't go to any of those activities...Bars were the only places I could really meet people...It was like circumstances were forcing me into the other pathway [toward heterosexuality].

Often worse than lack of a partner, however, was the lack of lesbian friends. A lesbian-who-returned (from Philadelphia) began recognizing her feelings for other women when in high school. Yet when she tried to come out in college, the isolation soon overwhelmed her and she conformed (temporarily):

I came out alone and had no support. The first people I told expected me to change. It was unspeakably lonely to think I was the only woman who felt this way...I gave up. I decided to be het...

Even where two compatible women were lucky enough to meet and fall in love, being a closeted couple isolated from other lesbians was stressful. One former lesbian described the effects of her ex-lover's fear of discovery:

I felt isolated in my relationship with Karen – isolated from the whole world, including other lesbians. Karen wasn't out – she didn't want to be out and she didn't want me to be out. She wanted to keep a secret. This was a stress between us. See, part of loving her was being proud of the whole thing...I always wanted to go to lesbian events, find other lesbians and see what was happening. She'd say no, no, no. She was too afraid... Her fear put a lot of stress on our relationship.

Ironically, it was Karen who embraced lesbian identity and

community when they broke up. Meanwhile, her lover, left alone with her pain, turned to male lovers.

Their experience was not unusual. Many lesbians had their first intimate relationships with other women in total isolation. One lesbian in her forties wrote:

> I was lovers with my best girlfriend from the time I was in seventh grade until my freshman year in college (approximately 5 years). We did not use the "L" word but we knew enough not to tell anyone. We both dated and slept with men also. In 1968, she decided that it was "just a stage" and I went straight (because I believed her) until 1976.

When she got involved with a woman again, she was still isolated:

> I didn't know any other lesbians for the first one and a half years of the relationship. I guess I still didn't quite identify as a lesbian until I met other dykes.

Such isolation was felt most keenly when relationships were ending. A heterosexual former lesbian from the Bay Area had known other lesbians, but only at a distance. Thus, she found herself with no close friends to turn to when she broke up with her lover. She explained what that was like:

> I felt isolated and alone. I was dealing with all this stuff. I didn't have anyone to discuss it with.

Soon, she began dating men again.

A lesbian living in a rural part of California described her own isolation from the few lesbians that she knew:

> My last two years have been lonely, lonely, lonely. In this community, a single, political out-of-the-closet lesbian is seen as a threat to established friendship networks – the only way lesbians here relate to each other…

Just as isolation from other lesbians leads to conformity in some women, lesbian connection can make it easier for many women to come out. One lesbian-who-returned, a former bisexual, told me how changed circumstances helped her come out as a lesbian the second time:

> I felt less isolated. I knew more people who were gay like me – men and women but mainly women. They were open about it – maybe not at work, but when 5:00

comes, everybody was back to normal, whatever that normal was. I was able to pick up copies of The Lesbian News, seeing all the things going on across the country. The Gay Movement was starting and I realized I'm not really alone.

Isolation from the World

But sometimes the lesbian community, however supportive, was not enough, if it meant being cast out by the world at large. The desire for social acceptability – to "fit in" with the larger society – was mentioned time and again by the lesbians-who-left as a reason for leaving.

For example, one bisexual former lesbian in her forties (from Maine) began pursuing sexual involvements with men because:

As I went through different growth experiences, I began to feel the importance of integrating the rest of the world into my life.

Often former lesbians felt most ostracized from other women. This was the case for a heterosexual woman from Colorado who explained her motivation as follows:

I felt I was missing something being a lesbian and it has to do with my relationships with heterosexual women as much as it did with men. Just somehow feeling – out of touch with the mainstream of society.

A bisexual former lesbian from Connecticut blamed this isolation on other lesbians, rather than on the lesbophobia rampant among heterosexual women:

The lesbian community has really set itself apart from the straight female community. And that's what bothers me. They've really chosen to segregate themselves off from other women who are not lesbians.

Her lesbian identity had made her feel "ghettoized" in a way that being bisexual did not:

In the last four years, I began to feel that I was ghettoized and that I want to live in the world...When I came out as bisexual, I didn't feel like I had lost one community to gain another. I feel like I had added...I feel more connected to the world.

Other lesbians-who-left also felt "more connected to the world" once they had modified their lifestyle. I asked Bisexual

Barbara (whose story is told in Chapter II) whether becoming bisexual made her feel more connected with other people. She replied:

> Yeah, I'm not going to be married, have kids, be monog-amous. So there's three big things eliminated right there, other than heterosexuality...So it helps to have some things where I can relate.

Another bisexual former lesbian living in the Boston area told me how cut off she had felt from friendships with a wide variety of people:

> After a while I started feeling I wasn't a part of the world – just a part of this [lesbian] community...I felt I was cutting myself off from a source of great enjoyment, i.e., friendships with men, gay or straight, and from a lot of my straight women friends.

Why did she feel cut off from these friendships? She explained:

> I didn't want to deal with anyone who wasn't a lesbian at the time because no one else could understand.

In other words, it was the prejudices of non-lesbians that had compelled her to choose between the possibility of such friendships and her lesbian life. Ultimately, it was her lesbianism that was sacrificed.

Sometimes, dissatisfaction with isolation from the larger society took the form of complaints about the small in-grown nature of the lesbian community. A bisexual from the Boston area told me that one reason she made the decision to be involved with a man was because the lesbian community was, as she put it, "incredibly small". "Everyone had been lovers with everyone else", she explained. "It felt a little crazy to me..."

Similarly, another former lesbian, now heterosexual and living in the Bay Area complained:

> The whole scene had become claustrophobic ...I began feeling stifled and limited. It was taking up too much of my time to have to go to specific places to be a lesbian. When could I go to a bar in a better neighborhood or hear a variety of interesting music or take a class? I was burnt out.

She acknowledged that she still has feelings for women, but "deliberately chose" not to live as a lesbian. "I had given up too much to gain too little", she said.

I asked what it was that she had given up. She replied:
Everybody takes it for granted that everybody else is
straight... – my husband this, my boyfriend did that and
even if you did say my girlfriend did this, they wouldn't
know what to say probably...I don't think I'd get a lot
of sympathy or discussion. All they would think was
hey, lesbian, ugh...If you're having trouble with your
boyfriend, you could talk about it. If you're having
trouble with your girlfriend, where can you go?

A lesbian in her twenties from the midwest wrote about her
ex-lover's decision to stop being a lesbian in similar terms:
She decided she could no longer do this. She started
freaking out and being really paranoid about people
finding out – what would people think. All of a sudden
it was a real priority to get married and have kids.

Isolation from Minority Communities

For women who are members of racial, ethnic, and/or religious
minorities (Jews, Latinas, Asian-Americans, African-Americans,
Arab-Americans, Native-Americans, etc.), the decision to live as
a lesbian can mean isolation not only from one's cultural roots,
but also from the only source of solace and support in a White,
Anglo-Saxon, Protestant-dominated world.

Among African-Americans, the bigotry of white society and
the homophobia of their own community makes a lesbian choice
doubly difficult. I asked Doreen, whose story is told in Chapter
II, whether she thought being Black made it easier or harder to
be a lesbian. She replied:
I think it makes it harder. In my experience, compared
to Anglo cultures, the family is more important,
including the elders...There's even less role models in
terms of Black lesbians than white. And as my father
once said, Black people are generally more conservative
about sex...

Likewise, an African-American lesbian in her forties described
her own experience with family and community:
My mother associated homosexuality with deviance and
poverty. Only the standard American model of being
married to a man led to a bourgeois middle class lifestyle
and that was the values she had...My lover's mother

(when she told her that she was a lesbian) said well
Linda, white people do that. There are no Black lesbians.
That's almost a direct quote...During my coming out
process...I found few Black women. White women
were in the bars; white women were in the classes. My
first sexual relationships were with white women.

However, I finally went to a Black lesbian support group and
found thirty-three Black lesbians! ...In my travels, I found Black
lesbians and I found Black lesbian bars which were much fewer
and farther between and harder to find than white lesbian
places.

I asked her why she thought that was the case. She replied:
The first reason is economics – there are fewer women's
places than men's and then when you add racism to the
economics, there are fewer Black women's places...

She also suggested why being an "out" lesbian was problematic for many Black women, despite the emphasis in African-
American culture on strong self-sufficient women:
If you're already on the fringe of society and barely
holding a job because you're Black, you don't want to
add anything to that like homophobia.

Stigma

Lesbians are not only isolated from the world for being
"different", they are also vehemently condemned by the majority
of the population as "sick", "unnatural", or "immoral". Indeed,
bigotry against lesbians and gays is the only prejudice that has
retained widespread respectability. A 1992 Gallup poll found
that 57% of Americans say that homosexuality is an unacceptable
lifestyle. Even among liberals, 40% agreed that homosexuality
was unacceptable. According to the same poll, almost half –
44% – believe that gay sex should be illegal.

Living under such stigma is never easy; there are few lesbians
who at one time or another did not internalize the stigma and,
at the same time, modify their behavior to lessen its impact.
Sometimes this involved creating a public image that was increasingly out of sync with one's actual, personal life. Other times a
lesbian's dislike of hiding led her to change in a heterosexual
direction.

Both the lesbians and former lesbians in this study revealed that they had been deeply affected by their stigmatized status. This was especially the case for the lesbians-who-left.

One former lesbian from Northern California in her forties who now considers herself heterosexual described the anti-gay violence and lesbophobia she knew as a young woman:

> When I was first exposed to lesbianism in girl scout camp, I saw it as an enjoyable lifestyle. But I also knew that you cannot tell – it's got to be kept secret because so many people just seem to go nuts, off the wall. I was a victim of gay-bashing at least twice. I used to go to a gay bar...a bunch of low brows decided to "kill the fags"...and would come swinging chains and sometimes they'd have knives and rocks and stuff...you couldn't talk about things like that, because if you got caught, you could get killed, you could get fired...It was total repression in the 50's. In the 60's, things got a little easier, because you could always be bi, bi was OK because that meant a guy would be there so he could watch and that made it all right...It was just not safe to be a lesbian. Just to be labelled something meant total isolation.

A lesbian-who-left from Maine wrote that she was "ecstatic" when she finally got involved with a woman who considered herself a Dyke in a situation men were not orchestrating. "I wanted to tell the whole world", she said. But soon she discovered that the world was not too pleased with her decision. Her ex-boyfriend threatened a custody suit, but that was not all:

> My father told me I was crazy and my daughter should be taken from me. My (straight) friends shook their heads and called it a "phase". People on the street gave us dirty looks when we held hands.

Other former lesbians also indicated that they were extremely troubled by the social consequences of being openly affectionate.[20] One bisexual from the mid-west wrote:

> The other thing that is difficult for me [about being a lesbian] is the cultural attitude toward homosexuality. I am a demonstrative person and the consequences for that – kissing, hugging, etc. – between women in public – is a very high price to pay.

Similar comments were made by another bisexual former lesbian, this one from New Mexico:

> I feel uncomfortable and anxious when I walk down the street holding hands with a woman lover...I'm uncomfortable about other people's reactions – their hostility – and I've experienced some of that...It's the same anxiety I sometimes have with women who look obviously lesbian.

A lesbian-who-left (from New York City) told me how she had been afraid to bring her relationship with her woman lover out into the world because of people's reactions. I asked her what she was afraid of. "I guess just awkwardness and offending people", she said.

From these and other comments, it appeared that the lesbians-who-left had a greater fear of stigma than the lesbians or else were somewhat more likely to internalize that stigma. This difference between the two groups of women was also reflected in responses to the multiple choice questions. For example, 29% of the former lesbians agreed with the statement, "Women who look obviously lesbian or who publicly flaunt their lesbianism make me uncomfortable", while only 12.4% of the lesbians agreed. In addition, many former lesbians acknowledged that their turn toward male lovers was a conscious attempt to escape stigma and win social acceptance. As one lesbian-who-left, now with a dual identity, explained:

> My fear of being gay pushed me into exploring relationships with men even though I had no sexual attraction to men specifically or in general...Those fears get in the way of me having the life I'd like to have.

In her case, however, the fear was not a result of internalized anti-lesbian beliefs. Rather, she feared other people's reactions:

> There's nothing about being a lesbian that's wrong, bad, or problematic...but it gets in the way of being comfortable in the outside world. It's fitting into the dominant culture as a gay person, not fear of my own lesbianism.

Similarly, another lesbian-who-left, unsure of her identity, wrote:

> It seems too hard to be gay...I don't want to put out the effort...I feel that as a lesbian I always kept myself once removed from straight people because I was fearful of questions they might ask and I am not a quick on the

spot talker.

A bisexual former lesbian (from the Bay Area) told me why she felt it was easier being with men:

> One thing I hated about being a dyke is the edge of paranoia that is often apparent... The fact that we weren't allowed to touch in public...I'm not a good hider, I guess, and I think it was very oppressive...It was just easier with men. Men are more available, there's more of them on the shelves and you can do more things with them in public. It's more acceptable and less stressful. It's hard work being a lesbian.

One lesbian-who-left (from the midwest) presently heterosexual, told me why she got married after more than fifteen years of lesbianism:

> I simply got tired of clingy women. I got tired of playing the game...this was a small town...I got tired of not being able to hold hands in public. I got tired of living in the closet. I felt I was cutting half of life off – half the world off.

Though many former lesbians emphasized the oppressiveness of the closet, others feared the consequences of coming out. For example, a heterosexual-identified woman living in the relatively supportive environment of the Bay Area, decided that being a lesbian "just wasn't worth it". She explained why she felt that way:

> There was pressure at the time that everybody should become uncloseted. I thought, I don't want to discuss this with my family. I don't want to discuss this with my co-workers...You'd see how they'd talk about the other gay people at work.

Many of the lesbians reported that they, too, had, at some time in their lives, modified their sexual behavior in order to avoid the hostility of the larger society. A lesbian-who-returned (in her forties from Northern California) described how she tried to conform as a teenager:

> I had my first woman lover in high school. She broke up with me after two years. She was getting a lot of pressure being called queer – both of us were...I tried to overcompensate. I wanted to fit in so I did everything that was cool... After my girlfriend and I broke up, I

had a major boyfriend…We were together for about a year…

Another lesbian-who-returned described the events leading up to her twenty year marriage:

I had experience with young women when I was in high school for two years and was very frightened by that experience – having to be secretive and being afraid if people saw us, especially my parents. We didn't identify as lesbians. I didn't tell my other women friends about it. When I got to college, I was too afraid to go on doing that even though I was running around with people who were sometimes lesbians or secret lesbians…My ex-husband identified as being gay and was having relationships with men when we met…We both wanted to be married and have children.

Likewise, another lesbian-who-returned conformed for several years:

At sixteen, I moved out on my own and moved in with Judy, my first lover…my grandmother made sure to let me know that I shouldn't be "funny". My aunt would ask me more forthrightly, are you two doing funny things. And because of Judy's denial, I said well no. But at the same time if I wasn't going to be able to be with a woman, I would not be happy with myself. I felt that being a lesbian was too difficult for people to accept…So after Judy and I broke up, I tried to be heterosexual for about a year. Then, for the next two years I lived a bisexual life.

Why did she choose a bisexual identity at that time? She replied:

Because I could have the best of both worlds. I could be "normal" when I wanted to go out with men and at the same time, I could go to bed with women and have what I really felt in my heart was what I wanted.

I also asked why heterosexual relationships had appealed to her. Her response emphasized that it was the absence of stigma that had made all the difference:

It was more socially acceptable, it was safe…you could go out and hold hands or kiss in public and you wouldn't be called names or roughed up. I tried to show affection in public to a woman and it didn't work at all – we probably could have gotten killed.

Religion

Patriarchal organized religion is one of the largest purveyors of sexist and homophobic ideology in this culture, an effective form of social control. Because of the influence of religion, not only do many women and men suffer overwhelming guilt over their homosexuality, but also others around them – parents, employers, co-workers, teenage gay bashers, etc. – are encouraged to discriminate.

Studies have shown that the greater one's religious involvement, the greater one's biases against "out" groups – women, people of color, and homosexuals.[21] A study published in the May 23, 1990 edition of the *San Francisco Chronicle* found that half of Northern Californians who attend church on a weekly basis oppose the ordination of homosexuals. Of those who attended church less than annually, only 18% opposed the ordination of gays.

Though Christian fundamentalists and the Catholic Church hierarchy have been the most actively anti-gay in the United States, leading campaigns to repeal gay rights laws, censor pro-gay materials in schools, etc., other religious denominations are far from blameless. Nearly all mainstream Protestant denominations – as well as conservative and orthodox Judaism– forbid the ordination of gays. As recently as June of 1992, the Southern Baptists overwhelmingly approved an amendment to their constitution barring any churches that "affirm, approve, or endorse homosexual behavior", and voted to oust two congregations that had sanctioned homosexuals. The record of eastern religions is not much better; witness the treatment at her Buddhist University that led "Doreen" to leave a lesbian life.

The phenomenon of gays becoming "straight" for religious reasons has been openly discussed in both the gay and mainstream press. In 1990, both the *San Francisco Chronicle* and the *San Francisco Examiner* featured articles on "reparative therapy", part of an effort to "preserve heterosexuality as the norm for the USA".[22]

Lesbian-who-left Jeannette Howard, a "counselor" dedicated to changing gays, told the *San Francisco Chronicle* that she believes emotional and sexual abuse causes lesbianism. In addition, she implied that a large part of her problem was that she had not known her "place" as a woman:

Five years ago, as a lesbian, I was in competition with men. I thought there was nothing a man could do that I couldn't. Now I am looking to complement a man.

Few of the women in my study (4% of the lesbians-who-left and 18.1% of the lesbians-who-returned) stated that they had left for religious reasons. This is most probably because subjects were found primarily through advertisements in feminist, gay and bisexual publications and through lesbian contacts. Women who make this change because they are convinced that lesbianism is "sinful" are unlikely to consider themselves feminists or bisexual, or to maintain contact with lesbian friends.

Some lesbians, however, reported that they personally knew women who had conformed for this reason. But more commonly, the religious influence was indirect and subtle. Sometimes it was felt through other family members who continued to be regular church or synagogue goers; other times the former lesbians simply internalized prejudices, at least partly religious in origin, even though they themselves were no longer religious.

More of the lesbians, particularly the lesbians-who-returned, reported conscious struggles with religious issues. One lesbian from a Protestant background described her difficulty:

I tried to come out when I was twenty-eight...Since I come from such a religious background, it was very difficult for me. I finally got scared and went running right back into marriage...

She became a lesbian five years later though immediately thereafter, she made one more attempt to be heterosexual:

In order to prove that I was not [a lesbian], I went out with a man I had been involved with before I came out...I could not perform at all. I hyperventilated and became quite ill. It was the last time I ever tried to be sexually involved with a man.

Another lesbian-who-returned, also Protestant, suffered such severe religious conflict that she became suicidal:

When I was in high school I dated a few boys...At one point I did get very seriously involved with a guy and we began talking about marriage. The relationship ended though after we fought about sex. (I still wouldn't sleep with him.) That's about the time I started dating women. I swayed back and forth about my sexuality, mainly because of Christianity, and when I would decide that I was not gay, I would try to go out with guys. Other than that, I had no desire to be with them. In my first three semesters of college, I was admitted to the psychiatric hospital four times for being suicidal. I could only see my life as an awful denial of the total person I really am.

She explained that she had not resolved the conflict between Christianity and her lesbianism but decided she wanted to live long enough to figure it out.

Another Protestant lesbian-who-returned described her guilt and attempt at heterosexual conformity:

I always felt I was called to the ministry...That was my motivation in trying to live a heterosexual life.

When I was nineteen, I had my first total sexual experience with another woman...I felt very guilty...And that was directly related to religious messages I was getting. When it first happened, I had to be hospitalized – I became comatose for two weeks...I just didn't see how I could go on with life...

Then I became an atheist...I made lesbian friends and started going to bars. But I still had nagging guilt...I became involved in a relationship with a woman that lasted five and one-half years...During the relationship, I had the born-again experience – speaking in tongues. I once again felt the call to the ministry and also the guilt. I left my lover to go into seminary. I decided to give up the lesbian person to become the religious person...

After five years of celibacy, she married a man "in order to fit in" and because she was "damn tired" of being alone. But because she was unable to have sex with her husband, she was ex-communicated:

My husband was calling up the minister every morning to let her know whether or nor he was successful in having sex with me the night before. Because I couldn't have sex with my husband, I was ex-communicated. She determined that if I wasn't able to have sex with a man, I was still a lesbian.

Thrown out of her church, she returned to a lesbian life. Though she occasionally attends services at the Metropolitan Community Church (MCC), a gay church, she found it necessary to distance herself, at least to some degree, from organized religion.

"While I still consider myself very spiritual," she explained, "I do not consider myself religious in institutional terms…"

Footnotes

[1] I use the word "family" with some trepidation, because of its common meaning – as an economic unit composed of a heterosexual couple and children, and as an institution that perpetrates class divisions and patriarchy.

[2] This means, in the short and medium term, fighting for the right of same-sex couples to marry, as well as for the passage of domestic partnership legislation. Ultimately, it will require the elimination of marriage as we know it, in favor of a simple system of registration available to all couples, and the recognition of all partnership and familial relationships.

[3] Pay discrimination against women continues to be rampant, as a result of the both the segregation of jobs by gender and the devaluing of "women's work" or "men's work" when it is done by females. An article in the 3/28/93 *San Francisco Examiner* based on the 1990 census returns in California for all full-time workers, reported that women earn only 60 cents for every dollar men earn. The gap is even wider for lawyers, physicians, engineers and other (predominately male) professions, where women take home barely more than half of what men do. Nationally, the figures are even more dismal; according to the U.S. Census Bureau, the average woman earns only 53 cents for every dollar paid to a man.

[4] See Marilyn Frye's insightful 1987 article, "Lesbian Sex" republished in *Willful Virgin – Essays in Feminism* (The Crossing Press, 1992.)

[5] Ann Muller, *Parents Matter – Parents' Relationships with Lesbian Daughters and Gay Sons* (The Naiad Press,Inc., Tallassee, 1987) p. 161.

[6] Ibid., p. 108.

[7] I was particularly interested in this woman's story because I come from an almost identical background. But unlike the woman interviewed, I am a second generation American and my parents are unusually supportive. These differences, perhaps more than anything else, explain why I am still a lesbian and she is not.

[8] Another issue for Jewish lesbians who wish to remain childless is the idea that you are not doing your part to insure Jewish survival,

particularly in light of the mass slaughter of the Jewish populations of Europe that took place during the living memories of many of our parents and grandparents.

[9] Polikoff's essay appears in *Politics of the Heart: A Lesbian Parenting Anthology* Sandra Pollack and Jeanne Vaughn, eds. (Ithaca: Firebrand Books, 1987), pp. 48-65.

[10] Ibid., p.49.

[11] Ibid., pp.49-50.

[12] A disturbing example of this appeared in the April 11, 1994 *San Francisco Examiner* reviewing a study by Barbara DeFoe Whitehead, "an impeccably credentialed liberal" on the state of the family. Whitehead blamed "family diversity" – the increasing number of single mother and stepparent families – as a "central cause of many of our most vexing social problems", including poverty, drugs, crime, and behavioral and emotional problems in children, who become unhappy and unsuccessful adults. "It dramatically weakens and undermines society, placing new burdens on schools, courts, prisons and the welfare system", Whitehead contended. Rather than suggest women's wages be raised to the level of men's, and that society provide increased social supports for parenting, Whitehead advocated getting and staying married as the only "acceptable" and "economically viable" way of raising children.

[13] A 1989 Time/CNN poll found that 69% of the public were opposed to gay marriages and an even higher number -75% – felt that gay couples should not have children. (*Time*, 11/20/89)

[14] Pat Parker, "Gay Parenting, or Look Out, Anita" by Pat Parker, appearing in *Politics of the Heart*, p. 98.

[15] Lesbian biological mothers continue to lose custody not only to fathers but even to other family members. For example, in 1995, after a long court battle, the Virginia Supreme Court denied Sharon Bottoms custody of her son in favor of the child's grandmother, solely on the grounds of Sharon's lesbianism.

[16] Martin B. Levine and Robin Leonard, "Discrimination against Lesbians in the Workplace" published in *Signs: Journal of Women's Culture and Society,* 9, no. 4 (Summer, 1984).

[17] See the stories of three such women who were imprisoned for homosexuality – Barbara Baum, Cheryl Jamison, and Joann Newak, in *Conduct Unbecoming: Gays sand Lesbians in the U.S. Military* by Randy Shilts (St. Martin's Press, New York, 1993.)

[18] During his first term in office, President Clinton issued an executive order mandating that security clearances no longer be denied based on sexual orientation.

[19] Her sexual history had been exclusively lesbian up to the time of the interview.

[20] It should be noted that being affectionate to a woman in public was difficult for lesbians as well. In response to the true/false question, "I often feel uncomfortable or frightened when a woman lover holds my hand or shows affection in public", the lesbians were almost equally

likely to check true as the former lesbians (72.1% of the former lesbians as compared to 68.5% of the lesbians.)

[21] See "Interrelationship of Sexist, Racist and Anti-Homosexual Attitudes" by Nancy M. Henley and Fred Pincus *Psychological Reports,* 1978, 42, 83-90, which found greater racism, sexism, and homophobia among regular church-goers. Of course, there are numerous religious persons who are progressive activists as individuals or through their churches, and who support women's and gay liberation. However, most organized religion is patriarchal, hierarchical, and homophobic.

[22] The campaign of Christians to "save gays' souls" reminds me as a Jew of a similar campaign of violence and coercion used over centuries to convert Jews into Christians.

V
SHE SWALLOWED THE LIE

Oddly enough, I don't think I've ever felt guilty about sleeping with women per se; I always felt that my real crime was not sleeping with men. After the first euphoria of discovery...what plagued me and still does is the nagging feeling that in not sleeping with men, I am neglecting a terribly important obligation.

– from "Not for Years But for Decades" by
Joanna Russ, published in *Magic Mommas,
Trembling Sisters, Puritans and Perverts,*
(The Crossing Press, New York, 1985), p. 30.

Anti-lesbian ideology permeates every institution in our society, from the schools to the mass media. While organized religion and the scientific establishment (including psychiatry, socio-biology, and other fields that purport to study human sexual behavior) provide these ideas with legitimacy. However, the purpose of this propaganda is not merely to justify discrimination against a sexual minority; rather, its primary goal is to insure that the overwhelming majority of women conform to the role laid out for them. Because the sexologists have played such a major role in perpetrating lesbian oppression – their ideas seeping into the subconscious of even the most politically aware among us – this next section will analyze their contribution to maintaining the heterosexist social order.

Part I - Sexologists as Social Police
Most sexologists – with the exception of feminists like Shere Hite and scientists like Alfred Kinsey who saw homosexual behavior as quite natural – are unabashed defenders of the heterosexual status quo, especially for women. Indeed, much of their work champions the traditional "feminine" role of wife, mother, and helpmeet to man as the key to female health and happiness.

There is essential agreement among them that heterosexuality is the natural order of things and that "something went wrong" if women become lesbians. However, they hold varying views on exactly what went wrong. Some believe that homosexuality is caused by congenital defects such as masculinizing hormonal imbalances in the womb; others speculate that neurosis-inducing life experiences like heterosexual trauma, or unhealthy family constellations are to blame. Many sexologists combine both "nature" and "nurture" approaches in their attempt to "explain" homosexual behavior, but usually the emphasis is on one view or the other.

Though these theories keep cropping up in new forms, their substance, has changed surprisingly little in the last hundred years. The "born that way" school of thought had its origins in the nineteenth century with writers such as psychiatrist Richard Von Krafft-Ebbing. Dr. Krafft-Ebbing, writing in 1882, had to go through mental gymnastics to reconcile the existence of widespread homosexual behavior among the population (which he acknowledged), with his theory that homosexuals were congenital freaks. He (as well as others both before and after him) accomplished this by attempting to distinguish between "perverse sexual acts" (ie., "acquired" homosexuality) and "perversion". The latter he defined as a "congenital reversal" of sexual feeling, and a "functional sign of degeneration", hereditary in character, originating in anomalies of the brains of the affected individuals.[1]

According to Krafft-Ebbing, normally constituted "untainted" individuals were quite capable of engaging in homosexual acts when in prison or in boarding schools, or as a result of the "contaminating" influence of masturbation. In the case of women, fear of pregnancy or hatred of men could also lead to such "temporary aberrations". "Congenital" homosexuality was thus distinguished not by homosexual acts or desires but by the relative absence of interest in the other sex – the most developed cases of abnormality manifested by exclusive homosexuality as well as gender role non-conformity – "femininity" in men, and "masculinity" in women.[2]

"Uranism", Krafft-Ebbing wrote, "may nearly always be suspected in females wearing their hair short, or who dress in the fashion of men, or pursue the sports and pastimes of their male acquaintances…The female urning may chiefly be found in the haunts of boys. She is the rival in their play, preferring the rocking horse, playing at soldiers, etc. to dolls and other girlish occupations…The consciousness of being a woman and thus to be deprived of the gay college life or to be barred out from the military career, produces painful reflections."[3]

In other words, a lesbian is a woman who resents, and rebels against, her subordinate position in society. However, since in Krafft-Ebbing's view, women's inferiority is biologically ordained, the "invert" was therefore "congenitally abnormal".

Notably, Krafft-Ebbing recognized that though "inverted sexuality" is as common in women as in men, in the case of women, society is more often successful in suppressing it:

> ...the chaster education of the girl deprives the sexual instinct of its predominant character; seduction to mutual masturbation is less frequent; the sexual instinct in the girl begins to develop only when she is, with the advent of puberty, introduced to the society of the other sex, and is thus naturally led primarily into heterosexual channels. All these circumstances often serve to correct abnormal inclinations and tastes and force her into the ways of normal sexual intercourse.[4]

To safeguard the heterosexual norm, Krafft-Ebbing advocated that the "congenital" cases be prohibited from reproducing.[5] For the "acquired" cases, he suggested protection from "injurious influences", especially masturbation.[6] Krafft-Ebbing also recommended co-education and appropriate gender roles in children. He wrote:

> An early preference for games, occupations and pastimes of the opposite sex ...should be strongly discountenanced and interdicted.[7]

Havelock Ellis, writing at the turn of the century, made a similar distinction between congenital homosexuality in women and the "spurious kind" such as the passionate friendships commonly found among school girls. Ellis believed that "spurious" homosexuality was fostered by employment that kept women in association with each other apart from men. Though Ellis claimed to support the Women's Movement, he emphasized that it carried certain "disadvantages", an increase in homosexuality being prominent among them. At the same time, Ellis characterized the female "true invert" with "a certain degree of masculinity".[8]

Like Krafft-Ebbing, Ellis also concerned himself with the the prevention of homosexuality. He believed little could be done about the small minority of persons who were "true inverts" except to prevent them from begetting or bearing children, (as they belonged to a "neurotic and failing stock"[9]) and from flaunting their "perversion" in society's face.[10] In contrast, he felt that "sound social hygiene" should be successful in preventing most cases of "acquired" homosexuality. Such a social policy would encourage an ideal of chastity among congenital inverts, "so that the invert's natural perversion may not become a cause of acquired perversity in others".[11]

Ellis also agreed with Krafft-Ebbing that single-sex schools were a major cause of "artificial homosexuality" and should be eliminated in favor of co-education.[12] He opposed sodomy laws, however, as unnecessary since "social opinion" would deter most people from embracing a homosexual life.[13]

Throughout this century, many other sexologists, following the lead of Krafft-Ebbing and Ellis, have attempted to find some physical abnormality in lesbians and gays, and in others who defy gender role stereotypes. In the 1940's, social biologists theorized that female homosexuals were genetically male and male homosexuals genetically female, though having lost the secondary sex characteristics appropriate to their genetic sex. By the 1950's and 60's, with the development of techniques whereby nuclear and chromosomal sex could be determined, new studies were conducted that found no evidence to support this theory.

Beginning in the 1940's, and through the post-Stonewall 1970's, socio-biologists attempted to prove that "hormonal imbalances" caused homosexuality. However, when studies of hormone levels in gay men and lesbians produced inconclusive and contradictory results,[14] the emphasis shifted to the study of pre-natal hormonal influences that might affect "sexual differentiation" in the brain. Thus, according to prominent researcher John Money, writing in the 1980's in language reminiscent of the musings of Krafft-Ebbing and Havelock Ellis, a strong proclivity for homosexuality and other "cross-gender" behavior stemmed from "prenatal brain hormonalization that bisexually combines masculinization with feminization either equally, in a 50:50 ratio, or unequally, in a disproportionate ratio such as a 60:40 or 20:80 and so on".[15]

Such conclusions were drawn from studies of rat behavior

where female rats, treated pre-natally and after birth with androgen, exhibited a higher incident of mounting behavior (mounting rats of both sexes) as compared to receptive "feminine" lordosis responses. This mounting behavior was considered equivalent to human lesbianism, while the females (and males) who were mounted, were, of course, still "normal". In most species, untreated females are known to mount other females (and males to mount males); comparing a lesbian preference in all its complexity to rat mounting behavior is on its face absurd.[16]

This theory – that lesbianism is caused by the hormonal "masculinization" of the female fetus – is further developed in John Money's book, *Gay, Straight, and In Between – The Sexology of Erotic Orientation*. There, Money discusses not only rat sexual behavior, but also that of canaries, lambs, and female rhesus monkeys. However, in the case of prenatally "masculinized" female monkeys, he reports that though they engaged in "tomboyish play" in childhood, they did not turn out to be "lesbians".[17]

Money also cites studies of human physical hermaphrodites in support of his theory. He describes a 1984 study of females with congenital adrenal hyperplasia, a condition in which a masculinizing hormone is secreted pre-natally and continuously after birth, inducing masculinization of external genitalia. Of the twenty-three cases reviewed in the 1984 study, 52% were heterosexual; 26% bisexual, and 22% lesbian.[18] Two earlier studies, done in 1968 and 1976, of groups of women with the same condition found somewhat different results. While a majority turned out heterosexual, and a few bisexual, none became exclusively lesbian.[19]

On the basis of this ambiguous data, Money does not hesitate to conclude that "prenatal brain masculinization alone is sufficient to predispose to a bisexual or lesbian orientation".[20]

Money's work interlinks sexual preference and gender roles and concludes that both are largely based on biology. "Normal" girls, in his view, are not only programmed pre-natally to be heterosexual, but, as a result of identical processes, are less inclined toward vigorous outdoor activities, have a lesser capacity for mathematical reasoning, and are more oriented toward "nest-building" and nurturing children than "normal" boys are.[21] Thus, a deviation away from traditionally "feminine" behavior and interests or the development of a lesbian or bisexual orientation equally signify that "something went wrong" in the womb.

However, like many of his nineteenth century predecessors, Money is also concerned with negative social influences after birth which might encourage a homosexual result. He writes that there is preliminary evidence that a "gender cross-coded course of events might be changed if a child can be relieved of the self-imposed responsibilities of keeping his feuding parents together".[22] He also points to "ethnographic evidence" that where heterosexual sex play is not punished or prevented, homosexuality is rare.[23] But the main impact of Money's theories is to perpetrate the view of lesbians as freaks of nature, thus "naturalizing" the sexual and heterosexual status quo.

Despite the reactionary nature of these theories – the fact that they both reflect and perpetrate sexist and heterosexist prejudices and assumptions – they have held a certain attraction for sections of the gay and lesbian community as holding the promise of greater tolerance. In the mid-nineteenth century, a gay German jurist, Karl Heinrich Ulrich argued that gay men and lesbians were a third sex, which he called "Urnings", – persons whose in-born sexual instinct, due to some imperfection in the process of development, does not correspond to their genitals.[24] Ulrich acknowledged that homosexual practices and desires could be found among "normal" people. He attempted to reassure his homophobic society that the heterosexual norm would not be threatened by a policy of tolerance toward homosexuality since such "acquired habits of inversion" were destined to be temporary.[25]

In the 1990's, another gay man, Dr. Simon LeVay, made a similar plea for tolerance, arguing that homosexuals had different brains than heterosexuals and thus their homosexuality was a matter of destiny, not choice.[26] LeVay conducted a study comparing the brains of nineteen homosexual men who died of AIDS, with those of sixteen men only six of whom also died of AIDS, whose sexual preferences were "presumed" to be heterosexual; and with the brains of six women, also presumed heterosexual. His finding of a sex and a sexual preference difference in the INAH-3 region of the hypothalamus provided

LeVay's proof that homosexuals were "born that way".[27]

LeVay's work is a take-off on studies that purport to show differences in the hypothalamus between men and women. LeVay claimed that this same difference is reflected in the gay/straight dichotomy, i.e., that gay men have brains similar to straight women's and lesbians have brains like those of straight men. Whether these differences exist is far from clear. And, more importantly, there is no clear understanding of their significance.

In Ann Fausto-Sterling's book, *Myths of Gender*, the author reviews five reports of sexual dimorphism in the hypothalamus, including LeVay's. She points out that three of the studies were unreplicated; one of the studies found a volume difference in what has been called the "sexually dimorphic nucleus" only after the age of five, with no differences between homosexual and heterosexual men. Only one study besides LeVay's reported a difference between men and women in the INAH-3 region of the hypothalamus, though there was a significant overlap between the sexes.

Fausto-Sterling also notes that the results of LeVay's study could have been effected by other factors. Some of the subjects may have suffered from brain damage as a result of AIDS; others may have been economically disadvantaged and consequently had less access to medical care. But even were these differences to be confirmed, this would not mean that biology is destiny. Recent studies have shown that brain structure can be altered by experience. Thus, such gender and sexual orientation differences in the brain could be a result rather than a cause of varied social experiences.[28]

Months after LeVay published his gay brain study, psychologist Michael Bailey published his study of male homosexuality in twins where he found that identical twins were more likely to be gay than fraternal twins. Two years later in March 1993, Bailey published results of a similar twin study on lesbians, finding that 48 percent of identical twin sisters of lesbians were gay, compared with 16 percent of nonidentical twins and six percent of adoptive sisters.[29] However, the identical twins were raised together,[30] and it is commonly known that no two people have as close a growing up experience as identical twins – often wearing the same clothes, hairstyles, and being confused for one another. Thus, far from proving the decisive role of genetics,

145

this study only confirms the importance of environmental influences.

The many holes in these studies have not prevented LeVay, Bailey, and other scientists from continuing their search for a genetic basis for homosexuality. Neither has it prevented segments of the gay community from relying on "born that way" theories in their struggle to win basic human rights.

But arguing for freedom for lesbians and gays on the ground that "we can't help it" is ultimately a foolish and dangerous strategy. By failing to challenge the idea that homosexuality is unnatural and undesirable – a result of "something going wrong" – lesbians and gays end up no safer than we were before. As Anne Fausto-Sterling reminds us, in Hitler's Germany, gays and lesbians were sent to death camps not because they were sinners but because they were deemed "biologically unfit". In the UK and the USA, lesbians and gays have already been subjected to shock treatments, hormone injections, and other "therapies" designed to make us "normal". If homosexuality continues to be viewed as a biologically abnormal condition, what horrifying "cures" might future scientists come up with? Or will lesbians and gay men simply be prevented from having children so that future generations will be spared our "genetic defect"?

Countless women who love and prefer other women have been temporarily, or permanently, deterred from a lesbian life because they were convinced by psychiatrists, parents and others that they could not possibly be those biological freaks – "real lesbians". Such views do nothing whatever for lesbian self-esteem while insuring that most women continue to conform to the expectations of the heterosexual institution, regardless of whether their individual needs are met within its confines.

The other wing of sexology – that of Freud and his followers – is equally pernicious in its effects on women. Though Freud, writing in the early part of this century, rejected the idea that homosexuals were physical degenerates he worked to discover what might result in a homosexual "deviation". The causes he identified included "primitive psychical mechanisms" such as narcissism, the absence of a strong father, heterosexual frustration or fear, a fixation on the mother, and, in the case of girls, "penis envy" culminating in the wish to be a boy.[31]

His analysis in 1920 of an eighteen year old lesbian whose

father wanted her "cured" is especially revealing. Freud explained that at puberty, the girl experienced a revival of her "infantile Oedipus complex" and wished to have her father's child. But when her rival, her mother, bore a son, she turned against her father and men altogether.[32] However, Freud also noted that his patient "had taken a specially lively interest in a number of young mothers long before her brother's birth".[33] This he blamed on an "infantile fixation on the mother" but also on "penis envy", Freud's code word for girls who were not satisfied with the secondary role assigned to them by society. Freud wrote:

> ...she was not at all prepared to be second to her older brother; after inspecting his genital organs, she had developed a pronounced envy of the penis...She was in fact a feminist; she felt it to be unjust that girls should not enjoy the same freedom as boys and rebelled against the lot of woman in general.[34]

Freud was generally pessimistic about the prospects of an effective "therapy of inversion" and continued to emphasize the "universal bisexuality of human beings".[35] But he was willing to "help" where he could and put considerable thought into the "causes" and "prevention" of homosexuality. Despite his prejudices, Freud understood the connection between feminism and lesbianism; he also recognized that human beings' choice of object is originally (in childhood, primitive cultures and early history) independent of biological sex[36] and that homosexuality would be common were it not for "its authoritative prohibition by society".[37]

Freud's followers were considerably more rabid. Frank Caprio, writing in the 1950's, claimed not only that lesbians suffered from "deep-seated neurosis which involves narcissistic gratifications and sexual immaturity",[38] but that they were basically unhappy people, emotionally immature and unstable, insecure, insanely jealous, possessive, sadistic, hostile and violent.[39]

"Crime is intimately associated with female sexual inversion", wrote Caprio. "Many crimes committed by women, upon investigation reveal that the women were either confirmed lesbians who killed because of jealousy or were latent homosexuals with a strong aggressive masculine drive". According to Caprio, lesbian relationships were "at best mutual masturbation". "I am convinced that lesbians would not be healthy persons even if they lived in a society where sexuality with their own sex was socially acceptable. There is seldom any permanency to a lesbian alliance. Lesbians become dissatisfied, jealous and change partners frequently".[40]

With none of Freud's ambivalence and hesitation, Caprio expanded on Freud's list of "what went wrong" to "cause" lesbianism. Caprio claimed that many lesbians had psychopathic, alcoholic or tyrannical fathers or mothers who instilled a fear of (hetero)sex in their daughters.[41] Often the parents were divorced, separated, puritanical, or sexually maladjusted.[42] He also maintained that many lesbians had turned away from men as a result of having experienced sexual abuse:

> It is not too difficult to understand how a young girl, who during her puberty years is sexually accosted by her father or brother, an uncle or some elderly man, may develop an aversion to men and sex. I have encountered a good many lesbians who gave a history of some unpleasant sexual experience in adolescence.

In addition, Caprio cited the "harmful" effects of feminism and female independence on women, expressing concern that this new freedom, along with a "slavelike devotion to a career" might cause some women to "replace heterosexuality with an exploitation of sexuality amongst themselves which is contrary to women's basic needs".[43]

Caprio claimed that women were often "seduced" into lesbianism. He mentions the case of a woman in prison for killing her husband who had purportedly seduced dozens of high school and grade school girls by warning them against men. "In this case", Caprio wrote, "the lesbian expressed her extreme anti-male rebellion by beating her husband to death".[44]

"Manhating" was thus, for Caprio, both cause and evidence of lesbianism, and led to a woman "cheating herself" out of a "happy marriage".[45] From Caprio's perspective, only loving a man, marriage and motherhood held the promise of fulfillment for women.

Caprio was somewhat less condemning of bisexuality. "It is understandable that a child wishes to be loved by both parents", he wrote.[46] He was also not particularly worried about sexual relations between young girls at boarding schools which he deemed "a purely transitional phenomenon which in no way prevents a later development into fully normal hetero-sexuality".[47] However, Caprio differed from sexologists like Albert Ellis who regarded bisexuality as "by no means necessarily neurotic", in contrast to exclusive homosexuals who were "heterophobic" and sexually "fixated" on their own sex.[48] For Caprio, anything short of a complete sublimation of homosexual desire was likely to be a symptom of a personality disorder.

Since lesbianism is "an acquired or psychogenic disorder and not a congenital condition", Caprio was confident of the ability of psychoanalysis to render a complete "cure" – even in the case of what he termed the "exclusive" or "compulsive" types. This personality overhaul consisted of: renouncing "the wish for masculinity"[49] and learning to limit one's life to the constraints of the feminine. "Many patients of mine who were former lesbians have communicated long after treatment was terminated informing me that they are happily married and are convinced that they will never return to a homosexual way of life", Caprio boasted.[50]

Unfortunately, Caprio's stridently homophobic views are not unique to him or to the era of the early 1950's. In 1962, the Research Committee of the Society of Medical Psychoanalysis published a study of male homosexuals which concluded that homosexuality is a pathological response to heterosexual fears and inhibitions. "We assume that heterosexuality is a biologic norm and that unless interfered with, all individuals are heterosexual".[51]

A female member of that Committee, Cornelia B. Wilbur, writing in 1965, applied the Committee's "findings" to women, identifying a number of likely "causes" of female homosexuality. They included a "seductive father", the "prolonged absence of the mother", a "weak ineffectual father and strong domineering mother", isolation from peers, and especially "heterosexual trauma" or the treatment of heterosexuality as "taboo" by the parents, resulting in the development of "fears and inhibitions associated with heterosexuality".[54]

Wilbur's view of lesbians is similar to Caprio's – they are "compulsively preoccupied with sexuality" and their relation-ships are unstable, violent and destructive. "Female homosexual relationships are characterized by great ambivalence, by great longing for love, by intense elements of hostility, and by the presence of chronic anxiety. These relationships are unstable and often transient. They do not contribute to the individual's need for stability and love", wrote Wilbur.[55] Also, like Caprio, Wilbur believed a "cure" was possible, but warned that lesbians needed many years of psychoanalysis before a change to exclusive heterosexuality could be effected.

Years after the Stonewall rebellion and the birth of lesbian/gay liberation, the theories of the neo-Freudians were still given considerable credibility by psychiatrists[56] and by much of the general population. That they have been taken seriously in recent times is evidenced by the fact that the Kinsey Institute in 1981 devoted a whole study to testing their validity.[57] The Institute's research found a lack of support for most of the neo-Freudian notions of "what went wrong" to cause homosexuality. For example, they found that homosexuals had as many opportunities for heterosexual involvement as the heterosexuals they studied and were no more likely to have had negative experiences such as rape or parental punishment for heterosexual sex play than were heterosexuals.[58] Neither was seduction by opposite sex parents or by an older person of the same sex shown to be a "cause" of homosexuality.[59] Moreover, the Kinsey Institute found that a lesbian's relationship with her mother or her father had little effect on the development of her sexual preference.[60] Though the relationship between parents was more likely to have been negative or at least unconventional in the lesbians as compared to the heterosexuals, this also did not appear to be very useful in predicting sexual preference.[61]

An important link was discovered, however, between gender non-conformity in childhood and the development of homosexuality.[62] There was also a tendency for the lesbians to have been more isolated from their peers when growing up, but this, too, appeared to be connected with gender non-conformity.[63] No other significant "causes" of homosexuality were uncovered.

Rather than simply concluding that homosexuality is a natural aspect of human sexual expression, or exploring why traditional gender roles tend to channel people into heterosexuality, the Institute's researchers reverted to congenital explanations: "...indeed, homosexuality may arise from a biological precursor (as do left-handedness and allergies, for example), that parents cannot control", they concluded.[64]

Thus, mainstream sexology, even the more "liberal" among them, has focused almost exclusively on "what went wrong" theories of homosexuality while avoiding any study of heterosexuality and gender as political institutions that help maintain the subordination of women. Neither have any alternative theories been put forward identifying positive influences that might make a woman choose to be a lesbian. If we recognize that lesbianism is as natural and healthy a way of life as any other, offering its own unique possibilities for intimacy and female self-definition, why not ask "what went right" to encourage the development of a lesbian preference?

I can think of some positive contributing factors from my own upbringing: a particularly spirited and intelligent mother who was not satisfied with being "Mrs. Somebody" but asserted her own personhood, a father who took a strong interest in me, sharing his hobbies and intellect; love and nurturing from both parents who urged me to explore whatever interested me, whether it was traditionally "feminine" or not (from dolls to train sets to stamp and coin collections), leading me to believe I could grow up to be whatever I wanted, a family atmosphere where reading books, debating ideas and asking questions was encouraged, and lastly, the good fortune to come of age during the radicalization of the sixties and seventies and the beginning of the powerful, transformative second wave of feminism.

No studies of what went right are being funded and despite the Kinsey Institute's debunking of the homophobic and woman-hating theories of the neo-Freudians, they are, even today, far from dead. As recently as 1987, an article on "the Neo-Freudians" by Manny Sternlicht complained that the sexual revolution had obscured the "true nature of homosexuality" and referred favorably to theories of "causation" such as "fears of the opposite sex", "narcissism", "fixations", and an unresolved "Oedipal complex".[65]

What effect do these ideas have on our self-image as lesbians? How often do they deter women from even considering the possibility of a lesbian life? And, most importantly for our purposes, do some lesbians stop being lesbians because they believe the lies of the sexologists? As will be seen in Part II below, this appears to be the case for a significant number of lesbians-who left.

Part II - "She swallowed the lie"
> There was a young woman
> Who swallowed a lie
> I don't know why
> She swallowed that lie
> Perhaps she'll die.[66]

Therapist JoAnn Loulan calls it the "lesbian snot". She explains, "It's the feeling that there is something wrong with being a lesbian. We all have it. Why else aren't we shouting our love from the roof tops?...We can tell ourselves it's because of external oppression, but we also believe their lies".[67]

This internalized prejudice can be manifested in a number of ways: through alcohol or drug abuse, by an inability to take our own intimate relationships seriously, or by a refusal to recognize our partner or former partner as the other parent of our children. Our self-hatred can contribute to problems we experience being sexual with a lover especially in long-term relationships. It can lead to being overly critical of other lesbians in a way that we would never be toward heterosexuals. Our own homophobia may also cause us to live a more closeted existence than our external circumstances really require, or to take responsibility for our parents', friends' or co-workers' negative responses to lesbianism. Our negative feelings about ourselves as lesbians may even play a role in lesbian battering. And "lesbian snot" can sometimes lead to a decision to leave a lesbian life.[68]

This study uncovered a disturbing amount of lesbophobia in both the lesbians and former lesbians. However, the lesbians-who-left were somewhat more likely than the lesbians to have "swallowed the lie", thus strongly suggesting that anti-lesbian ideology has an important role to play in securing conformity to heterosexual norms.

What did the women in this study tend to believe? I've identified four main "lies".

Lie #1 – (Normal) Women Need Men
Sexologists of both the "born that way" and neo-Freudian schools, most religions, and the mass media all agree on at least

one thing: that all biologically normal, mature, and emotionally healthy women need men. Heterosexuality is deemed to be the natural state of things. Men are essential to women's lives, we are told, for sexual satisfaction[69] and psychological completion, in order to be a "real woman" and to achieve adulthood. Men are held out as the key to women's happiness and fulfillment, as necessary for our physical protection,[70] and as our only hope of obtaining financial and emotional security and a family. We are also taught that "our job" as women is to take care of men emotionally and sexually. We learn that we are valued to the degree that we do this job well and if we do not, we are doomed to a miserable and lonely life.[71]

This study included a number of true/false questions to help measure the respondents' beliefs. However, as always, statements taken directly from interviews proved to be most revealing.

An overwhelming majority of both groups – 95.1% of lesbians and 90.2% of the lesbians-who-left checked "true" to the statement, "Most women who have intimate relationships solely with other women are happy and fulfilled and are neither limiting themselves nor missing anything". At the same time, many women had become convinced that they were limiting themselves by being lesbians: almost half (44%) of the former lesbians (and 13.6% of the lesbians-who-returned) gave as at least one of their reasons for leaving, the feeling that they were "missing something" by not being with men and/or by living as part of the lesbian community. Indeed, the idea that something vital is lacking in a lesbian life, that only a heterosexual relationship can provide a sense of wholeness, came up repeatedly in the statements of the lesbians-who-left.

One bisexual-identified former lesbian in her thirties, living in Canada, explained her feelings this way:

Felt I was limiting myself by identifying as lesbian only. It was no longer empowering. Still feel women were the stronger sex, but wanted to expand my options...

A woman in her forties, describing her transition from lesbian to bisexual wrote, "I feel whole now..."

In a similar vein, a bisexual living in New Mexico stated that her new boyfriend, "helped me see men from the human side and this has taken down many walls and divisions in my heart.

I feel like a whole person in a way I didn't before". She considered her heterosexual involvement part of her "healing" despite the fact that she continued to prefer women.

Another bisexual, also in her thirties, explained:

> After five or six years of being a dyke, I felt kind of cut off from something, something I never really had an opportunity to experience…There's a different perspective on the world I get from men…There were things I wanted to learn from men. In the lesbian community I had the feeling of being cut off…

Sometimes what women felt they were "missing" was the possibility of a fulfilling sex life, even where (as was the usual case) they strongly preferred women emotionally and in every other way. As one former lesbian wrote:

> I think I am more attracted to men physically but like them less as people in general and do not usually have men in my life, preferring the company of women.

Often, the myth that heterosexual relationships were the only ones capable of fulfilling women's sexual needs caused a woman to continue such involvements even when the reality was quite different. For example, a lesbian-who-returned, in her thirties, told me that she continued to pursue relationships with men though she received neither sexual nor emotional satisfaction from them:

> I went back and forth from thinking I could be with women and I could be with men…I knew I wanted kids…People said, you're with women, but I know this nice man, do you want to meet him? And I'd say sure…why not…I did it a couple of times and I just kept thinking, this is boring…For a long time, I just lived with this really deeply ingrained sense that I should be with men, I should be with men. So I kept trying.

When she found herself sexually frustrated with her heterosexual relationships, she blamed herself:

> I always felt that I should do something different than I was doing. I always thought I was not doing it right.

Sometimes it was the promise of emotional and financial security in heterosexual marriage that held the primary appeal. In this study 94.6% of the lesbians and 82.8% of the lesbians-who-left checked "false" to the statement, "A good marriage to a decent, loving man offers women a greater possibility of satisfaction and security than any other lifestyle". However, the ideological "pull" of heterosexual marriage was much more powerful than is apparent from these statistics.

A lesbian-who-returned, over fifty, presently divorced, described the pressures to get married when she was growing up during the 1930's and 40's:

> I grew up in a very poor time...I think that women, if they were very wealthy and very well educated, they could be doctors or something like that. Any other option was just waiting while you found a husband.

One lesbian who came out after several marriages, described the environment of the 1950's when she came of age:

> In that day and age, most women got married and had children. Those that didn't they called "abnormal"...I felt that my position in life or my duty or my destiny was to get married and have children. And that's exactly what I did...

Unfortunately, young women are not immune from feeling that they are "missing something" by not marrying a man or from blaming themselves for their lack of heterosexual "success".

A significant minority of respondents – 18.7% of the lesbians and 20.3% of the lesbians-who-left checked "false" to the statement "Lesbian relationships are generally no less stable or secure than heterosexual ones". In addition, approximately one-quarter (24%) of the former lesbians (and 13.6% of the lesbians-who-returned) gave the hope that a heterosexual relationship would be more stable, lasting and emotionally secure as a reason for leaving.

Moreover, validation from men in general was important to the lesbians-who-left, more so than for the lesbians. More than a third – 34.9% of the former lesbians (as compared to 20.4% of the lesbians) checked true to the statement,

> "It is important for me to know that men like me and find me physically attractive even when I'm not interested in a particular man or men."

Some women in this study, again more former lesbians than lesbians, stated that they felt dependent on men for physical protection in the outside world: 38.7% of the lesbians-who-left checked "true" to the statement, "I usually feel safer walking down the street with a man than by myself or with another woman" while only 16.5% of the lesbians did so. One such former lesbian (a woman who had been molested as a child and also experienced heterosexual date rape as an adult) explained that she feared street violence directed against her as a woman and as a lesbian:

> I've worked with domestic violence, with rape crisis, and
> so I'm hyper-aware of rape and assault...So when I'm
> alone, I'm scared. And when I'm with another woman,
> I fear the hostility directed at us for being lesbians.

Yet women who do not suffer such fears can also be influenced by definitions of "normal" womanhood that necessitate a male presence. Even women who have been exclusively lesbian throughout their lives are not necessarily exempt. For example, a woman in her late thirties, a long-time lesbian who is presently unsure of her identity, acknowledged that "from time to time" she felt like a "failure as a woman" because she had never been heterosexually involved.

Lie #2 – Women Don't Count

The idea that women are inferior to men is intimately connected with anti-lesbian ideology that ignores and trivializes relationships between women.[72] In fact, it is impossible to separate the two.

Among the mostly feminist lesbians and former lesbians I studied, overtly sexist attitudes were rare. Only a small minority of respondents stated that they found men more interesting than women (8.2% of lesbians and 9.4% of former lesbians). Subtle forms of internalized sexism were more common, reflected primarily in some women's inability to take their relationships with other women seriously.

Whether overt or covert sexism was involved, the result was the same: the weakening of a woman's commitment to a lesbian life, sometimes leading to a decision to leave.

The connection between sexism and compulsory heterosexuality for women was manifested in the comments of several of the lesbians-who-left. One such woman, in her forties and now heterosexual, told me why she preferred men as lovers:

> I really don't trust women enough to be truly intimate

sexually...Men are more predictable...Most of the women I've run across are weak and demanding. Men are not as clingy...I don't know a lot of intelligent women. I can't stand stupidity. So it makes it really difficult to enter into a lasting relationship because you get them out of bed, you want to talk to them and they can't say anything.

Similarly, a bisexual woman in her twenties blamed women for their lower social status. She wrote that men "do not degrade themselves socially as much as many of the women that I know – that is, the men maintain their dignity".

Another former lesbian, also bisexual, stated that she had a hard time finding a woman who could be her "equal":

I am a very skilled woman as far as carpentry, electrical, plumbing, automotive...and am highly educated and politically active...It is difficult for me to find a woman who can match my skill level, a woman who I don't feel I have to "do" for.

One lesbian-who-left wrote that she found men "more outgoing and fun than the women I've met in my life". Another simply stated, "I don't trust women". All these women found a lesbian life problematic because they doubted the worth and abilities of other women.

Some of the lesbians were also affected by the lie that "women don't count". A lesbian in her forties who considers heterosexual relationships a possibility described her own anti-woman prejudices:

As a lesbian, I've basically had one-night stands with women. The one long-term affair I had I broke off because I was afraid to commit...In the last two years, I've had no sex with either men or women...I've tried to make friends with women first...I'm overcoming a lot of brainwashing that I couldn't trust women and that women are stupid.

Lie #3: Lesbianism is Sick

Though several controlled studies during the last few decades have found that the mental health of lesbians is indistinguishable from that of heterosexual women except for the greater self-confidence and self-esteem of the lesbians,[72] the lie that "lesbianism is sick" has lost surprisingly little of its power. Not only do many heterosexuals still believe it, but so do a considerable number of lesbians.

It is impossible to measure the amount of psychological harm done to women during the past century by this most insidious of lies about lesbianism.[73] Every woman who has ever passionately loved another woman has had to struggle to free herself from the grip of this lie whether or not she ever read the sexologists' writings, or ever visited a psychiatrist. Certainly, in contemporary times, the counter-balance of feminist consciousness-raising and lesbian/gay liberation has helped tremendously, but we have not yet succeeded in silencing the voices in our heads.

These voices – echoing the words of Havelock Ellis, Krafft-Ebbing, Frank Caprio, John Money, and others of their ilk – tell us that women loving each other is biologically speaking, neither "normal" nor "natural" – only heterosexuality is that. Then, they provide us with a whole list of what could have gone wrong. And finally, in somber tones, they warn that lesbian sexuality is not only, by definition, pathological, but also inevitably unsatisfying. If we believe them, self-loathing follows. This is what happened to a disturbing number of the women in this study.

Though almost all the respondents considered themselves feminists, only 61.9% of the lesbians and 54.7% of the former lesbians answered "false" without equivocation to the statement, "Heterosexual relationships are more natural for the over-whelming majority of women than are lesbian ones", 25.9% of the lesbians and 39% of the former lesbians responded "true" and the rest were unsure. This means that close to half – 45.3% – of the former lesbians either firmly believed that hetero-sexuality is the biological norm or thought this might be the case.

As one Jewish bisexual lesbian-who-left (in her thirties) explained:

> Whoever or whatever it was that created human beings in the form of a man and in the form of a female did it in a way to insure the survival of the species…You've got the biological drive to reproduce the species that's present in all life…so in that sense it's more natural

being heterosexual.

Like many of the sexologists, she believed that homosexuality was explained by environmental factors that changed in the direction of the biological "instinct".

Consistent with this general view, a significant minority of the respondents distinguished between "real lesbians" and at least some of the women who became lesbians through feminism. While 90.5% of the lesbians gave an unequivocal "false" response to the statement, "Many women who used to date men and became lesbians during the Women's Movement of the 70's are not real lesbians", 73.4% of the lesbians-who-left did so. The balance, over a quarter of the former lesbians and close to 10% of the lesbians, gave credence to the distinction between "congenital" and "acquired" homosexuality first postulated by nineteenth century sexology.

For example, one lesbian-who-returned, who is from a strict Christian background, saw herself as a "born" lesbian, while doubting that other women she knew were truly lesbians:

> I do believe that some women who have been abused
> by men, or have been raped...or have been victims of
> incest move into a lesbian lifestyle simply to protect
> themselves against men. I don't believe that they're
> necessarily lesbians.

The idea that abuse "causes" lesbianism – found repeatedly in the sexologists' writings – turned out to be one of the most popular theories held by the respondents. A full half of the lesbians-who-left and 34.7% of the lesbians checked "true" to the statement, "Traumatic experiences with men such as rape and childhood sexual abuse are one reason that many women become lesbians". Typical were the comments of an African-American lesbian-who-left who wrote, "I related sexually to women due to early childhood sexual assaults by male cousins." She later attempted a serious relationship with a man.

Other "explanations" for lesbianism given by respondents in this study – most of which are drawn directly from the Neo-Freudians – included sex-negative messages from parents, alcoholic and violent father, passive mother, and the absence of love from the mother (causing a daughter to seek mother-love in another woman).

Sometimes these ideas came from a homophobic therapist,

who actively encouraged a heterosexual "adjustment". One heterosexual former lesbian in her forties, now in a primary relationship with a man, told me:

> What I discovered in the therapy work is how much fear I had around my father...As I started to regain a sense of power relative to men, then I started finding myself more sexually attracted to them.

She also came to blame her lesbianism on her problematic relationship with her mother:

> That kind of bonding that happens between two women, the emotional intensity was something I never had with my mother so I appreciated having it with another woman.

However, she believed that her exclusive lesbian orientation was a response to the negative things in her life, thus concurring with the opinions of some sexologists that while bisexuality is not necessarily pathological, lesbianism always is.

Those former lesbians who blamed heterosexual trauma for their lesbianism were likely to see involvements with men as a necessary part of their "healing". One bisexual former lesbian described her decision to return to heterosexual relationships:

> I was incested by my father when I was ten until about sixteen...I was raped by a man who I was sexual with previous to the rape when I was eighteen years old. I was also sexually assaulted by a man when I was out on a date when I was twenty...I came out as a lesbian out of a lot of anger toward men...I came out when I got active in a lot of feminist organizing...I stopped being a lesbian because I was not getting everything I needed from the lesbian community. I needed to work out this stuff around men with men. So I pretty deliberately found a man that I felt safe with...Making the decision to come out as bisexual was very connected...I don't think I would have come out as a lesbian if I had not been abused.

Una, the lesbian-who-left (in Chapter I), began to change her identity in response to the belief that "lesbianism is sick". As Una explained:

> Why after fifteen years am I giving up the lesbian label? Partly because I used that label to run away from my

fears of sex with men. My proclivity is toward the literal; when my parents and other adults got the message across that sex was dirty, shameful, evil, they meant sex with men. I took them literally so sex with women seemed more OK with me!...As I shed fears, gain a positive self-image, the need to identify solely as a lesbian changes...

Rather than seeing her spirited rebellious nature as all the explanation she needed for her lesbian preference, Una considered her lesbianism a result of "something going wrong", in her case, sex-negative parents. Fostering heterosexual interests was thus, as she perceived it, a form of "therapy".

Other former lesbians also emphasized the connection between their move toward male lovers and their desire to "heal" from child sexual abuse, rape, or "fear" of men. A total of nine women – 18%-stated that their desire to be "healed" was a reason for their leaving. In addition, one former lesbian (2% of the sample) stated that she left because she wished to be "cured" of her lesbianism. Of the lesbians-who-returned, 13.6% (three women) said that they sought heterosexual relationships for "healing", and 22.7% (five women), stated that they desired a "cure". This amounts to a total of 36.3% of the lesbians-who-returned and 20% of the lesbians-who-left who believed heterosexual relations necessary for their mental health.

In addition, 14% of the former lesbians and 9% of the lesbians-who-returned indicated that they had begun dealing with their personal history of sexual abuse immediately prior to their change of identity.

"Heterosexual therapy" can be bitter medicine indeed for the women involved. One lesbian-who-left (in her thirties) described extreme ambivalence:

I became a lesbian at eighteen although I always loved women. I was raped at twenty-one and after two years I decided I'd better learn to love men or I'd be crippled emotionally by the rape. Current male relationship is part of healing. (Still love women best.) I think I still see myself as a lesbian because I am woman-identified and love women, but because I occasionally sleep with men I'm called bisexual. It's like saying a vegetarian who eats meat once a year due to anemia or something, doctor's orders, she'd still be a vegetarian at heart. I am working hard emotionally to heal the rape and letting a man love me and learning to love and be responsible and not abusive to him is part of my healing, but I don't see it as a lifestyle. I love women and want to grow old with the woman of my dreams.

Ironically, despite the bigoted ravings of neo-Freudians, there is no real evidence that rape and incest leads to lesbianism, as the Kinsey Institute and others have shown.[74] Neither is there any evidence supporting consensual heterosexual relations as a "therapy" of choice for such trauma.

If violence and sexual abuse have any impact on a woman's sexual preference, it might be just the opposite: by undermining her self-esteem, she may find it more difficult to resist society's lesbophobic messages (including the idea that abuse "causes" lesbianism), and to avoid becoming dependent on male approval and "protection" in order to feel at all valuable and safe in the world.[75] In addition, since survivors of sexual abuse learn to split their minds from their bodies as a defense mechanism, sex may feel less threatening where there is little or no emotional connection. All these factors might make acquiring and, more importantly, *keeping* a lesbian identity problematic.

Other lesbian writers have commented on the important part male violence and other abuse during childhood may play in enforcing the heterosexual institution and conditioning women to accept the feminine role. One such woman, Susan Strega, a sexual abuse survivor herself, wrote with unusual insight on this subject in *Lesbian Ethics*:

> Despite the patriarchal myth that child abuse leads to lesbianism, most female incest survivors, like most females in general, are heterosexual. Indeed, the stated motivation and justification of many adults, male and female, who sexually abuse female children, aside from the satisfaction of immediate sexual needs, is to train and prepare females to be heterosexual, that is, not lesbians... During childhood rape, we learn to be submissive, terrified to say no or fight back, and to view the abuser, male or female, as dominant and superior... Overt sexual abuse is merely a more dramatic expression of the ongoing, day-to-day socialization/ abuse of female

children by the institutions of patriarchy – families, schools, religion, the media.[76]

In this study, both lesbians and former lesbians had experienced significant amounts of violence as children and as adults, primarily, though not exclusively at the hands of men. Given the high incidence of violence against women and children in the culture at large, however, the amount of violence reported does not appear out of the ordinary. In comparing the two groups of respondents, a higher percentage of lesbians reported childhood sexual abuse compared to former lesbians (38.6% compared to 29%).[77] Close to the same percentage of both groups were battered as children (30.9% of the lesbians; 33.3% of the former lesbians). At the same time, the lesbians-who-left were likely to have been raped: as adults (31.7% versus 19.9%), to be attacked on the street (33.3% compared to 16.4%), to have been battered in a heterosexual relationship (25.4% versus 14.6%), and also, were more likely to have been prostitutes (12.4% of lesbians compared to 20.3% of former lesbians) or to have worked as a model, topless dancer or stripper in the sex industry (4.8% of lesbians compared to 14% of former lesbians), groups with disproportionately high sexual abuse histories and a high risk of male violence in their work. However, substantially more of the lesbians than lesbians-who-left had been entirely free of experiences of physical or sexual violence throughout their lives (42.4% of the lesbians compared to only 27.4% of the former lesbians).

It is certainly possible that this greater experience of (mostly male) physical and sexual violence among the former lesbians contributed to their increased vulnerability to lesbophobic ideology. Thus some women may have become stuck in what Strega describes as "a nether-world of sexual identity confusion, unable to come out fully and leave self-destructive heterosexual reenactments of abuse behind, but unwilling to give up the dream of romantic and sexual love with a woman".[78]

Such experiences may also explain the somewhat greater submissiveness toward men of the lesbians-who-left. More former lesbians than lesbians responded "true" to the statement, "There have been times that I found it difficult to say no to men who wanted to have sex with me even though I didn't really want to have sex." (45.3% of the former lesbians compared to

38.3% of the lesbians).

One such woman, a former lesbian with a history of childhood sexual abuse and an ex-husband who had physically abused and raped her during most of their marriage, described the problems she had:

> A year and a half after I came out as a lesbian, a male friend and I arranged to go away together...After we got there, I discovered we were booked into the same room...I had said to him before we went, look, we've been flirting and I need to be clear that this is not a trip for the purpose of sexuality...Over the course of that weekend, I came out to him as a lesbian... However, very shortly after I came out to him, we began a sexual relationship. I had as much to do with initiating it as he did, although I would never have put myself into these circumstances and I hold him responsible for that and myself for not having the courage to get out of that situation.

Like the other former lesbians we've discussed, this woman viewed her heterosexual relationship, despite its coercive beginnings, as "therapeutic":

> Setting sexual limits with this man was actually a very helpful process for me in working through the abusive sexual relationship with my ex-husband.

When she became involved with this man, she also felt a strong attraction to a woman whom she described as "an ideal person for me". But because of "work" on abuse issues, she chose not to pursue the attraction.

Another lesbian-who-left, now heterosexual and married, described experiencing sexual abuse both as a child and as an adult. She also explained why it might be harder for a woman who had suffered in that way to become a lesbian:

> I would say a good third of abused women remain passive through their entire lives and drift whichever seems the easiest way to go through life...If they are married and have kids, it's easier to stay that way...I strongly suspect that more women would be in lesbian relationships if it were safer. It's still so against what society tells you to do especially if you've been abused. You just don't want to make anybody angry...If you've

been abused, you gave up original thoughts so young you can't remember having them. If anytime you expressed anything that was different than your family said was OK to think, you were smashed, so why risk being different?

Of course, as we have seen, it is not only women who have been abused who "swallow the lie" that lesbianism is sick and heterosexual relationships the "cure". Many women absorb these messages and, as a result, suffer from feelings of shame and disgust over their love for other women.

Internalized lesbophobia can not only destroy an intimate relationship (or prevent one from starting in the first place), it can also cause the woman involved to pursue relationships with men. Wrote one former lesbian:

At age 23, I had a guilty relationship with an equally guilty co-worker. The guilt between two first time lesbians prevented the relationship from going anywhere...I had no support and felt "crazy". I then began to date men.

Similarly, a lesbian in her forties became so convinced as a young woman that her sexual feelings for other women were sick that she married twice before coming out as a lesbian:

As a small child I was touching all my girlfriends and they liked it. However, when one girlfriend's parents found out, I was not allowed to see that friend again. I never knew why my friends had to stay away. I just knew there was something "wrong" with me...

Sometimes internalized lesbophobia, in women conflicted over their sexuality is projected outward in anger at other lesbians, especially those who are open about their lives and insist on rights heterosexuals take for granted. One of my lesbian contacts gave me the name and address of a woman she claimed was a former lesbian who might be willing to fill out a questionnaire. The response to my inquiry is a classic example of this psychological mechanism:

I do not know how you got my name. It may have been from a crazy "woman scorned". I am not now, have not in the past and do not plan to become a lesbian. I have been in a monogamous heterosexual relationship for twenty years. I do not think lesbianism is an alternative lifestyle. I think it is a pathological, immoral, abnormal lifestyle. If you plan to do a study on psychotic personality, especially narcissism, I can give you the name of a woman who could fill a textbook of pathology.

Other responses from lesbians-who-left were only slightly less hostile. Wrote one woman:

I have no objection to lesbian activities and women who prefer to make it their lifestyle. I do not understand why they seek public recognition…Why make it a public issue and insist on special rights?[79]

Prejudice against other lesbians was not as rare as one might expect. A disturbing number of respondents – 29% of the former lesbians and 12.4% of the lesbians – checked "true" to the statement, "Women who look obviously lesbian or who publicly flaunt their lesbianism make me uncomfortable".

Such feelings have been linked by a number of clinicians to the problem of lesbian sexual dysfunction. One such expert, Laura Brown, a psychologist and sex therapist, describes its basis in internalized lesbophobia:

…many problems in sexual functioning experienced by lesbian couples serves as the "fly in the ointment", the problem in the relationship that satisfies the demands of a homophobic culture which believes that no relationship between two women can be entirely satisfying. The sexual problem functions as a self-fulfilling prophecy, strengthening the internalized stereotypes regarding the lower value of lesbian relationships.[80]

Behavioral sex therapy of the sort described by Masters and Johnson has had little effect when the clients have persisted in strongly held, although often not overtly expressed beliefs, such as, "This won't work anyway because all lesbian relationships are short and shallow", or "Lesbianism is just another closet for celibacy, so why work on being sexual". It is astonishing how frequently and regularly these and similar sentiments occur in client and non-client populations of lesbians, including self-identified feminist lesbians.[81]

Among our respondents, almost a third – 32% – of the lesbians-who-left and 4.5% of lesbians-who-returned reported experiencing sexual dysfunction immediately prior to leaving. In addition, 20% of the former lesbians (though none of the lesbians-who-returned), stated that their personal difficulty in being sexual with a woman was one reason they left. As one former lesbian frankly explained:

What makes me think I'm bi is that I haven't had much sex with women and it's not been good when I have had it...It has fizzled quickly and I have turned it off, said no. Said no to women as I couldn't say no to men. With women I have had better relationships... but not good sex. I understand heterosex; I am afraid of lesbian sex. I am homophobic as well. I am proud to be a lesbian and tell everyone but I don't act it in bed.

One method lesbians commonly use to reduce the anxiety of internalized lesbophobia is to "self-medicate" through heavy use of alcohol, marijuana, and other drugs.[82] Researchers have found a greater tendency to abuse alcohol among lesbians who were in conflict over their homosexuality, compared to those who had a significant degree of self-acceptance.[83] Many avoid lesbian sex when sober and, upon entering recovery, experience a crisis over not only their sexual functioning but also over their sexual identity. As psychologist Kathleen O'Halleran Glaus explains, "In recovery, internalized homophobic feelings may surface in lesbians who, when drinking or using drugs, were unaware of them".[84]

In this study, 12% of the lesbians-who-left reported that they had gone into recovery from alcohol or drug abuse immediately prior to moving toward male lovers. For all of these women, upon entering recovery, issues arose concerning lesbianism that they had previously been able to avoid. I asked one former lesbian how her experience of lesbian sex changed once she achieved sobriety. She replied:

It was easier that way [drunk]. All that mind stuff didn't come into play...Something that was already difficult [being sexual with a woman] became more difficult.

Since becoming sober, what did she feel when making love with a woman?

Real distance, she told me. Like I don't want to be there with her, I don't want to touch her, and I don't want

167

her touching me. I just want to keep away.

Having swallowed the lie that "lesbianism is sick", touching another woman while free of the numbing effects of alcohol became just too threatening. So, like so many others, her lesbian relationship came to an end and she began looking for a boyfriend.

Lie #4 – Lesbians Are Bad People

A lesbian in her thirties described her own long and painful struggle with this lie:

I fell in love with a female in high school...We didn't have sex but we frequently held hands (in private) and professed our love for one another. That was in Tennessee where I grew up and where I learned that homosexual men and women were BAD PEOPLE, no two ways about it. So the love of my life and I believed we were not lesbians because we knew we were not bad people. We even thought we could run away and live together and we wanted to move to a more liberal place (like California) so people wouldn't think we were lesbians...Instead of running away together, I went to college and left my dear friend to date boys (much to my chagrin). And since I wasn't a lesbian, I tried to get interested in the boys in college...Then I picked one man to try to settle down with. A stormy three year relationship ensued...By the age of twenty-five, I was sure I was a lesbian, I was free of the abusive hetero-sexual relationship, I was involved in a sexual relation-ship with an older woman and I was addicted to heroin. I wonder sometimes if I wasn't trying to be as BAD as I could so that I could identify as a lesbian since they were BAD people.

Sometimes, "swallowing the lie" that lesbians are bad people can cause a woman to leave. One lesbian-who-left wrote:

I don't know any healthy lesbians. They are out for themselves, to look cool, see how many women they can ensnare, and don't share or develop feelings.

The very act of choosing women over men as romantic/sexual partners is evidence of being "bad", according to lesbophobic ideology. The large majority of respondents in both groups rejected this view – 93.2% of the lesbians and 85.9% of the lesbians-who-left giving an unequivocal "false" response to the statement, "Most lesbians hate men". However, this still leaves a significant number of women – 14.1% of the former lesbians (nine women) and 6.8% of the lesbians who either believe that this statement is true or that it might be true.

Ironically, at the same time that lesbians are accused of being "man-haters", we are supposed to be "just like men", apeing their least desirable characteristics, especially men's treatment of women. In reality, of course, most lesbians are emotionally and sexually similar to most straight women, in that a majority of both groups prefer sexuality in the context of emotional intimacy, emphasize the importance of friendship and are not aggressive sexually.[85] Yet a disturbing number of respondents – again more former lesbians than lesbians – answered true to the statement, "A lot of lesbians are just as macho and are just as oppressive and objectifying of other women as many men" (46.9% of the lesbians compared to 64% of the lesbians-who-left).

This tendency to be overly critical of other lesbians is one way lesbians express their own lesbophobia. Suzanne Pharr, in her book on homophobia, labels it "Horizontal oppression/hostility", which she describes as internalized prejudice turned against one's own kind:

Suffering the pain and damage of a world that despises us, we transform our pain into anger and turn it against one another instead of at the source of oppression. Instead of focusing that anger and energy in a unified way to make the changes needed in the dominant culture, where it is more risky and dangerous to confront oppression, we expend ourselves attacking and limiting one another. We become the harshest and most exacting critics of lesbian lives.

Such horizontal hostility was reflected in many of the comments of the lesbians-who-left. For example, one former lesbian with a dual identity stated:

The lesbian community in general is so anti-men and particularly prejudiced against bisexual women that I cannot comfortably share my growth/exploration process with other lesbians.

Another former lesbian, bisexual-identified (though at the time of the interview, she had never had sex with a man), told me that she had recently been fired from her job for being a lesbian and that anti-gay discrimination and gay-bashing were rampant in her city. She herself had been attacked on the street while holding hands with a lover. Yet, for her too, it was easier to project her anger onto the lesbian community rather than confront the primary source of oppression in her life:

> I began to identify as bi in 1986...A factor could be my increasing disillusion with lesbian separatism and the incredibly parochial and close-minded character of my local women's community... The last two years identifying as a lesbian...I was speaking out publicly about the biphobia, racism, anti-intellectualism, and anti-semitism in my lesbian community...It was the "politically correct" crap that got me really fed up with the lesbian community.

A number of other lesbians-who-left agreed with this negative assessment – 26% of the former lesbians (13 women) and 4.5% of the lesbians-who-returned (1 woman) gave as a reason for leaving that the lesbian community was "too narrow-minded". Apparently, the institutionalized bigotry of the straight community was preferable (perhaps because familiar).

One bisexual woman told me that when still a lesbian she took a job where she was required to dress "professionally" and stay closeted. She felt that the lesbian community did not understand her need to make these compromises and this was one reason she left. Yet, the resentment she expressed toward other lesbians also seemed, at least in part, misplaced:

> I had some negative feelings about the lesbian community at that time [during the transition from lesbian to bisexual]. A lot of it was that I felt there was a lot of negativism about the way I was living my life and the fact that I wasn't totally out at my office. There were professional lesbians in D.C. who could do that because they were protected by the D.C. laws and they worked for the government. They didn't have to worry about it as much. But I had no protection. I didn't see any reason to broadcast. I felt the lesbian community was very restrictive and not very accepting – that there

were good lesbians and bad lesbians. That good lesbians were out and looked kind of butch and not very feminine and the bad lesbians were the "lesbians for lipstick"...

A few former lesbians claimed to have been driven away not just from a lesbian life but also from the feminist movement (particularly its lesbian-feminist wing) because of "back-biting and trashing", and "star-tripping, internalized sexism and homophobia, racism and classism". Certainly these are real problems that have at times plagued our movement as they have all other progressive movements. In addition, our own self-hatred can cause us to treat other women very badly. Why are we so unforgiving, so lacking in generosity toward the all-too-human faults of other feminists, particularly other lesbians? Why do we judge our lesbian sisters more harshly than we would ever think of judging men, heterosexual women, or the dominant straight society? Perhaps we hold up such perfectionist standards for lesbians because we all have been/can be judged by the acts of those who fail to meet these standards. Perhaps, in the deep recesses of our subconscious, we have "swallowed the lie".

Footnotes
[1] Krafft-Ebbing, *Psychopathia Sexualis*, (Stuttgart, 1886) (English adaptation of last German edition) (Pioneer Publications, Inc., New York, 1941), pp. 286, 538-540.
[2] This is but one example of the dual nature of the taboo – that what is forbidden, perhaps even more than homosexual acts themselves, is the unwillingness to participate in the heterosexual institution, ie., a woman's refusal to carry out her "duty" to love and marry men and to play the subordinate, nurturing role.
[3] Krafft-Ebbing, *Psychopathia Sexualis*, pp. 398-399.
[4] Ibid., p. 397.
[5] Perhaps this reflects a concern not only for "bad genes" being passed on to future generations but also for the possibility of a "role-modeling" effect on children who are raised by overtly gay and lesbian parents.
[6] This obsession with the "dangers" of masturbation may, at first glance, appear to be merely an irrational nineteenth century prejudice. Yet, for many women, learning how to masturbate was the first step in developing an independent and self-defined sexuality. It is not too difficult to see how such self-knowledge – in both men and women but particularly in women – could begin to challenge the inevitability of heterosexuality.
[7] Krafft-Ebbing, *Psychopathia Sexualis* p. 448.

8 Havelock Ellis and John Addington Symonds, *Sexual Inversion* (NY: Arno Press, New York, 1975.), p. 94. *Sexual Inversion* was originally published in 1897.

9 Ibid., p. 146.

10 Ellis ideas are echoed in the debate on lifting the ban on gays and lesbians in the military which occurred while this book was being written. The biggest problem for maintaining the heterosexual norm in the military is not the existence of homosexuals themselves, but the existence of "open" homosexuals. Thus, we've seen the "compromise" of "don't ask; don't tell" that was ultimately imposed by President Clinton to allow homosexuals only so long as they remain in the closet.

11 Ellis, *Sexual Inversation*, p. 146.

12 The idea that the existence of women's colleges posed a threat to the heterosexual institution continued into the 1950's and 60's and was a large part of the motivation for many such colleges to admit male students. For example, at Vassar College in 1951, Dr. Carl Binger, a psychiatrist, resigned amidst much publicity, claiming that Vassar was a "matriarchy" with "too many unmarried women in supervisory capacities" and that he was concerned about the "sexual development of undergraduates" in such an unwholesome atmosphere. Within a few years, the first steps were taken to create a "normal" atmosphere at Vassar: a male President was appointed and plans were made to admit male students. See Ann MacKay, ed., *Wolf Girls at Vassar – Lesbian and Gay Experiences 1930-1990* (NY: St. Martin's Press, New York, 1993), pp. 16-17.

13 Ibid., p. 156.

14 John Hart and Diane Richardson, *Theory and Practice of Homosexuality*, (Routledge & Kegan Paul, London, 1981)pp. 10-16; See also B. A. Gladue, "Psychobiological contributions" published in *Male and Female Homosexuality* by Louis Diamont, ed., (Hemisphere Publishing, 1987), pg. 134, Gladue, reviewing the studies on lesbians, concluded that "the majority of adult female homosexuals appear to have testosterone and estrogen levels well within the female normal range".

15 John Money, *Gay, Straight, and In-Between – The Sexology of Erotic Orientation* (Oxford University Press, New York, 1988), pp. 80-81.

16 See Diane Richards, "Theoretical Perspectives in Homosexuality", published in Hart and Richardson, *The Theory and Practice of Homosexuality*, p. 19; see also Ruth Bleir, *Science and Gender – A Critique of Biology and Its Theories on Women* (Pergamon Press, Oxford, 1984) pp. 173-175.

17 John Money, *Gay, Straight, and In Between*, p. 26.

18 Ibid., p.36

19 Hart and Richardson, *Theory and Practice of Homosexuality*, p. 20; Hart and Richardson also point out that in cases where physical hermaphrodites are reared in a sex contrary to their chromosomal sex, hormonal sex, their internal organs and/or contrary to the appearance of their external genitalia, in most instances they develop a gender

identity consistent with their sex of rearing. (Ibid., pp. 6-9.)

[20] John Money, *Gay, Straight, and In Between*, pp. 58-61.

[21] Ibid., pp. 58-61.

[22] Ibid., p. 83.

[23] Ibid., p. 124.

[24] Few sexologists, gay or straight, would today refer to most homosexuals as a "third sex" (a man's soul born in a woman's body or a woman's soul born in a man's body). However, a sub-group of the lesbian/gay community, "transgenders", has now convinced themselves of the term's legitimacy. This term has come to embrace transvestites of both sexes – drag queens and women who pass as men (as were many lesbians in history) – as well as transsexuals, persons who become so convinced that their "problem" lies in their physical body that they take hormones and/or undergo "sex change" surgery to alter their body's appearance.

[25] See Appendix C, "Ulrich's Views" by JA Symonds, in Ellis, *Sexual Inversion*.

[26] "Born or Bred" *Newsweek*, February 24, 1992.

[27] The measurement of brains in order to provide pseudo-biological justification for social hierarchies of race, class, ethnicity, and sex, has a long and sordid history. LeVay fits squarely into this biological determinist tradition. See Stephen Jay Gould, *The Mismeasure of Man* (WW Norton & Company, New York, 1981) which successfully debunks the scientific bigotry of the last two centuries and provides the background necessary to analyze LeVay's work in its historical context.

[28] Anne Fausto-Sterling, *Myths of Gender* (Basic Books, New York, 1992), Chapter 8, "Sex and the Single Brian" pp. 223-259.

[29] Lisa M. Krieger, "Study cites a genetic basis for lesbianism" published in the March 11, 1993 *San Francisco Examiner*

[30] As Anne Fausto Sterling told *Newsweek* (Feb. 24, 1992), "In order for such a study to be at all meaningful, you'd have to look at twins raised apart. It's such badly interpreted genetics".

[31] Sigmund Freud, "Three Essays on Sexuality – The Sexual Aberrations", (1905) republished in *The Standard Edition of the Complete Psychological Works of Sigmund Freud* (The Hogarth Press, London, 1953), Vol. 7, p. 145

[32] Ibid., pp. 145-146; see also Sigmund Freud, "Psychogenesis of a Case of Homosexuality in a Woman" (1920) republished in *The Complete Psychological Works* Vol. 18, p. 168.

[33] Freud, "Psychogenesis of a Case of Homosexuality in Women", p. 157.

[34] Ibid., p. 168.

[35] Ibid., p. 169.

[36] Ibid., p. 157.

[37] Sigmund Freud, "The Sexual Aberrations", *Complete Psychological Works*, p. 145.

[38] Freud, "Three Essays on Sexuality – Transformation of Puberty" *Complete Psychological Works*, p. 229..

[39] Frank S. Caprio, *Female Homosexuality – A Psychodynamic Study of Lesbianism* (N.Y.: The Citadel Press, 1954) p. 120.

[40] Ibid., pp. 61, 171, 174, 180.

[41] Ibid., pp. 61, 302-304.

[42] Ibid., pp. 121-122.

[43] Ibid., p. 122.

[44] Ibid., p. 132

[45] Ibid., pp. 132-133.

[46] Ibid., p.148. Of course, Caprio does not ask what might have driven the wife to murder.

[47] Ibid., p. 169.

[48] Ibid., p. 120.

[49] Ibid., p. 74.

[50] Ibid., pp. 117-118.

[51] Ibid., pp. 298-299.

[52] Ibid., p. 169.

[53] Ibid., p. 299.

[54] See Cornelia B. Wilbur, "Clinical Aspects of Female Homosexuality", *Sexual Inversion – The Multiple Roots of Homosexuality*, Judd Marmor, ed. (Basic Book, Inc., New York, 1965) pp. 268-277.

[55] Ibid.

[56] A 1978 survey of 2,500 members of the American Psychiatric Association found that 69% believed being gay was pathological. 73% viewed homosexuals as less happy than heterosexuals and 60% felt that homosexuals were less capable of mutual and loving relationships. See Rothblum & Cole, eds., *Loving Boldly: Issues Facings Lesbians* (NY: Harrington Park Press, New York, 1989.) p. 5.

[57] See Alan P. Bell, Martin S. Weinberg, Sue Kiefer Hamersmith, *Sexual Preference – Its Development In Men and Women* (Indiana Univ. Press, 1981).

[58] Bell, et al., *Sexual Preference*, p. 185; Likewise, a study done in 1973, also found no significant difference between lesbians and heterosexual women in parental rigidity and negativism toward sex. In that study, sexual traumas in childhood occurred in only a small minority of the lesbians. (See Marcel T. Saghir, MD and Eli Robins, M.D., *Male and Female Homosexuality – A Comprehensive Investigation* (The Williams & Williams Co., Baltimore, 1973).

[59] Bell, et al., *Sexual Preference*, p. 185.

[60] Ibid., pp. 1225, 133.

[61] Ibid., p. 139.

[62] Bell, et al., *Sexual Preference*, pp. 188-189; 149-151. However, this connection was not absolute. While 62% of homosexual females considered themselves very "masculine" when growing up, compared to 10% of heterosexual women, only a third of heterosexual women (compared to a fifth of lesbians) were highly "feminine" as children. This means that most women were to some degree gender non-conforming in childhood. In addition, retrospective accounts of child-hood by adult homosexuals may be colored by present identity and

are thus of questionable reliability. See Hart & Richardson, *Theory and Practice of Homosexuality*, p. 34.

[63] Bell, et al., *Sexual Preference*, p. 189.

[64] Ibid., p. 192.

[65] Manny Sternlicht, "The Neo-Freudians", *Male and Female Homosexuality – Psychological Approaches* Louis Diamont, ed. (Washington: Hemisphere Publishing Co., 1987) pp. 97-106.

[66] Feminist lyrics by Meridith Tax (1971) (from original folksong by Rose Bonne and Alan Mills) published in Rise Up Singing (Sing Out Corporation, 1988).

[67] JoAnn Loulan, *Lesbian Passion: Loving Ourselves and Each Other* (Spinsters/Aunt Lute, San Francisco, 1988) p. 33.

[68] See the excellent discussion of internalized lesbophobia in *Homophobia – A Weapon on Sexism* by Suzanne Pharr (Charden Press, 1988), pp. 65-91.

[69] Two recent Hollywood films that feature lesbian and bisexual women characters – *Basic Instinct* and *Three of Hearts* – both portrayed heterosexual men as impossible for women to resist. This is true whether the man is a brute as in *Basic Instinct* or a seductive charmer as in *Three of Hearts*. As Kathy Maio explained in her review, "Three of Hearts, The Lesbian Loses Again" (June, 1993 *Sojourner*), "Like *Basic Instinct*, *Three of Hearts* ends up endorsing the notion that the straight man is the only true (undeniable) sexual force on this planet".

[70] The "male protection racket" as it has been named by some, is essentially a fraud: most rape, battery, and murder of women is carried out by men women know – husbands, fathers, boyfriends, dates, etc., rather than by strangers. The most "chivalrous" of men often hold traditional sexist attitudes toward women and are frequently the most violent. (See Stephanie Coontz, *The Way We Never Were* (Basic Books, New York, 1992), pp. 279-280.)

[71] The message that women are to blame if their heterosexual relationships fail or are unsatisfying comes through loud and clear in a number of books in the self-help genre, including *Women Who Love Too Much*, *Smart Women/Foolish Choices*, and more recently *Ten Stupid Things Women Do to Mess Up Their Lives*, all aimed at an exclusively female audience. In the world of self-help books, any unhappiness women experience in our relationships with men is our own fault; if we are just smart enough and chose our men wisely, heterosexual bliss will follow. There is thus no need to examine men's sexism or the patriarchal structures of society, and, of course, lesbianism doesn't exist even as a possiblity.

[72] See Rothblum & Cole, eds., *Loving Boldly*, p. 4, where Esther D. Rothblum mentions a 1971 study by Thompson, McCandless & Strickland and more recent research reported in J. S. Hyde's book *Half the Human Experience* (3rd ed., 1985) (MA: C.L. Heath & Company). Rothblum remarks, "Given the extremely homophobic societal views, it is amazing that lesbians have coped so well".

[73] Of course, the parallel and closely related religious condemnation

of lesbianism as "sinful" is equally destructive and results in many of the same conflicts that are described in this section. However, standing alone, it lacks the aura of "scientific objectivity" that "lesbianism is sick" has, and does not have the same universal appeal.

[74] In Joann Loulan's study of 1566 lesbians, 38.6% reported that they experienced childhood sexual abuse before the age of eighteen. Loulan points out that Diana Russell's random sample of 930 women came up with the same statistic of 38%. *Lesbian Passion*, p. 148. The lesbians in our study also had approximately the same rate of abuse – 38.6%.

[75] Ellen Bass and Laura Davis in *The Courage to Heal* (NY: Harper and Row, 1988), p. 34, described how abuse affects self-esteem: "When you were abused, your boundaries, your right to say no, your sense of control in the world, were violated. You were powerless. The abuse humiliated you, gave you the message that you were of little value".

[76] Susan Strega, "Breaking the Ties that Bind: Healing as Political Process" published in Lesbian Ethics, Vol. 4, No. 3 (1992), pp. 21-22.

[77] Since incidents of sexual abuse in childhood are not always remembered, it is unclear whether the difference between the two groups represents one of incidence or merely of recollection.

[78] Strega, *Lesbian Ethics*, p. 18.

[79] The idea that lesbians, by fighting for equality and for laws prohibiting discrimination on the basis of sexual preference, are thereby seeking "special rights", has been a main theme of the religious right in its anti-gay initiative campaigns around the country. Such rhetoric twists reality since it is in fact heterosexuals who are granted legal and social privileges (including public recognition of their relationships) under the present system.

[80] Laura S. Brown, PhD. "Confronting Internalized Oppression in Sex Therapy with Lesbians", *Historical, Literary and Erotic Aspects of Lesbianism*, Monica Kehoe, ed. (NY: Harrington Park Press Inc., 1986), p. 103.

[81] Ibid.

[82] Ibid., p. 101.

[83] See Sagher & Robins, *Male and Female Homosexuality – A Comprehensive Investigation*, p. 285; See also discussion of the issue of alcoholism and internalized lesbophobia in "Alcoholism, Chemical Dependency and the Lesbian Client" by Kathleen O'Halloran Glaus published in Rothblum and Cole, eds., *Loving Boldly, Issues Facing Lesbians.*

[84] Ibid., p. 139.

[85] This does not mean that women are incapable of mistreating or abusing their women partners. Inter-women violence, battering, and even sexual abuse occurs among a significant minority of lesbians (though, in my view, it is unlikely that it approaches the scale of male violence against women). In the present political climate, violence and abuse in lesbian relationships may even be on the increase as feminism loses its influence in the lesbian subculture and both sado-masochism and butch-femme roles become more commonplace. At the same time,

deep cultural differences between the sexes and the fact that there are no gender-based institutionalized power differences involved when two women are lovers, often gives relationships between women a different quality than heterosexual ones. See *Women and Love* by Shere Hite (NY: Alfred A. Knopf, 1987), particularly the section, "Are Love Relationships Between Women Different?" For example, Hite found that 86% of lesbians found talking and affection their number one pleasure in the relationship, 61% are and have always been monogamous with their lovers, and 64% remain long-term friends with their most serious lovers.

VI
FEMINISM AND WOMEN'S CHOICES

The modern movement of emancipation, the movement to obtain the same rights and duties, the same freedom and responsibility, the same education and the same work – must be regarded, on the whole, as wholesome and inevitable movement. But it carries with it certain disadvantages. It has involved an increase in feminine criminality and in feminine insanity, which are being elevated to the masculine standard. In connection with these, we can scarcely be surprised to find an increase in homosexuality...having been taught independence of men and disdain for the old theory which placed women in the mooted grange of the home to sigh for a man who never comes, a tendency develops for women to carry this independence still further and to find love where they find work...

– Havelock Ellis, *Sexual Inversion*
originally published in 1897

Only women can give each other a new sense of self. That identity we have to develop with reference to ourselves, and not in relation to men...Our energies must flow toward our sisters, not backwards toward our oppressors...It is the primacy of women relating to women, of women creating a new consciousness of and with each other which is at the heart of women's liberation, and the basis for the cultural revolution.
– from "The Woman Identified Woman" Radicalesbians, 1970.

An angry woman is a beauty
She's chosen to be a Dyke like me
She's a lesbian...
Any woman can be a lesbian.

-from "View from a Gay Head" song by
Alix Dobkin, *Lavender Jane Loves Women*, 1974

The intimate connection between lesbianism and feminism has been long recognized by both the enemies of women's liberation and by many of its most passionate proponents. From Adrienne Rich's observation that there is "a nascent feminist political content in the act of choosing a woman lover or life partner in the face of institutionalized heterosexuality"[1] to Jill Johnston's controversial statement that "until all women are lesbians there will be no true political revolution"[2] to non-lesbian Ti Grace Atkinson's acknowledgment of the "strategic importance" of lesbianism to the feminist struggle,[3] many radical feminists of varying sexual identities have understood that lesbianism is not merely about sexual practices, but about a "commitment of one woman to others of her class".[4]

This does not mean that the second wave of feminism began untainted by the lesbophobia that plagued the rest of society. Quite the contrary. Most straight feminists of the time internalized powerful prejudices against lesbians whom they deemed "the lavender menace" who would discredit feminism by their very presence. Such hostility was primarily responsible for the gay-straight split that the Movement suffered in the early 1970's and the earliest attempts by lesbian-feminists to organize separately through such groups as Radicalesbians and the Furies Collective.[5]

Yet, at the same time, something else was going on within the Feminist Movement as a whole that brought the lesbian issue to the forefront. Through feminism's support of women's autonomy and self-organization, active encouragement of female bonding and sisterhood, questioning of traditional gender roles, and biting critique of heterosexual relationships, heterosexuality became less compulsory for those women touched by the Movement. For the first time in many women's lives, loving another woman seemed both desirable and possible. The Stonewall Rebellion of 1969 gave further impetus to this changing social environment. Thus, by the mid-1970's, there were many thousands of new "political" lesbians, many having left behind heterosexual marriages or long-term relationships with men. Some of these women were returning to a lesbian life that they had experienced in their younger years; others had never before considered the possibility of loving another woman. Prominent lesbian-feminists such as Charlotte Bunch and Alix Dobkin (both of whom had been married), and lesbians-who-left like Holly Near were among those who made this personal transformation to a lesbian identity under the impact of feminism. The flood of women coming out appeared so overwhelming (for those of us caught in the middle of it), that Sally Gearhart, in the 1977 lesbian/gay documentary "Word is Out", claimed with only slight exaggeration that "Women are leaving men in droves".

The stories of the five women – Billie, Carol, Sue, Dian, and Nelly – who made up the Womanshare collective in rural Oregon in the mid-1970's were typical of the times. All of them considered themselves Lesbian separatists which they defined as "giving our primary emotional, sexual, economic, political, and work energy to women". Of the five, two, Billie and Carol, had been married and two others, Dian and Nelly, had been in long-term relationships with men. Only one woman, Sue, had never related sexually with a man.[6] For Billie, Carol, and Dian, lesbian relationships were completely new and arose directly out of their experiences in a feminist consciousness raising group. As Carol explained in a coming out letter to her mother:

> I had been in a consciousness-raising group for a year, and felt myself moving more and more toward women. I was beginning to think I could trust and maybe even work with women. The question of really loving women had been in my mind for a couple of months. I had read articles, etc. but I felt afraid of becoming a lesbian, or being called one, being considered sick and a misfit in society…but as the summer wore on Billie and I realized that we were really drawn to each other. We were both in relationships with men…but found them lacking. The men just weren't really able to understand us and feel as we did about a lot of things…Why? Because they were men and did not have the same experiences as we had. They were even sympathetic at times to our feelings of oppression, but it was not as good a feeling as when I shared with my women friends. I knew that I wanted more than what men could offer, but what could I have with women? It was so unknown to me, so scary! Billie felt the same and one night in Nova Scotia we decided together that we needed to find out…and we made love. What can I tell you about it?…It felt like a freeing experience. Like I was a virgin all over

again...Like I was no longer dependent on men for my emotional gratification. Women could be there in all ways for me too! It blew my mind".[7]

Nelly, on the other hand, had seen herself as basically bisexual prior to her involvement in the Women's Movement. In a coming out letter to her parents, she wrote:

I got involved in the Women's Movement through the Gay Women's Movement. It just made sense that when I loved someone dearly of whatever sex, it became physical and sexual...Anyway, over the years, as I got more and more involved with the Women's Movement it became clear to me that having close emotional relationships with men was a drain on my energy. Men have not been given a strong emotional constitution by our society. They are taught to deal with the physical world and often lean on women for their emotional support. I did not need to be leaned on. I needed to stand on my own two feet and be strong...And I need to be apart from men to do this.[8]

Though many of the early radical feminist groups that had focused on consciousness-raising and political action disappeared during the mid-1970's, casualties, at least in part, of the Gay-Straight split, the new lesbians that they had created began building feminist cultural and political institutions. These included: feminist presses and publications, women's bookstores, women's centers and coffeehouses, rape crisis centers, battered women's shelters, lesbian-feminist record companies; women's studies programs at various universities, women's music festivals, etc. At the same time, specialized feminist groups were born: women's health organizations, women's trade union groups such as CLUW (Coalition of Labor Union Women) and Union WAGE (Union Women's Alliance to Gain Equality), groups focused on violence against women, the National Welfare Rights Organization, Tradeswomen, Inc. for women entering the trades, the Older Women's League, and local coalitions struggling for childcare – among others. The National Organization for Women also experienced monumental growth during the period of the mid to late 70's as it campaigned publicly for passage of the Equal Rights Amendment. A base of support for female independence and self-definition was thereby established and, as a result, women coming out as lesbians through feminism continued as a mass phenomenon throughout the late 1970's and into the early 1980's.

Considering the period in which this study was conducted (1988 to 1990), it is therefore not surprising that the women who participated were not only overwhelmingly feminists (89% of the lesbians; 91.8% of former lesbians)[9] but also acknowledged that they were influenced by feminism, at least to some degree, in their coming out process (59.2% of lesbians and 65.6% of the lesbians-who-left.)

Notably, however, in the case of the former lesbians, feminism was more likely to have played a major role in their decision to become lesbians, than was true for the lesbians (29.9% of the lesbians as compared to 54.7% of the lesbians-who-left.) Rather than conclude that this means one group contained more "real" lesbians than the other (a theory that relies on heterosexist assumptions and biological determinist mystifications), this merely shows that the former lesbians were somewhat more dependent on a favorable social climate. Perhaps the lesbians-who-left were more traditional women to begin with or simply had less self-confidence; perhaps their families and communities were less tolerant of difference or had less exposure to the lesbian possibility prior to feminism. Whatever the case, it is clear from the comments of the lesbians-who-left that feminism was universally a liberating experience for these women, freeing them for other sexual possibilities and ways of viewing themselves and the world, (rather than, as some have suggested, a coercive environment that "required" lesbianism as a badge of "political correctness"). Though certainly some lesbians argued that women who engaged in heterosexual relations were "collaborating with the enemy" and only a lesbian could be a feminist, this "pressure", to the extent it existed, could never do more than weaken the powerful pull of the dominant culture toward heterosexuality.

One lesbian-who-left in her forties described how her involvement with feminism influenced her to become a lesbian:

> I came out in 1974 in Boston when I was in a Women's Studies graduate program...I was living with my boyfriend in upstate New York and his friend was a writer for Ms. Magazine so I started becoming more

aware of feminist stuff...There was a woman I knew who was going to a women's studies program and I said to myself now I know what I want to do with my life...I got accepted into the program and moved to Boston and my class was all lesbians. So I was around lesbians all year and that encouraged me to be completely comfortable with that.

Likewise, a former lesbian, now heterosexual, told me how the progressive social climate of the 1970's and her exposure to lesbians in the movement helped her to come out as a lesbian:

The early 70's was a time that there was a lot of social change going on. I was being introduced to a lot of new ideas – feminism, separatism, anti-war, androgyny, everything...All of a sudden, everything just blew open...There was this atmosphere of change that made me look at myself...I see these people, these lesbians – they're not part of the psychology books -they're not weird or deviant or abnormal – telling everybody how superior they are and how they are advancing their consciousness and I would like to check this out...I guess times were ripe.

A lesbian-who-returned explained how feminism had changed her sense of herself:

I think I just got much more of a sense of women as very powerful people who could make their own choices...I felt it was really my choice who I wanted to be with, it wasn't the culture's choice. And that definitely came out of feminism.

I asked her if she believed she would ever have found a lesbian life without the feminist movement. She replied:

No. Feminism offered me the support I needed to make those choices. And I don't think I was strong enough or could have broken out of my insular community without it.

I also interviewed a bisexual former lesbian about how feminism had helped her to overcome lesbophobia and come out in 1978.

Q. How did feminism play a role in your coming out as a lesbian?

A. I think it provided a community and a method of

meeting people and shared goals. Without feminism and its embrace of lesbianism, I don't think I would ever have considered it.

Q. Why is that?

A. It was nothing that was ever in my childhood. It wasn't on TV or in the newspapers. So it took a while to accept it...My early experiences with lesbianism - sleeping with a couple of women in college were fine, but I couldn't deal with it.

Q. Why couldn't you deal with it?

A. I didn't know where to put it...It was scary. It wasn't something I could really talk about with anybody. I didn't even know what to say to myself about it.

Q. So did feminism change that somewhat?

A. I think it changed it because it made it more acceptable and more prominent – it made it like it was a normal thing – it gave it a place...It made it more OK for a woman to be without a boyfriend.

Another bisexual lesbian-who-left told me the story of how she came out in 1974 as a result of her exposure to feminist ideas and institutions. In the early 1970's, she had pioneered a women's studies major at U.C. Berkeley and met her first lesbian. "But, I didn't think I was one", she explained. However, her experience living in a hippie commune in the mountains where she felt she didn't "fit" made her question her sexuality further. She continued:

Around 1974, I read Jill Johnston, *Lesbian Nation* and it clicked for me...Then I spent the summer in Seattle and found the Women's Bookstore. By that time, there was institution building [among lesbians]...I picked up this women's radio programming and I said, "that's it".

It all just fit together. To me, this was the way to fight patriarchy – women bonding on every level and forming communities...I started going to women's festivals. I plunged into it. I went from being a heterosexual to being a separatist...When I heard that women's radio, I thought that wow, I can do that too.

During this transition, she had become "utterly bored" with her role of "helping" a man. In contrast, her lesbian identity brought a new sense of self:

When I became part of the lesbian community, I
suddenly had a whole context, a whole world. I had an
audience. I became a writer. I did radio programming...I
developed my identity as a person. Before that, I was
following this heterosexual model because that was
what you fell into.

She confessed that she had come "full circle" in her present
relationship with her boyfriend where she again finds herself
playing the caretaking role.

Another former lesbian told a similar story:

In 1974, I went to a CR [consciousness raising] group. I
was living in Los Angeles at the time, certainly a hotbed
of feminism. At this time, I met many women who were
lesbians...All around me, women were coming out...In
an attempt to understand my lesbians sisters more, I
bought a copy of *Sappho Was a Right-On Woman.* I still
remember sitting up in my black wicker chair until four
in the morning, unable to put the book down. When I
was finished, I said "So that's what's wrong with me.
No wonder I don't fit in. I am a lesbian". Within weeks,
I had gone to a CR Convention in San Francisco and
had a clumsy encounter with another woman. But I was
thrilled anyway...Feminism and the women's movement
played a major part in my coming out and became the
center of my life.

Again and again, women emphasized how feminist books, CR
groups, and political activism were intertwined with their
lesbianism. One lesbian-who-returned described her feminism
as being "on a parallel track to my lesbianism – Feminism:
political, social, intellectual; Lesbianism: romantic, sexual and
emotional".

A heterosexual identified former lesbian explained how
feminism and lesbianism had been linked in her own life:

I first identified as a lesbian in 1976. My coming out and
feminist political activity happened hand-in-hand. I got
involved in a women's center and women's bookstore...
in Portland at the same time I had my first woman lover.

Her participation in the women's movement also changed her
feelings about attractions to women:

Feminist literature which said "The only true feminist is

a lesbian" did influence my thinking, but it was my sexual feelings for women which lost their disgusting quality through exposure to other lesbians, lesbian literature and films, etc. which were the deciding factor in my taking women lovers.

Similarly, Leslie, whose story was featured in Chapter I, found that her attitudes were changed by the feminism of the 1970's:

I finally relaxed. It was OK not to have a boyfriend... There could be a world that wasn't centered around men, one that was centered around women...women could have power and do anything...I wouldn't have to play all kinds of female games that I saw women do.

An African-American lesbian in her thirties described how the Feminist Movement, particularly the influence of Black lesbian writers, made it possible for her to come out in 1982:

I would never had the courage to acknowledge my attraction for women if I had not had access to books by Black lesbian-feminists like Audre Lorde, Barbara Smith and Anita Cornwell. In the Black fundamentalist world I was born into, lesbians were "mannish," called "bulldykes" and always white. Polite older relatives (parents, aunts, etc.) never mentioned lesbians at all. Before I read these and other authors, I had no concept of a Black lesbian community.

Even those women who stated that feminism had played only a minor role in their coming out indicated that it was not an insignificant one. One such woman, a lesbian in her thirties, who had married five times and had five children before coming out in 1983, wrote:

As I learned that I deserve to be in a relationship that is not abusive, I learned that I was an OK person in myself. I did not need a man to complete my life. This came about through the female therapist that I had and the counselors at two different battered women's shelters that I was in with my children. Learning that women were exciting and whole individuals was wonderful for me.

Similarly, another lesbian, in her twenties, stated that her feminist political involvement strengthened her previously acquired lesbian identity:

When I became a feminist, it helped me to understand my role as a lesbian and helped relieve any guilt or doubts I felt and made me proud of being a lesbian. It changed my perspective from protecting heteros from my gayness or trying to fit into their homophobic culture to expecting people to accept me as I am and not cater to their homophobic fears.

There can be little doubt that a feminist consciousness and Movement support makes it easier to be a lesbian. For example, an African-American lesbian-who-left in her twenties told me that she felt that the lack of such a consciousness contributed to her leaving. She explained:

I did not take feminism seriously enough when I first came out. I was only beginning to comprehend it. I think for lesbianism to really work as a liberation rather than just a variation of the same old shit, you need feminism.[10]

Likewise, a white lesbian in her forties, who had come out in 1984, found that feminist ideology was essential for a lesbian life:

I grew up despising women, despising my mother, hating the feminine, hating my own body, and valuing men and the masculine. As a child, I fantasized growing up to be a man. My most clear and consistent ambition was not to be like my mother. I think overcoming "anti-feminism" was a necessary prerequisite to my becoming a lesbian.

Whether or not women credited feminism, their experience of a greater degree of equality and mutuality in lesbian relationships was often a reason the lesbians in this study preferred women. One such woman, a lesbian-who-returned, in her thirties, described why she chose to be a lesbian:

I felt much more nurtured in relationships with women; much more cared about…women are my comrades; I have much more in common with them…I'm much more myself, much more comfortable, my self-esteem is higher with women than with men. I always feel there is an objectification with men and I hate that…

Another lesbian, this one over fifty, also found that the increased possibility of equality and intimacy made lesbian relationships more attractive:

> The possibility of equality in a relationship between two women is so wonderful and so important to me that it's overriding....I think men in our culture have a very hard time being intimate partners...I think they are encul- turated to be strong and silent and not too emotional...I can fantasize about a world where boys and girls would be brought up with a full range of possibilities and no heavy prescriptions of what their role should be because of sex. I think it's virtually impossible in today's society...In this culture, my need for intimacy and caring and sharing...couldn't be met by a man.

Similarly, a lesbian in her thirties (who works in women's studies) wrote:

> My lesbianism is an integral part of my feminism. I continue to live as a lesbian because it gives me a great deal of pleasure, satisfaction and power to change the heterosexist system...There are men that are caring and decent enough individuals, but under the present social situation, I don't see any way my lesbian consciousness could possibly deal with the shit I would have to deal with to be with men.

Sometimes, for the women in this study, a lesbian choice was not based on a conscious feminism, but solely on a personal rebellion against the restrictions of the feminine role. Typical of such personal rebellion is Una, whose story was reviewed in chapter II. She was also one of the few women in the study who did not consider herself a feminist.

For women who had made monumental changes in their lives in an era when radical change seemed eminently plausible, what happened when the climate grew more conservative and economically uncertain? As would be expected, those who were most dependent on the support of feminism in order to be "different" found their lesbianism increasingly problematic.

One bisexual-identified former lesbian in her twenties (who had come out in 1980 toward the end of the wave of new "political" lesbians) described how both her political activity and her optimism had eroded immediately prior to leaving:

> After late 1983, I got pretty burnt out as an organizer...I definitely felt like social change work was hard, you

didn't see a lot of results, that this was sort of a waste of time – you know – two steps forward, three steps back – that it wasn't really rewarding...I definitely was much more optimistic and excited earlier...

She began sleeping with men again in 1984, a few months after the "burn-out" had set in.

Her story was not unusual: 28% of the lesbians-who-left reported a decrease or cessation of feminist political activity immediately prior to leaving and 18% stated that they had become less optimistic about feminism right before they left. This demoralization was also reflected in the fact that during the last two years of lesbian identity, the former lesbians were less likely to be involved in lesbian and/or feminist organizations than were the lesbians (61.4% of the former lesbians compared to 74.3% of the lesbians) and also less likely to be reading lesbian and feminist theory, literature and poetry (64.4% of the lesbians-who-left as compared to 75.3% of the lesbians).

Another former lesbian, now heterosexual, described her process of disillusionment this way:

I thought we were going to save the world. I thought we'd have an amazon society...But you start getting a deeper look at things and I found that some people don't want male domination eliminated – they are offended by some mild form of feminism, no less lesbian separatism...Now I think some women like it the way it is and always will...When the ERA got defeated, I felt the conservatives run the country and it seems that any progressive ideas just get shoved down...

Often isolation from other lesbians and pessimism about the prospects for Women's Liberation went hand-in-hand, sometimes precipitated by a move to a more conservative locale. As one Jewish lesbian-who-left explained:

I was much more hopeful about feminism in the late 70's and early 80's than now...In Boston I was very involved with Jewish feminist activities...Then I moved to Atlanta and that doesn't exist here...I learned that non-Jewish feminists didn't know much about anti-semitism or much about racism and so I didn't move in that community, and the women in the gay/lesbian synagogue didn't know doo-da about being feminist. I felt very isolated as a Jewish lesbian-feminist.

However, the loss in feminist activism and vision was far too common to be explained merely by geography. For example, a bisexual former lesbian from Washington, D.C. stated that in the 70's she had started a few feminist groups, produced a few women's concerts and organized a socialist-feminist conference. Though she saw her present AIDS work as an outgrowth of her feminist politics, she also acknowledged that "the vehicles and momentum that propelled me into feminist activism are no longer obvious in my life".

The women in this study disagreed about whether or not it was actually harder to be a lesbian during the late 1980's (the time the study was conducted) as compared to the decade of the 1970's. Those who said it was harder mentioned the decline in lesbian-feminist community and activism, the conservative climate of the Reagan/Bush years and the growth of the religious right; others felt that it had never been easy being a lesbian. Some felt lesbianism was actually more accepted now than it had been a decade earlier. An African-American lesbian in her thirties from the Boston area who had come out in 1979 wrote tellingly, "No, it's not harder to be a lesbian...but it is harder to be a separatist".[11]

How easy or hard a lesbian life may seem to an individual depends on a number of factors including where she lives, her job, her family and friends, her life experiences, and her sense of herself, not merely the politics of her time. Yet, there can be little question that for many lesbians-who-left, the choice to remain a lesbian had become more difficult because of changes in the economy and social climate that placed feminism and all radical movements and ideologies on the defensive. As one bisexual former lesbian described it:

> [In the 70's] we were in the first rush and thrill of discovery – this new world of possibilities that we could create and empower ourselves as a group of women... Now we're reverting to old forms...I think social context makes a really big difference...

She also observed that:

> Instead of creating women's businesses and institutions, businesses were going under.

The life history of a lesbian-who-returned provides another

example of the importance of the Feminist Movement in the development and maintenance of a lesbian identity:

> I came out again with the Women's Movement starting in the late 60's and early 70's...Feminism made it possible for me to come out again and particularly the separatism part had a big influence on my life. My husband and I decided to separate and later got divorced because it seemed to make the way we were living together impossible...

> ...One of the reasons I didn't want to stay a lesbian in the 50's was there wasn't anything except a few gay bars and they were always being raided. There wasn't any other kind of life for lesbian and gay people. So that if those things were removed, if it were harder, I'm not sure what I would want to do...

She, also noted the losses of recent years:

> I think that AIDS has affected the whole gay community very profoundly, making it harder for everyone...I think I know many more women now who either have tried experiences with men or might want to be bisexual than was true in the early or mid 70's...

> In general, I think so many wonderful things have happened and I'm surprised how quickly we take them for granted until they are lost. In New York, there's not a women's newspaper anymore, so there's no way of finding out what's going on in the community, so lesbian life in New York City is very hidden...Here in San Francisco, we do have many gay papers but no women's newspaper. I see how important it is that we not lose our ways of communicating.

Feminism and lesbianism clearly need each other. A feminism that fails to openly acknowledge its lesbian activists and leaders, or to embrace lesbian issues as its own, is doomed to failure. At the same time, the more women dream big dreams together of creating a peaceful, just, and women-centered world; the more we fight for the complete emancipation of all of our sex (including the poorest and most oppressed among us); and the more we create bonds of friendship and community with other women, the more we are able to free ourselves from the constraints of compulsory heterosexuality.

Footnotes

[1] Adrienne Rich, "Compulsory Heterosexuality and Lesbian Existence" (1980) republished in *Powers of Desire*, Ann Snitow, Christine Stansell & Sharon Thompson, eds., (Monthly Review Press, New York, 1983) p. 201.

[2] Jill Johnston, *Lesbian Nation* (Simon & Schuster, New York, 1973), p. 271.

[3] Ti Grace Atkinson, *Amazon Odyssey* (Links Books, New York, 1974), p. 138.

[4] Ibid., p. 132.

[5] This is one way that the Feminist Movement of today is leaps ahead of the beginning of the Second Wave. In the early 1970's, NOW had conducted a purge of open lesbians. In 1993, Patricia Ireland, president of NOW spoke at the Lesbian/Gay/Bi March on Washington on behalf of her organization in a way that few feminist groups, mainstream or radical, would have spoken twenty or twenty-five years ago: "We march because we know homophobia is a very powerful weapon used to keep women – all women – in our place". (*National NOW Times*, 6/93.) In addition, Ireland, who is married, has acknowledged publicly that she has a woman "companion". However, she has refrained from identifying as a lesbian or even as bisexual.

[6] *Country Lesbian, the Story of the Womanshare Collective* by Sue, Nelly, Dian, Carol, Billie (Womanshare Books, Grants Pass, 1976), pg. vii.

[7] Ibid., p. 174.

[8] Ibid., p. 177.

[9] One striking exception was a former lesbian who wrote: "I am not a feminist. I feel that aggressive feminists do more damage to male/female relationships. However, I do support equal rights...I detest men who batter women...On the other hand, I have seen many women who badger men, who lie and cheat, who are greedy, lazy and sloppy and, worst of all, use their sex to punish their men by withholding themselves or expect special rewards".

[10] Perhaps it is not a coincidence that the weakening of feminism in the lesbian community (reflected in decreased activism, the revival of butch-femme roles, the growing popularity of lesbian sadomasochism, and the depolitization of lesbian identity itself) has coincided with an apparent increase in heterosexual behavior patterns.

[11] "Separatist" has become a loaded word. However, this statement probably means that it is not lesbianism per se but female independence, whether economic, ideological, or sexual, which has become both less acceptable and more difficult to achieve.

VII
RETURNING TO THE LIFE

After twenty-two years of marriage, I felt like a stranger in my skin; I was emotionally empty. I'd been ignoring my feelings year after year. Patching up a relationship in which neither of us were happy or satisfied...Finally we were divorced...The four year gay relationship I'd had before my marriage – the one I thought I'd put out of my mind – became an anchor for me. The realization that my life was half over finally helped me accept my lesbianism.

> – Nancy Roberts, "A Gift to Share", in *Long Time Passing: Lives of Older Lesbians*, ed. Marcy Adelman,Phd, (Alyson Publications, Boston, 1986), p. 94.

The stories of the lesbians-who-left that have appeared in this book may be distressing for lesbians and other supporters of lesbian/gay liberation to hear. Some may even fear that these stories could end up encouraging bigots who want nothing better than to win "converts" to heterosexuality. I have chosen to record them because we, who are challenging the hetero-sexual institution, must understand the dynamics of lesbian oppression. In the long run, knowledge can only strengthen us.

Lest our own efforts at analysis cause us to sink into despair, we should recognize two things. First, though society's efforts to enforce conformity are effective, they can never be completely so. The liberation movements that reshaped the second half of this century are not so easily reversed. These movements are still a living force for progressive change and the experiences and insights that came from them make it virtually impossible to return to the rigid gender roles and impenetrable closets of the pre-Stonewall era.

Second, we should remember that the lives of the former lesbians are not yet over. Times change; women change. Some women who love other women need to do what is expected of them before they reject society's demands. That is why a large number of lesbians come out in middle age or beyond, after having done a heterosexual "stint" through marriage and child-rearing. As one lesbian-who-left told me, the hardest thing is to be different your whole life.

Thus, it is not unreasonable to expect that many of the lesbians-who-left may return. We can predict some of the paths they will take because we know the stories of women who have already travelled those – the lesbians-who-returned. Of the 147 lesbians who participated in this study, I was able to identify 27, or 18% as lesbians-who-returned.

My definition of a lesbian-who-returned was originally quite strict: a woman had to both identify as a lesbian and be involved exclusively with women as sexual partners for some significant period; subsequently change her sexual behavior and/or her identity to a non-lesbian one; and finally, return to exclusive self-identified lesbianism. A number of younger women fit this pattern nicely, but for women older than fifty, I found my criteria too narrow, excluding lesbians who felt coming out was a return to the lesbian passions and relationships of their youth. Prior to the second wave of feminism, a lesbian identity was rare and even some sort of gay identity was uncommon.[1] Most women who loved other women did so in isolation and did not discuss their feelings even with their lovers. Thus, dating men often continued simultaneously with their lesbian affairs.[2] I, therefore, decided to expand my definition of lesbians-who-returned to include women for whom the idea of returning made sense in the context of the time they came of age.

As we have already observed, the lesbians-who-returned left for many of the same reasons that the former lesbians did so. There were, however, some differences between the two groups (many more lesbians-who-returned – 19% – were over fifty years of age while only one lesbian-who-left – 1.6% of the total – was over fifty); the lesbians-who-returned view their past conformity from a lesbian perspective while the former lesbians speak from their present point of view as non-lesbians.

In summary, the lesbians-who-returned originally moved away from a lesbian or women-centered life toward hetero-sexuality for the following reasons:

1) They fell in love with a man or felt a compelling heterosexual attraction – 9% (compared to 28% of the lesbians-who-left). (None of the lesbians-who-returned gave this as the only reason for their leaving.)

2) to win approval from family members – 31.8% (compared

to 24% of the former lesbians).

3) to have or raise children in a heterosexual family – 22.7% (compared to 16% of the lesbians-who-left).

4) to heal from child sexual abuse, rape, or "fear" of men - 13.6% (compared to 18% of the former lesbians).

5) to fit in at work – 9% (compared to 20% of the former lesbians).[3]

6) to be able to express affection publicly – 18.2% (compared to 20% of the lesbians-who-left).

7) to conform to religious doctrine – 18.2% (compared to 4% of the former lesbians).

8) Lesbian community was too small or claustrophobic – 4.5% (compared to 22% of the lesbians-who-left).

9) Lesbian community too narrow-minded – 4.6% (compared to 26% of the former lesbians).

10) as a lesbian, felt isolated from other lesbians and/or the rest of the world and wished to fit in better with the heterosexual majority – 40.9% (compared to 48% of the former lesbians).

11) no role models for a lesbian life – 18.2% (compared to 34% of the former lesbians).[4]

12) economic security or "perks" – 9.1% (compared to 14% of the former lesbians.)

13) as lesbians, felt they were missing something by not being with men and/or by living within the lesbian community – 13.6% (compared to 44% of the former lesbians).

14) difficulty in finding a satisfactory woman lover – 4.6% (compared to 42% of the lesbians-who-left).

15) relationships with men would be easier, less painful, less emotionally demanding – 18.2% (compared to 20% of the former lesbians).

16) felt that heterosexual relationships would be more stable, lasting, and emotionally secure – 13.6% (compared to 24% of the lesbians-who-left).

17) demoralized by imperfections of lesbian relationships – 9% (compared to 28% of the former lesbians).

18) to be cured or have lesbianism go away – 22.7% (compared to 2% of the lesbians-who-left).[5]

Notably, none of the lesbians-who-returned gave as a reason for leaving any difficulty in being sexual with a woman, while 20% of the former lesbians did so. Similarly, there was a substantial difference between the former lesbians and the lesbians-who-returned regarding sexual dysfunction in lesbian relationships: 32% of the lesbians-who-left reported such difficulties while only 4.5% of the lesbians-who-returned did the same.

In addition, none of the lesbians-who-returned gave as a reason for leaving difficulty finding women for casual sex (compared to 12%, or 6, of the lesbians-who-left). Neither did any of the lesbians-who-returned mention difficulty finding lesbians for casual sex prior to leaving though 16% of the former lesbians said they experienced such problems. However, access to casual sex is not of major importance to most women in this study.

There were some additional differences between the two groups worthy of mention. Fewer of the lesbians-who-returned than the former lesbians experienced anti-gay discrimination prior to leaving (9% compared to 20%). This probably reflects a generational difference since lesbians had less visibility prior to Stonewall and the Second Wave of feminism. Thus, being fired from one's job for being gay, for example, was probably a rarer occurrence. None of the lesbians-who-returned reported getting sober or experiencing a decrease in feminist activity before leaving.[6]

Despite these distinctions, the stories of the lesbians-who-returned are echoed in the lives and choices of the former lesbians. This becomes most clear when we listen to their own words. Thus, with only minimal editing, here are three of the interviews I conducted with lesbians-who-returned:

Alice's Story
(Alice lives in Omaha, Nebraska, is in her thirties and works as an economist. She is white and from a German, Scottish, and Irish working class background. Our interview took place on March 1, 1989.)

Question: Let me ask you a little about your childhood. Were you raised in any particular religious faith?

Alice: Not really. Protestant.

Q: I noticed that you had gone to a religious college.

A: Yeah. I got offered a scholarship and it was the only way I could go...

Q: Did you become more religious in college?

A: Yeah, I did.

Q: What did you like to do as a child?

A: Read. Play sports – baseball, softball.

Q: Would you consider yourself to have been a tomboy?

A: Yeah, somewhat. Not to the extent that I know some people are, but, you know, I didn't play with dolls.

Q: Did you feel you fit in with your peers?

A: No. [said with feeling]...I just thought I was different than everybody else...I didn't make friends very easily.

Q: Please tell me about your first coming out.

A: The first time I was ever with anybody I was maybe thirteen.

Q: And that was with another girl?

A: Yeah. And that just happened a couple of times. And then the next girl that I met when I was about fifteen; we were together for two years. And I didn't date any guys during this time.

Q: Did she?

A: No.

Q: Were you in love with her?

A: Oh, I think so. First love.

Q: Did you consider yourself a lesbian? Were you familiar with the term?

A: Yeah, I was familiar with the term. I was probably more familiar with the term queer or homo, or you know, the derogatory terms. But I knew what a lesbian was. I guess I thought that's what I was.

Q: Did your lover think that too?

A: I'm really not sure.

Q: Did you ever talk with her about what it all meant?

A: Not really, I don't think...We didn't have any consciousness at all...It was pretty much a butch-femme thing. I was the butch. This was in 1966.

Q: Did you have anybody to talk to about your relationship besides each other?

A: No.

Q: Did anybody know about it?

A: No. Well, probably suspected, but...

Q: How did that make you feel?

A: I was scared that someone would find out and that there

would be some kind of price to pay. In fact, I know I was scared. There were a couple of times when we almost got caught and I remember the fear.

Q: Were you scared of your parents?

A: Yeah.

Q: How about your peers?

A: Them too. You know, fear of rejection.

Q: Did you feel guilty at that time?

A: I don't remember ever feeling guilty in my life...

Q: Did you think at that time that you wanted to spend the rest of your life being with a woman or with this particular woman?

A: Well, I think being with her but at that point I don't think I was able to conceive that women could be together for the rest of their lives.

Q: Why couldn't you?

A: Well, 'cause there's so much pressure. I went to a high school that was pretty working class. A lot of Mormons, a lot of Catholics, a lot of Hispanics, and there was a real strong pressure, y'know, you got married and you had kids. I guess I just didn't realize that women did that.

Q: How about your parents? What kind of messages were they giving you while you were growing up?

A: I think they expected I'd go to college and then I'd meet somebody there to marry. It would be good to have some kind of skill or profession in case I might have to work at some point, but I should really find a man who could provide for me.

Q: So what happened between you and your girlfriend?

A: Her parents found a letter I had written and foolishly signed "your loving husband"...So she was sent off to college and we weren't supposed to ever see each other again but I snuck over to her dorm and we saw each other.

Q: So you continued having a relationship?

A: Yeah. Until toward the end of her second semester, her parents didn't like the way things were going and they put her in a mental institution.

Q: Wow. Do you know what happened to her?

A: I'd love to find her. I don't have any idea where she is.

Q: So, during all this time did you have anybody to talk to about what was going on?

A: No, no one.

Q: So you were still in high school then, is that right?

A; Yeah. I was at the end of my senior year.

Q: So how did you cope?

A: I decided I'd better straighten up…I decided, number one, that the whole ending of the situation had hurt me so much that I had to protect myself. I figured that when I went to college, I would be in a new environment and could just be a different person. So as soon as I got to college, I tried to be straight.

Q: Why did you decide to do that?

A: Because I was in a fairly restrictive environment. Because I think my parents expected me to find someone and get married. And I think I was feeling some – I don't know if it was guilt or not. I said I'd never felt any guilt but maybe it was guilt. I thought, something that ended up that badly, maybe it's wrong. Maybe I'm not really this way.

Q: You said you were starting to get more religious.

A: Yeah, I think a lot of it was that. But I continued being sexual with women in college. Probably six months before I met the man that I later married I was still sleeping with women.

Q: Had you dated men before that?

A: Some yeah. But I hadn't slept with any of them.

Q: So you'd never slept with a man until you met the guy you married?

A: Yeah.

Q: Did you feel pressures or lack of acceptance from family members at that time?

A: Pressure, yeah. They couldn't accept because they didn't know.

Q: Did you have any problems being sexual with a woman?

A: No.

Q: Was there any feminism going on around you?

A: This was in 1969 to 1970, the beginning of feminism, but it certainly wasn't there at the Baptist College I attended.

Q: So you weren't exposed to any feminist ideas?

A: No. I was exposed to submit yourself to your husband stuff.

Q: Were you thinking about having children?

A: Yeah. That's something I always wanted.

Q: Did you have any lesbian friends at that time?

A: No, not that I knew of.

Q: But you were having affairs with women who were.

A: That didn't know [they were].

Q: They were undefined?

A: Right. If I had found any lesbian friends it could maybe have made a difference.

Q: Was any of the reason you went straight that you fell in love with a man or felt a compelling heterosexual attraction?

A: No, I don't think so.

Q: Was one of the reasons that you married that you felt isolated from other lesbians or from the rest of the world?

A: I think some of that, yeah.

Q: Did you get married in order to gain economic security?

A: Definitely.

Q: Did you think that heterosexual relationships would be more stable, lasting, and secure?

A: Probably security yeah...I felt I needed a man socially and economically...

Q: Did you feel that your relationships with women didn't count?

A: Yeah, because they weren't recognized. It wasn't something that society embraced and said was good.

Q: Did you ever feel that women were not the equals of men, that they were less smart, less interesting, less capable?

A: No. No. No. Never. My grandmother got a Master's degree in 1919...I come from a long line of strong women. Now it seemed to have skipped my mother and my aunt's generation. They're the apron and "Father knows best" generation. But the older generation, my grandmother and her two sisters were all very strong women. In fact, I have suspicions that one of my great aunts was a lesbian.

Q: How long were you married?

A: I was a military wife for fifteen years.

Q: What was that like?

A: Well, my kids were great. And I wasn't the greatest mother at that time because of the internal conflict. I knew I shouldn't be married, but I couldn't figure out a way to get out of it and keep my kids and support them because I wasn't willing to do without things and I wasn't willing for them to do without.

Q: Were you being supported by your husband?

A: Oh yeah.

Q: And you were staying home?

A: Yeah. And having affairs with the neighbors. I started sleeping with women about twelve years into the marriage. But I always had real real strong attachments to women friends.

Q: When were you convinced that the marriage wasn't working?

A: I was convinced that something was wrong after the first year when he came back from Vietnam and he was just not the same person I had known...And then I still tried for it to work...About seven, eight , nine years into it, I made a couple of suicide attempts. I was just totally depressed. And I know it was because I shouldn't have been there...I still had nobody to talk to.

Q: What kinds of things changed that made it possible for you to come out again?

A: Well, I went back to school, a state college, and I started seeing a lot of lesbians around me and a lot of women getting degrees and being able to support themselves. And I started seeing what was possible.

Q: Did you start knowing any lesbians personally?

A: I knew one at the first school I went to and then I knew lots when I moved to Omaha and went to school here.

Q: And was seeing women going to school and getting careers new to you?

A: Yeah. Military officers' wives at that time didn't work. We took care of the home and kids, went and played bingo...And when I moved to Omaha from having lived at the military base it was a major difference. There was just a lot more available here where feminism was active and there is a gay and lesbian student organization, a women's resource center, out lesbians on the faculty...I started reading feminist and lesbian books...I started making lesbian friends...

Q: So did that help?

A: Yeah, it helped a lot. I think the final straw that made me come out was meeting my current lover. I felt I just can't take it anymore. I just have to be with her. So that's what finally did it. But it was happening, it was coming to that point. It was an evolution.

Q: So did you meet your present lover before you actually got divorced?

A: I met her in August, the divorce was final at the end of the

following May. And we're still together. It's been four years...
When I came out, my husband threatened me about the
children, that he'd bring it all out in court, and, you know,
Nebraska's pretty conservative. So I gave up custody...I didn't
want the kids to be hurt.

Q: How old are your children?

A: Fourteen and eighteen.

Q: Have you come out to them?

A: Oh yeah. My husband threatened to tell them, so I told
them...Both my children have problems with it. My daughter
kind of overdid it trying to be the perfect heterosexual teenager...
their Dad is a good southern Baptist and he told them it's
immoral and it's a sin and it's sick...

Q: How long did the period that you were more religious last?

A: Probably from about 1969 to 1978.

Q: Do you think loosening that tie helped you come out?

A: Oh, I'm sure it did. Had I never left the church, I probably
would have never come out.

Q: While you were married did you consider yourself a lesbian
that just couldn't handle doing that, did you consider yourself
straight, did you consider yourself bisexual, or did you just not
think about it at all?

A: Well, I thought I must be bisexual, but I never ever enjoyed
sex with my ex-husband. I don't really think I had an identity.
I was just Mom.

Q: What things do you prefer about women?

A: They're not on ego trips, they don't have to prove
anything...Women are gentler and stronger; with a woman you
can be on an equal basis. Just by the nature of your gender,
you're not put in a power position over another person.

Bonnie's tale

(Bonnie is a twenty-nine year old Jewish woman living in
Colorado whose grandparents are from Poland and Russia. Both
parents worked while she was growing up. Her father
(deceased) was employed as a factory foreman; her mother
works as a school administrator. Bonnie's interview occurred
on June 22, 1989.)

Question: What did you like to do when you were a kid?

Bonnie: Sports. I loved to be outside, I loved to run around.

Q: Would you describe yourself as a tomboy?

B: Yep.

Q: Any scholastic interests?

B: Not early on. In college I did…

Q: Did you feel you fit in as a child?

B: I always felt like I was kind of on the border. All the girls I knew were dating boys and I was on all the teams with the boys. The girls wanted to marry the boys and I wanted to be with the girls.

Q: I think you indicated on your questionnaire that you were sexually molested as a child?

B: Yes, by a male cousin ten years my senior…

Q: Please tell me about your coming out process.

B: From what I remember, I was first with a woman when I was seventeen and my Dad had died and I was in the rebellious stage anyway…I was with that girlfriend for about four months.

Q: Did you consider yourself a lesbian at that time?

B: I identified myself as a lesbian two years before. So it was just a matter of time for me. I was struggling and this woman said to me, are you gay? I said yeah, why? She said, well, I'd like to start dating you. That was really nice for me.

Q: Were you out with your family during that first time?

B: If that means sitting down and saying I'm a lesbian, no.

Q: Were you connected with other lesbians besides your lover?

B: Yeah, I marched in the first Boston Gay Pride parades and was at rallies and all.

Q: So how long were you just with women before you started getting involved with men?

B: After I broke up with my first lover, the next person who asked me out was a man. Then I dated women and three years later, I had just started a relationship with a woman when I met this man who become my husband. There was something about him that I needed to work out…I was very torn. I very much wanted to be with women and I wished he was a woman and one result was that our relationship wasn't sexual.

Q: What did you feel you needed to work out at that time?

B: I was just starting to deal with my father's death and Mike reminded me a lot of my father…Then I thought I'm also supposed to grow up and get married…I guess the shoulds that I grew up with started coming into play.

Q: So you were thinking that you should try to see if you could do what you were supposed to do?

B: Yeah, that's basically it...

Q: Did your mother have some intuition about you being a lesbian the first time around, even though it wasn't openly discussed?

B: Yeah.

Q: How did she respond to you getting involved with this man?

B: She didn't like him because he wasn't Jewish and he wasn't from the same socio-economic background. And I remember distinctly a conversation with her where I said would you rather have me bring home a nice Jewish girl? She said, wait a minute, nah...She probably thought I wasn't serious.

Q: Was there a lot of emphasis in your family about getting married?

B: No, there wasn't. Not overtly anyway, it was subtle. But I feel strongly that the message was there.

Q: Did you say your relationship with this man was not sexual?

B: No. It was sexual the first month and then the novelty wore off. I knew him for five years before we got married when I was twenty-five. It made it even better that I would be with this man and not be sexual...I got married after I graduated from graduate school and I didn't want to go back to Boston to my family and I didn't know what to do...When I felt really strong about myself, I'd tell him to take a walk. And when I felt really weak, somehow I needed that solid rock.

Q: Did you feel at the time you were involved with him that a relationship with a woman wouldn't last?

B: Yeah, I felt that a heterosexual marriage was more emotionally secure. I feel a lot more vulnerable in a relationship with a woman and it's too frightening for me to think of being in a long-term relationship with a woman. And I had to know somehow that it wouldn't work with a man.

Q: Do you mean it was more of an opening up with a woman?

B: Yeah, yeah. And I was just starting to feel what emotions were all about. It's pretty darn overwhelming...Also, commitment is a very scary thing for me...It's really hard to be in this [lesbian] relationship I'm in now because it feels like it's going to be around for a long time...If it was a heterosexual relationship, we'd be talking about marriage. We're not heterosexual and we're not talking about marriage. I think it's just scary to start thinking in terms of "we's" because there is no external thing, no legally sanctioned marriage, holding us together. That's a lot of my insecurity talk. I need some external thing because why would someone want to be with me for so long?

Q: Were you involved in the feminist movement in college?

B: Yeah. I always marched with everything and majored in women's studies as an undergraduate...Even when I was with Mike, I still went to Gay and Lesbian student union dances, I still marched in Take Back the Night and abortion rights. If there was a rally, I was there...That's why I consider myself a lesbian, because that's a woman-identified woman, a feminist, as opposed to a gay woman who behaviorally is with other women, but not necessarily politically or conscientiously.

Q: Did you still see yourself as a lesbian while you were married?

B: Well, after a couple of months, I knew it wasn't going to work out, so what I'm saying is I didn't identify as a lesbian while I was married to him. Yet I knew that should this marriage not work out, I would be with a woman.

Q: Why did you decide to identify as a lesbian and get involved with a woman?

B: Because I was tired of being miserable and tired of not feeling good about myself. And I was willing to take the risk. It didn't matter what I did, I could never please my mother, and it was time to please myself...I've been giving myself permission to follow my heart...And I'm really starting to feel alive, as opposed to just living on the earth...

Q: Did you think you were with a man because you were trying to please your mother?

B: Yeah. Yeah.

Q: Do you foresee any intimate sexual relationships with men?

B: I don't foresee it...I still think that if I was ever to be married to a man, it would be to Mike. He and I are really good friends. But it doesn't do anything for me.

Q: Are you out to your family now?

B: Yeah.

Q: Did you talk about it, did you do it officially this time?

B: Right. Uh huh.

Q: What was your mother's response?

B: She acted like it was the first time she ever heard anything about it...I said I'm dating this woman and my mother paused and then she said, well I didn't know that two women dated.

Last year, my mother marched with my sister and I in the Boston Gay Pride March and that was an incredible experience for all three of us. So intellectually, she's accepting, but emotionally, it's hard for her...The difference between now and ten years ago is that ten years ago I'd be talking about a woman lover and she'd feel like it was a knife stuck in her back and twisting around. And now I'm talking about Linda because I want to share my life with her. My mother can choose what she wants to do with the information.

Q: So your sister's also a lesbian?

B: Yeah. She's been living with the same woman for three years...I came out to her before she came out to me, but she came out to the family first. And I'm not out to my other family members – grandparents, extended family...I'm not planning on hiding anything...My aim isn't to blow people away; my aim is to be myself...

Carole's Herstory

Carole is a sixty-year-old white woman from a Protestant Italian background who grew up in New Orleans and now makes her home in the San Francisco Bay Area. Her father was an entrepreneur, working mostly as a clerk, and her mother had been a kindergarten teacher prior to marriage. However, her mother sought and obtained Federal government employment running a recovery house to teach girls housekeeping skills. Her mother worked all during the time that Carole was growing up. I interviewed Carole on February 6, 1990.

Question: When were you born?

Carole: 1929.

Q: Were you raised in any particular religion?

C: Methodist. We were very religious.

Q: So what did you like to do when you were a kid?

C: Tomboy, play, very physically active. When I couldn't get a bicycle because of economic reasons I arranged to sell my long thick braids. I got $35 for my hair and went out and bought a bike.

Q: Did you have ambitions of what you wanted to do when you grew up?

C: I think the usual girl things, nurse, teacher, doctor.

Q: Doctor? That's not a usual girl thing.

C: Then when I got to college, I couldn't pass calculus. I gave up the idea of being a doctor.

Q: What kind of messages did you get from your parents concerning marriage, sexuality, what a girl could do when she grew up, what were suitable careers?

C: Well, definitely to be a virgin. That meant you weren't supposed to be sexual at all. You were supposed to marry for life and have children. I was also taught I should be able to support myself.

Q: Did you have any awareness of gay people or the existence of homosexuality as a child or adolescent?

C: Absolutely none. A lot of my friends went to parochial schools but we didn't tease about the nuns beings lesbos, we didn't know anything about that stuff. Sex was just not referred to...I had very good girlfriends growing up and they were very important to me. I went to an all-girls high school. But sex, physical intimacy, never crossed my mind.

Q: Did you start dating boys at some point?

C: Not until I went to college. I was interested, felt attracted to boys – wanted to be asked out. But I wasn't. I was going to a girls high school and there was a war going on. And church was a lot of my life.

Q: So where did you go to college?

C: Louisiana State, Baton Rouge. I wanted to go where it was co-ed, to meet boys. Also, I wanted to major in PE.

Q: So did you major in PE?

C: Yes. My first year at Louisiana State, I had two roommates and started falling in love. I had a crush on one roommate especially. One time I was lying in bed with her, fondling her all over. It just happened. I never thought about it. My room-mates said I needed a boyfriend. So they got me a boyfriend. And I just pushed what happened out of my mind.

Q: What happened to the other girl?

C: She was going with some guy and got pregnant.

Q: Was this the first time you were conscious of your feelings for other girls?

C: Yes, but afterwards I just blocked it out. It wasn't until I went back to graduate school in Washington State that I remembered...I was attracted to two old maid sisters. I used to watch television at their house. I remember feeling desirous of them. But I never expressed it.

Q: What did you think about your feelings? Did you think they were bad, weird, sick, or anything like that?

C: I thought more about how they would be rejected. I guess I thought about it the way my roommates in college had taught me, namely that I needed a man...Then in graduate school, I met my husband-to-be playing softball. He liked the fact that I was so good at athletics...I had an affair with a woman student at the same time I was getting engaged to him.

Q: Tell me about that relationship.

C: We didn't talk much, it was very physical and so hidden. We knew it would be dreadful if anyone ever found out.

Q: What messages had you picked up at that time about what it would be like to make your life with another woman?

C: You would be lonely and miserable. The unmarried women I knew were successful professionally and financially, but their lives seemed incomplete. I didn't want to be that way.

Q: Was this the first time you had ever been sexual with a woman?

C: Yes.

Q: How about with anyone?

C: No, I had been sexual with my fiancé. So I could compare them. My desire was stronger for the woman. But I don't know that I was any more satisfied. My husband was pretty good sexually.

Q: How about emotionally?

C: He wasn't there. Maybe a little bit before we got married.

Q: Were you in love with her?

C: Yes. I would have built my life around her. I wanted her to get a job the same place I did. But she couldn't go through with it.

Q: How long were you seeing each other?

C: Six months.

Q: And that's while you were still seeing your fiance?

C: Yes...She was supposed to come see me and she didn't

make the trip. She sent word that she didn't want to see me anymore.

Q: Did she ever tell you why?

C: No. I couldn't get through to her...My heart was broken... Somebody years later told me she was married and wasn't particularly happy.

Q: Do you think she left you because she didn't want to be gay?

C: Yes. I assume she had the same feelings I had. Once she had rejected me, I decided that I didn't want that lifestyle, I couldn't do it. I felt it was impossible.

Q: Why did you feel it was impossible?

C: From what I saw around me. The people, the Dean of Women, and the other unmarried women I knew. I saw them as unhappy and I didn't want to lead that kind of life. There were no role models for liking what they were doing.

Q: Were you familiar with the term "lesbian" at that point?

C: No, I had heard the word "queer."

Q: Had you heard of "gay?"

C: No. This was the 1950's.

Q: Had you ever gone to a Gay Bar?

C: No.

Q: How did you think your family would respond if you had embraced a lesbian life?

C: I would have been a total outcast...My mother once told me about my father's reaction to a cousin who was gay. It was like he's not in the family anymore.

Q: What kind of work were you doing at the time you got married?

C: I was running teen groups and young adult groups, combining physical education and social work.

Q: Did your salary give you enough security or did you feel economic pressure?

C: I think I felt economic pressure.

Q: Did you ever talk to anyone about any of your fears about being with a woman, having this kind of lifestyle?

C: No, not with anybody, not even my girlfriend.

Q: How long after she broke up with you did you get married?

C: We broke up in June and I got married in August.

Q: Were you thinking about having children at that time?

C: That was the main reason for wanting to get married. I wanted to be a mother...I felt economically I needed a man to help support the children. I didn't want to have to work the whole time I had children.

Q: Had you fallen in love with the man you married?

C: No. I did it for children and for social acceptance, to be part of society. I don't think I fell in love. The sex was good.

Q: Could you conceive of being a mother without being married at that time?

C: No. I never knew anybody who could do it. All you had were these images of a single mother having to go someplace to have a child and hide it or be forced to give it up. There was no possibility without a man.

Q: Did you have any religious conflict over being sexual with a woman?

C: Well, it was strange. My religion didn't approve of any sex before marriage. So I didn't feel any more condemned for being a lesbian than for being sexually active with a man. But one reason I did get married was to legally have sex.

Q: Did you also feel that if you got married, it would be more secure, more lasting?

C: Yes, the whole society was built around it.

Q: Did you think at that time that women-loving-women was unnatural?

C: I must have thought it was unnatural, but it didn't feel unnatural...I remember studying psychology a lot in graduate school and looking for what they said about homosexuals. I remember disagreeing when they said that it's a psychological problem.

Q: Did any part of you think they could be right?

C: I'm sure I must have.

Q: When you decided to get married, did you hope your feelings for women would go away?

C: Yes, I did.

Q: So how long were you married?

C: Twenty-two years. I had three children.

Q: And what was that like?

C: I felt very close and satisfied with my children. I like the intensity of the tug of war between us at times. But I also felt a distance from my husband. He was unfaithful almost all the time and never admitting it...I never was jealous of the women he was with. I never really disliked them, It was him, he was the one telling the lies, breaking the vows. He was the one keeping me waiting.

Q: Did you work during your marriage?

C: No.

Q: Did you have feelings for women while you were married?

C: Not sexually. I didn't allow myself to feel that.

Q: You indicated in your questionnaire that feminism played a major role in your coming out process. How did it do that?

C: Feminism taught me that a woman has a right to be true to herself and her feelings, rather than this role, this patterned life you adopt. I knew that my true feelings were lesbian. I loved women. It's just the culture that puts a taboo on it. I refused to give that much power to the culture anymore...I decided to be true to myself and, to do so, I had to be independent. I had to get a job...At the community college, there was a woman, a counselor, who was very inspiring to me...I gradually worked into a semi-professional job and that was in 1975, the height of the feminist movement. It was just going on all around me...That same year, my husband had an opportunity to get his second masters...and that took him out of the house all week and hopefully on weekends too. And so then I was free to have a girlfriend...So after a year of playing house while he was away, I decided I didn't want to be dishonest like he did. So I just told him, I said, I'm leaving, I love women now and I'm going to make my own home...But as soon as I got free and really broke away, my girlfriend started breaking away...She just didn't want to get that close.

Q: Do you think she felt ambivalent at all about being a lesbian?

C: It could be. She had barely come out...Two months later, I met Judy...By the end of that year, I was getting a divorce and I took the settlement money and put it into a house. Judy and I lived there for five years.

Q: Did you live with your kids?

C: No. I left the kids with him because they wanted to stay in their house and in their neighborhood...The children were big enough – 11, 15, and 20 – so he couldn't keep them from seeing me. And I made a point to live within three miles of where he lived.

Q: Did your children accept your being a lesbian?

C: The youngest one was disappointed; she told me later that she was hurt by the fact that I didn't tell her in street language that I was a lesbian, I was a queer, I was a homosexual, because her friends called me that. I said no, I was just loving a woman. I didn't give her the words. She was hurt by that. And my son's girlfriend told me years later that he was pretty unhappy for a couple of weeks after I moved out. But then they saw how much better off we both were, both me and my ex-husband. No more nagging and fighting.

Q: Before you came out this second time, did you believe that women who made their lives with other women were man-haters or "just like men"?

C: Yes, they didn't like being women.

Q: And why did you think that?

C: Because the ones I recognized as gay were pretending to be men. I didn't know many women outside those stereotypes. That was the gift of feminism, you could like being a woman and still love a woman.

Q: Did you also used to feel that if a woman didn't have a man she was a failure?

C: I think so, yes.

Q: With feminism, did your feelings about being a woman change?

C: Yes, it was hooray, other people are agreeing with me.

Q: The isolation changed?

C: Right. I was the only one who'd felt that way and suddenly, there was such community.

Q: Did you feel more powerful as a woman as well?

C: Yes.

Q: What is it that you prefer about women?

C: On the feeling level, caring, the fact that it goes deep…And women seem to appreciate me. They catch on to what I'm feeling. Men are threatened because I'm smarter, bigger…

Q: Is part of what you prefer about women then the potential for equality?

C: Oh definitely, yes. That's a great feeling. Not one trying to be superior to the other…

Q: Do you think that if the feminist movement hadn't

happened, you would ever have come out?

C: Yes, I think so, but it would have been more difficult.

Q: Do you think there is still pressure to get married or to be heterosexually involved?

C: Yes. All around us...My oldest daughter who's about to get married told me she has been with women. She has never really talked much about it. I know she lived in a women's household. I think she was in love with one of her roommates whom she doesn't see her anymore.

Q: She never talked to you about it?

C: Yes, she could talk about her boyfriends...So even when she went to El Rio [a gay bar], I didn't think of her being with women, as being a lesbian, even as being bisexual because she has been so much with men. I was really surprised.

Q: And she's about to get married?

C: Yes...She wants to have children, a child at this point. She's a school teacher; her younger sister is married and going to have a baby.

Q: So do you think she's following in your footsteps?

C: Yes.

Q: Do you want to add anything else?

C. I think one thing that's important is how unhappy I was when I was married; I've never been so unhappy, before or since. So for sure, I should tell my daughter this if she's anything like me...

Q: Let me ask you one other question. Do you think it is easier or harder now being a lesbian than in the mid to late 1970's?

C: Some of the joy – the joy of life – is missing.

Q: So do you think it is harder?

C: Yes. Maybe it's just because I'm older but for me it's harder.

Footnotes

[1] Of course, there were many exceptions to this, in the bar culture and in groups like DOB (Daughters of Bilitis) that were pockets of female homosexual identity. In addition, exposure to sexologists' writings led to some degree of homosexual identification, though it often had the opposite effect.

[2] There were women who never married (at a time when virtually everyone did so), and who spent the bulk of their adult lives as lesbians. However, even among these courageous pioneers, it appears that a majority had at least some heterosexual experience. (Information

obtained from discussions with San Francisco members of GLOE – Gay and Lesbian Outreach to Elders.)

[3] The possibility of being "out" at work would probably not have existed prior to Stonewall.

[4] Perhaps lack of role models is an issue of which only the post-Stonewall generation would be consciously aware.

[5] Few younger women who have been affected by feminism and gay liberation would use the word "cured" in this context or expect their homosexual feelings to go away. However, as we have seen, they frequently do talk about "healing" from sexual abuse, etc. through heterosexual relationships.

[6] Many lesbians-who-returned experienced their first coming out either before the feminist movement or outside the context of organized feminism.

VIII
FREEDOM TO LOVE
(Conclusion)

Don't wanna be in the dark
Wanna turn on the lights
wanna love you baby
I know our love is right
What I want is the freedom to love
  – "Freedom to Love" song by Faith Nolan (1989)

This is a difficult appeal to make in what are dangerous times, but it is made without hesitation or apology. For women to have our full dignity and humanity, we must have the freedom to love. As long as women's lives are defined and circumscribed by the heterosexual imperative; as long as we need men to survive economically, socially, psychologically; as long as the stories of the lesbians-who-left keep repeating themselves – stories of oppression, isolation, self-hatred, and fear – no woman, whatever her sexual identity, can call herself free.

What would the world be like if women were no longer terrorized into heterosexual relations. How would it be if women's value was not measured by whether men approved of us? What if having a husband or boyfriend was no longer a badge of normality or respectability? What if women were never taught that lesbianism is unnatural, unhealthy, sinful or unful-filling? What if, instead, women's passions for other women became as much a part of social life as the air we breathe, recognized and celebrated, equally with heterosexual love, by the entire culture? What if, in such a world, men no longer had an "edge" because of their gender, and were judged solely on their own individual merits? Would they become better friends, better parents, better intimate partners, better people? Would we see an end to male violence? How much more power would women have in our personal lives, and in the larger society?

In such a world, a young woman who found herself preferring the company of her girlfriends or falling in love with a female classmate would not be forced to hide or deny her feelings and would not feel compelled to date and marry men. And women of whatever age who found relationships with men unsatisfactory or oppressive would no longer blame themselves for their difficulties or believe they had no other options for sexual intimacy. And in such a world, women would not leave a lesbian life in order to "fit in" with family and society. Such externalities would not be considerations, were women truly free to follow their hearts.

But to dream of freedom, we must first acknowledge the ways in which we are not yet free. This is what this book, by highlighting the lives of the lesbians-who-left, has tried to do. Yet, at a time when many substitutes for freedom are seductively offered, it is not easy to honestly confront the breadth and depth of our oppression. Lesbianism is "chic" we are told, we've made the cover of *Newsweek*, we have our own sex clubs and sex magazines, we have lesbian judges and politicians, a lesbian was even appointed to high office by a U.S. President. So, we have nothing to complain about; we've made lots of progress, and we must be patient and not too demanding about the rest.

But should we be so easily placated? The media's version of lesbianism as fashion statement, divorced from feminism and radical politics, a lesbianism trivialized as the kinky sexual practices of a tiny minority who were probably "born that way", may be a boost to consumerism but poses little threat to the heterosexist structures of patriarchal capitalism. And as long as these structures are in place, we are not safe and we are certainly no where near liberated.

It is true that a few lesbians have "made it" within that system (often by adapting to, or not actively opposing the values that dominate society), but how about the rest of us? How many lesbians still face terrible discrimination or stigma or have decided to stay in the closet in order to keep their jobs, their children, their status in the community?

How about the lesbians-who-left? Can we forget those women who found lesbian oppression too overwhelming to risk being different (or at least that different) any longer? What emotional price will they ultimately pay for having swallowed the lies of the homophobes?

Finally, can we forget the untold numbers of women who keep following the heterosexual script even when it consistently fails to meet their needs? Just how many such women there might be in this category was suggested by an unlikely source, a mainstream women's magazine. In its August 1992 edition, *New Woman* published a study on friendship in which over 4,000 of its readers participated. When asked whether their husbands or boyfriends were their best friends, 60% of the married women, 72% of married mothers and 81% of single women answered "no". Women reported that they usually experienced greater equality, intimacy, and mutuality in their female friendships. One divorcee was quoted as saying, "My best friend has put more effort into our friendship than my ex-husband ever did in our marriage".[1]

Sadly, though many women wished they could have with a partner what they had with their female friends, the heterosexual institution had successfully removed the lesbian possibility from their lives. As one single woman in her twenties wrote to *New Women*: "My best friend and I kid each other by saying, 'if you were a man, we'd definitely get married.'"[2] As long as there is even one woman on this earth who has her choices as constricted as does this reader of *New Woman*, the tasks of women's and gay/lesbian liberation are not yet completed.

Our vision of liberation must be a collective one, inclusive of all women. It must be a vision that seeks not just individual female self-confidence and assertiveness, not just power for a few, but an end to the structures of discrimination, inequality, and compulsory heterosexuality that continue to deny women our full humanity. We must reject the heavily promoted "create your own reality" backlash with its emphasis on individual responsibility. The media darlings of this backlash include not only self-proclaimed feminists like Camille Paglia and Kate Roiphe (both of whom mockingly reject fundamental feminist concerns like ending rape, sexual harassment and other forms of male violence as "Victorian" and "prudish") but also respected feminist writers like Naomi Wolf who now holds that women's attitudes, especially their "fear" of power and money, are the main obstacle to women's liberation. It is not surprising that the new "successful" Wolf also warns against "man-bashing", is concerned with women maintaining their "femininity", and touts heterosexual relations as the way to "greater knowledge of self". For success in a man's world still by and large requires being accessible to men; it requires a woman to be, in a word, heterosexual.[3]

To put an end to compulsory heterosexuality will require much more than the passage and enforcement of anti-discrimination laws based on sex and sexual preference, as important as these are. It will necessitate the radical transformation of society to a peaceful egalitarian one consistent with feminist values;[4] and an overhaul of popular culture – books, movies, music, television – in order to bring lesbianism into the center, into the light. No one will carry out these changes for us; we must do it ourselves by rebuilding radical feminist and lesbian political/social/cultural movements from the grass roots, making alliances where necessary, but never losing sight of our goal: that women secure the freedom to define the most intimate conditions of our lives. As we enter into the next century, can we demand any less for ourselves, for our sisters, for our daughters, for the generations of women to come?

Footnotes

[1] Victoria Secunda, "The New Woman Friendship Report" *New Woman* (August, 1992).

[2] Ibid.

[3] For a biting critique of Paglia, Roiphe and Wolf, and of Wolf's new book, *Fire with Fire: The New Female Power and How It Will Change the 21st Century* (NY: Randon House, 1993) see "Feminism for the Few" by L.A. Kauffmann, published in *San Francisco Weekly* November 24, 1993; see also my review of Wolf's book, "When Feminism Joins the Establishment", published in *Off Our Backs* (April, 1994).

[4] I would also describe my vision of a future just society as "socialist", an idea that has unfortunately been discredited by the male-run autocracies that formerly ruled the Soviet Union and Eastern Europe. With the moral bankruptcy of capitalist patriarchy becoming more and more apparent, both socialist and radical feminist ideas need to be reborn.

When you respond to the questions on this page, Onlywomen Press, Ltd. will give you a special mail order disount on any Onlywomen title ordered direct from us (*not bookshops*). We've been publishing literary and popular (Sci-Fi, Romance, Crime) fiction and poetry as well as non-fiction theory since 1974.

How often do you read feminist theory?
rarely ☐   occasionally ☐   never ☐   often ☐

How often do you read queer theory?
rarely ☐   occasionally ☐   never ☐   often ☐

Did you like this book (*Leaving The Life*)?
yes ☐   no ☐   in parts ☐

Why did you buy (or borow) it?
Friend's recommendation ☐   Interesting topic ☐
Catchy cover design ☐   Something else ☐

I understand that response to the above questions, at the back of *Leaving The Life*, entitles me to a 10% discount on an Onlywomen book purchased by mail-order before 31 December, 1999.

Name...
Address..
....
....
....

Please send me an Onlywomen mail-order catalogue ☐

Tear out or copy this page and post to:
ONLYWOMEN PRESS, 40 St Lawrence Terrace, London W10 5ST.